Latin Political Propaganda in the War of the Spanish Succession and Its Aftermath, 1700–1740

BLOOMSBURY NEO-LATIN SERIES

Series editors: William M. Barton, Stephen Harrison,
Gesine Manuwald and Bobby Xinyue

Studies in Early Modern Latin
Edited by William M. Barton and Bobby Xinyue
Volume 2

The 'Studies in Early Modern Latin' strand of the *Bloomsbury Neo-Latin Series* showcases the latest research on aspects of early modern Latin literature from around the globe. Volumes include monographs and collected volumes covering all aspects of the Neo-Latin world, illustrative of the field's wide-ranging literary, chronological, geographical, social and cultural span.

Aimed primarily at the international research community, scholars and students alike, these studies offer up-to-date critical perspectives from the flourishing field of Neo-Latin Studies. The strand's monographs and collected volumes address Neo-Latin both as a self-standing literary phenomenon as well as its role within the dynamic literary and cultural developments of the early modern period more generally. They offer thought-provoking analysis of significant moments and themes in Neo-Latin literary history of the period *c.* 1500–1800.

Alongside the series' 'Early Modern Texts and Anthologies' strand, these studies aim to bring Latin literature of this period to greater prominence among students and scholars of a wide range of academic disciplines, and thus contribute to the continued growth of Neo-Latin Studies.

Also available in this series:

Baroque Latinity: Studies in the Neo-Latin Literature of the European Baroque
edited by Jacqueline Glomski, Gesine Manuwald and Andrew Taylor

Latin Political Propaganda in the War of the Spanish Succession and Its Aftermath, 1700–1740

Alejandro Coroleu

BLOOMSBURY ACADEMIC
LONDON • NEW YORK • OXFORD • NEW DELHI • SYDNEY

BLOOMSBURY ACADEMIC
Bloomsbury Publishing Plc, 50 Bedford Square, London, WC1B 3DP, UK
Bloomsbury Publishing Inc, 1385 Broadway, New York, NY 10018, USA
Bloomsbury Publishing Ireland, 29 Earlsfort Terrace, Dublin 2, D02 AY28, Ireland

BLOOMSBURY, BLOOMSBURY ACADEMIC and the Diana logo
are trademarks of Bloomsbury Publishing Plc

First published in Great Britain 2024
Paperback edition published 2025

Copyright © Alejandro Coroleu, 2024

Alejandro Coroleu has asserted his right under the Copyright, Designs
and Patents Act, 1988, to be identified as Author of this work.

Cover design: Terry Woodley
Cover image: Louis Laguerre (1663–1721), *The Battle of Malplaquet*, 1709.
© The Picture Art Collection/Alamy Stock Photo

All rights reserved. No part of this publication may be: i) reproduced or
transmitted in any form, electronic or mechanical, including photocopying,
recording or by means of any information storage or retrieval system without prior
permission in writing from the publishers; or ii) used or reproduced in any way for
the training, development or operation of artificial intelligence (AI) technologies,
including generative AI technologies. The rights holders expressly reserve this
publication from the text and data mining exception as per Article 4(3) of the
Digital Single Market Directive (EU) 2019/790.

Bloomsbury Publishing Inc does not have any control over, or responsibility for,
any third-party websites referred to or in this book. All internet addresses given
in this book were correct at the time of going to press. The author and publisher
regret any inconvenience caused if addresses have changed or sites have
ceased to exist, but can accept no responsibility for any such changes.

A catalogue record for this book is available from the British Library.

Library of Congress Cataloging-in-Publication Data
Names: Coroleu, Alejandro, author.
Title: Latin political propaganda in the War of the Spanish Succession
and its aftermath, 1700–1740 / Alejandro Coroleu.
Description: London ; New York : Bloomsbury Academic, 2023. |
Series: Bloomsbury Neo-Latin series: studies in early modern Latin literature |
Includes bibliographical references and index.
Identifiers: LCCN 2023018991 (print) | LCCN 2023018992 (ebook) |
ISBN 9781350214897 (hardback) | ISBN 9781350214934 (paperback) |
ISBN 9781350214903 (ePDF) | ISBN 9781350214910 (ePub)
Subjects: LCSH: Latin literature, Medieval and modern–History and criticism. |
Spanish Succession, War of, 1701–1714–Literature and the war. |
Spanish Succession, War of, 1701–1714–Propaganda. |
Literature in propaganda–Europe–History–18th century. | LCGFT: Literary criticism.
Classification: LCC PA8040 .C66 2023 (print) | LCC PA8040 (ebook) |
DDC 870.9/004—dc23/eng/20230807
LC record available at https://lccn.loc.gov/2023018991
LC ebook record available at https://lccn.loc.gov/2023018992

ISBN: HB: 978-1-3502-1489-7
PB: 978-1-3502-1493-4
ePDF: 978-1-3502-1490-3
eBook: 978-1-3502-1491-0

Series: Studies in Early Modern Latin

Typeset by RefineCatch Limited, Bungay, Suffolk

For product safety related questions contact productsafety@bloomsbury.com.

To find out more about our authors and books visit www.bloomsbury.com
and sign up for our newsletters.

Contents

List of Illustrations	vi
Preface	vii
List of Abbreviations	viii
Introduction	1
1 Praise and Blame: Legitimizing the New Kings' Old Dynasties	11
2 'Bellonae et Martis genitus': Mapping the Spanish Conflict in Latin Verse and Prose (1701–1712)	43
3 Latin Writing between Court, Church and Academia during the War of the Spanish Succession	89
4 Latin Propaganda beyond the Dynastic Conflict (1715–1740)	121
Conclusions	143
Appendix 1: The Spanish Succession: A Dynastic Table	147
Appendix 2: Texts from Chapters 1 and 2	149
Appendix 3: Two Eighteenth-Century Latin Poets at Work	157
Notes	163
Bibliography	199
Index	217

Illustrations

Unless otherwise stated all images are in the public domain.

1. *Le Roy accepte le Testament de feu Roy Catholique Charles II et declare Monseigneur le Duc d'Anjou Roy d'Espagne sous le nom de Philipe V à Versailles le XI Novembre MDCC*, 1701, BnF, Estampes, Hennin 6667 — 15
2. Title page etching for a tract entitled *Europe Nooit voor Een* ('Europe never for one', Amsterdam, 1702); in the centre, a lioness (Britain) and a fox (the Netherlands) clipping the claws of the French tiger while two other lions approach from the right. The inscription on the monument reads: *Sic pax cum tigribus esto* ('How to make peace with tigers'). Reproduced in Cilleßen 1997: 351 — 44
3. *Elogia heroum Caesareorum in Italia*, Vienna, 1702, p. 10; ÖNB, 303026-B. Adl. 3 — 47
4. *Carolus III invictissimus Hispaniarum rex*, s.l., s.d. (but surely 1706), title page, reproduced by kind permission of the Biblioteca de l'Abadia de Montserrat, Res. 4º 1/32 — 64
5. *The Battle of Malplaquet*, oil on plaster, by Louis Laguerre (1663–1721) and assistants, *c.* 1713–14, reproduced by kind permission of the Royal Collection Trust / © His Majesty King Charles III 2023 — 78
6. A medal minted for the city councillors of Amsterdam in 1714, bearing the inscription *Diva tegens Batavos, qua cuspide reppulit hostes, / nunc oleas pacis surgere signa iubet* ('With the spear with which she repelled the enemy the goddess protector of the Dutch commands the olive tree, symbol of peace, to rise'). Reproduced in Van Loon 1717: 249 — 112
7. Rector Anton von Öttl's entry in the main register of the University of Vienna for the year 1708. Reproduced from the History of the University section of the Universität Wien website (accessed on 1 July 2022) — 119
8. Francesc de Santacruz i Gener, *Barcino magna parens*, engraving, Arxiu Històric de la Ciutat de Barcelona, reg. 18265 — 125

Preface

The present offering began in the Herzog August Bibliothek at Wolfenbüttel. It was during my time there that I first stumbled across some of the sources on which my study is based and decided to investigate the uses of Latin in the War of the Spanish Succession. The project took shape at the Ludwig Boltzmann Institute for Neo-Latin Studies (Universität Innsbruck), where, as Research Fellow in the spring of 2021, I had the great privilege of reading and writing freely. I am most grateful to its director, Florian Schaffenrath, as well as to the rest of the LBI staff for providing a most hospitable and stimulating research environment. The democratization of rare books via the internet has greatly facilitated the research for this volume, yet I owe an enormous debt of gratitude to the staff of four libraries who have always assisted me personally and answered my queries promptly and efficiently: the Biblioteca de l'Abadia de Montserrat, the Österreichische Nationalbibliothek, the Bibliothèque nationale de France, and the CRAI Biblioteca de Fons Antic at the Biblioteca Universitària de Barcelona. In addition, I would like to acknowledge in particular the patient assistance of Joan Miquel Oliver in Barcelona, whose catalogue of the special collection on the War of the Spanish Succession held at the BUB is an indispensable tool for anyone interested in the literature produced during the conflict. Several individuals have contributed to this project through their friendship, generosity, and conversation: Cristina Fontcuberta, Elisabeth Klecker, Maria Paredes, Barry Taylor, and José Luis Vidal. I am grateful to the two anonymous readers for their critical comments and encouragement. I also wish to thank the staff of Bloomsbury for their interest in my project and for their friendly and efficient handling of the publication process. This book would not have reached its current form without the discerning eyes of David Barnett, who copy-edited the volume and offered precious advice on how best to organize my material. Any errors and infelicities that remain are, naturally, my own.

This book is dedicated to Vroni, David and Laura, without whose support and inspiration nothing would have been possible.

Abbreviations

BC	Biblioteca de Catalunya, Barcelona
BL	British Library, London
BNE	Biblioteca Nacional de España, Madrid
BnF	Bibliothèque nationale de France, Paris
BUB	Biblioteca Universitària de Barcelona, Barcelona
CRAI	Centre de Recursos per a l'Aprenentatge i la Investigació (Biblioteca de Fons Antic, Biblioteca Universitària de Barcelona, Barcelona)
ECCO	Eighteenth Century Collections Online
ELTE	Eötvös Loránd Tudományegyetem, Budapest
HAB	Herzog August Bibliothek, Wolfenbüttel
MBSB	Bayerische Staatsbibliothek, Munich
NuBIS	Digital library of the Sorbonne, Paris
ÖNB	Österreichische Nationalbibliothek, Vienna
RCIN	Royal Collection Inventory Number
sign.	indicates the signature (A, B, C, etc) and folio number in pre-1800 unpaginated printed books
SJ	Society of Jesus

Introduction

Among the first military conflagrations to be waged on a global scale, the War of the Spanish Succession was fought between 1701 and 1715 to decide who should inherit the Spanish throne – and with it, the Spanish overseas territories –, vacant since 1700 when the last Spanish Habsburg king, Charles II, died without producing an heir. The conflict pitted France under Louis XIV, who supported Philip, duke of Anjou (Philip V of Spain), against the Habsburg contender, Archduke Charles of Austria (or Charles III of Spain, as he styled himself), who was favoured by the countries in the so-called Grand Alliance. In Spain this international struggle degenerated into a civil and regional war, with the Crown of Castile in support of Philip and the Crown of Aragon (especially Catalonia) behind Charles, with a few exceptions on both sides. At the end of this dynastic feud between the Austrian Habsburgs and the French Bourbons, neither of the two claimants to the throne was able to gain full control of the Spanish Empire: the Peace of Utrecht of 1713 acknowledged Philip V as king of Spain but also conceded territories in Italy and the Spanish Netherlands to Charles. As a result of the conflict Britain emerged as the dominant European colonial power to the detriment of the Dutch Republic, whilst French political and military influence in Europe, though still formidable, returned to limits more acceptable to its neighbours. The end of the War of the Spanish Succession also represented a political and administrative turning point in Spain as the Crown of Aragon was stripped of its legal status by the new Bourbon regime. As aptly summarized by Hamish Scott, 'the war marked an important stage in the transition from an international system dominated by attempts to restrain one leading state, first Spain and then France, to a competition between a number of powers which were more equal in status and potential' (2018: 59).

Despite the historical significance and enduring political and economic impact of the conflict, the War of the Spanish Succession has long been regarded as a 'forgotten war'. By and large scholarship has been concentrated on issues of a military and diplomatic nature and been heavily influenced by the many national and largely unconnected historiographies. In recent decades, however, this conventional framework has opened up, and scholars have gradually recognized the need to include the public and cultural dimension of warfare.[1] Like any other early modern conflict, the War of the Spanish Succession was fought on the battlefield and in diplomatic circles, yet it was also one of the first wars to be staged 'in the printed press and on the ceremonial stage' (Pohling and Schaich 2018: 12). The present book contributes to this new approach by bringing to light a range of Latin texts produced during the war and providing a sense of the extent of the political role of Latin within the propaganda machines employed by both sides and the span of remits in which the learned language was deployed.

The reign of Charles II of Spain (1665–1700) was characterised by the monarch's ill health and lack of descendants. The question of who should succeed him was therefore the motive for active diplomacy among European powers in the last decade of the seventeenth century. There were three contenders for the crown: Prince Joseph Ferdinand of Bavaria (b. 1692), whom Charles II had named in his first will, Archduke Charles of Austria (1685–1740), and Philip, duke of Anjou (1683–1746), second grandson of Louis XIV of France (1638–1715). The death of Joseph Ferdinand in 1699 led Charles II to sign a new will – on 2 October 1700, shortly before his death on 1 November – naming as his universal heir Philip of Anjou, who was proclaimed king of Spain with the name of Philip V in a ceremony held in Versailles on 16 November. The ascent of a Bourbon to the Spanish throne was greeted with hostility in most other European states, and the first military encounters between the two sides took place in northern Italy a few months later. In May 1702 the Grand Alliance, a coalition formed of England, the Holy Roman Empire and the United Provinces of the Low Countries, officially declared war on the Bourbons of France and Spain, and, in a ceremony held in Vienna in September 1703, Emperor Leopold I of Austria (1640–1705) and his firstborn son Joseph (b. 1678) formally asserted the dynastic rights of Archduke Charles, proclaiming him king of Spain as Charles III. The new Habsburg monarch, accompanied by the English ambassador George Stepney (1663–1707) and by Prince Anton of Liechtenstein (1656–1721), visited his Grand Alliance partners in Holland and England, before setting sail for Lisbon, where he arrived in March 1704 to open up a new front on the Iberian Peninsula. In the following summer, with a large contingent of Allied troops, he landed near Barcelona, and captured the city in October.[2]

Seven months later a Bourbon army led personally by Philip V attacked the Catalan capital, but the arrival of the Allied fleet forced the assailants to abandon their siege. This successful defence of Barcelona in May 1706 coincided with important victories by Charles's armies elsewhere in Europe. By March 1707 the French had been forced back to their borders, but the Allies were unable to break their lines. Meanwhile, lack of popular support in Spain meant Charles's forces were unable to hold any territory gained outside Catalonia. Between 1706 and 1711 Charles established his royal court in Barcelona and it was also where, in August 1708, he married Elisabeth Christine of Brunswick-Wolfenbüttel (1691–1750). In 1710 a new parliament was elected in Great Britain with a Tory majority. Unlike the Whigs, the Tories were in favour of abandoning the war in return for trading concessions in Spanish America, a plan which was also supported by Philip V. The death of Emperor Joseph I in April 1711 and the election and coronation later that year of his brother Archduke Charles as emperor of the Holy Roman Empire under the name of Charles VI added impetus to the peace negotiations. The treaties signed in Utrecht, Baden and Rastatt between April 1713 and September 1714 acknowledged Philip V as king of Spain, but Charles VI was in turn granted Spain's continental possessions in Italy (Naples, Sardinia and Milan) and in the Spanish Netherlands. For their part, Great Britain and the United Provinces recognised Philip V as king of Spain in return for important political and economic concessions. Despite the succession being no longer an issue, Catalonia continued to wage war against Philip in order to defend Catalan liberties. After a long siege by French and Spanish troops, Barcelona finally surrendered on 11 September 1714. The conquest of Majorca and Ibiza ten months later put an end to the hostilities. After this comprehensive defeat between 25,000 and 30,000 people were forced into exile from Spain. This group of mostly Catalan clergymen, scholars, nobility and high-ranking officials established itself in Italy, the Low Countries and Austria. The end of the dynastic feud at the heart of the War of the Spanish Succession was sanctioned by the Treaty of Vienna in 1725.

The conflict whose major events I have just summarized was also waged on the printed page, in text and images, leading to a veritable 'war of written words'. The war set the scene for a major upheaval in the relationships between European powers and the need arose for a propaganda offensive aimed, initially, at legitimizing Philip V as the new king of Spain. Later, in 1702, this then became a real conflict when the Allied powers joined forces to launch a counteroffensive in support of Archduke Charles. Both sides used all the means at their disposal to win over followers to their respective causes to such an extent that the propaganda war was fought in parallel with the confrontations on the battlefield. Victories were exploited to consolidate positions and increase the number of supporters; defeats were used to call for more prayers as well as finance and arms. It is in this context of the parties vying for consensus and public support that we must view all the literature produced, inseparable from its primary function as publicity.

A greater interest in the means of diffusion, in the context, in the people who commissioned these works and their target audience, and in their final objective has led some scholars to speak of three propaganda fronts: genealogy, war and religion. Between 1700 and 1704 there appeared any number of literary works in praise of Philip V, produced, logically, before the conflict escalated, and promoted by the higher social classes who supported the consolidation of the Bourbon's power base. The diffusion of these messages relied not only on encomiastic writing and chronicles, but also on visual images – in paintings, prints and battle plans – all framed with mythological and religious references (Cilleßen 1997: 342–51; Miralpeix 2012; Mínguez Cornelles et al. 2014: 125–40). The unfolding of events on the ground determined the duke of Anjou's profile – initially he was the 'legitimate king', then the 'bold king' or the 'soldier king' and then finally the 'despotic king' – and was complemented by the distribution of popular pamphlets against the Archduke. On the other side, the Habsburg camp promoted Charles's image throughout Europe in much the same way: using positive literature on the one hand to build up his image and, on the other, an altogether more popular form aimed at discrediting his rival.

Beyond the propaganda focused on the images of Philip and Charles, there was another particularly fruitful strand centred on the action on the battlefields, in the physical theatre of war, which was always expressed in the language of power struggles and religion. One approach that sheds invaluable light on this strand is the study of some of the paintings and prints that depict battles or sieges, often with the aid of plans and diagrams. They tend to be large-scale works that present the viewer with a broad panorama; in the foreground are the senior military figures directing the manoeuvres, just behind the victorious general, shown on horseback; in the middle ground, there is the cavalry (the nobility); and then in the background, a well-disciplined army, drawn up in formation (infantry and artillery) framed by a backdrop of the fortifications or geographical features that are being defended or attacked. The typology of the literary works is diverse: books commemorating battles, with maps and sketches of clashes at sea or on land, but the so-called 'reports', detailed chronicles that recount a battle to entertain and to move the readership, are especially noteworthy.

As noted by several scholars (Casarotto 2020, González Cruz 2002, Martínez Gil 2011), preaching (recorded in sermon books) played a central role in spreading information to congregations, the vast majority of whom were illiterate. The clergy were by no means impartial: numerous witnesses show to what extent they gave their support to one or other side, exploiting both the victories (which tended to be linked to the protection of a saint, a patron saint or the Virgin Mary) and the defeats (which prompted calls for public prayers). Examples of this religious dimension to the conflict (some speak of a 'religious war') can clearly be seen in the way the clergy on the Habsburg side imposed obedience to the cause, accusing the Bourbon camp of being in 'mortal sin', while Cardinal Luis Antonio Belluga (1662–1743), a supporter of Philip, dubbed the conflict a 'holy war'. Loyalty to king and nation often prevailed over membership in a particular religious order.

During the War of the Spanish Succession the literary and visual propaganda strategies outlined in the previous paragraphs found their expression largely in the various vernacular languages of Europe. Political power and dynastic legitimacy were discussed, debated and promoted in a broad spectrum of genres, lofty and popular alike, from historical and legal tracts, to engravings, pamphlets, gazettes, periodicals, satirical and laudatory poems, plays and songs. Aimed at different audiences according to the format employed, all these literary and artistic resources were exploited as vehicles of a political message, designed to confirm or subvert relations of power and authority (Pérez Picazo 1966 and Oury 2020: 387–408). In the course of the conflict and in its immediate aftermath Latin was also used as a medium of political communication through which victorious rulers and generals were exalted, enemies derided, and propaganda campaigns were effectively countered. Contemporary military episodes gave rise to a considerable amount of propaganda writing in Latin which praised the valour of Philip's or Charles's troops and helped raise support for both contenders' claims to the Spanish throne. Texts written in Latin with the same aim as those composed in the vernacular have, however, often been neglected, if not squarely dismissed, by historians of the War of the Spanish Succession. All too often there is an assumption that Latin has been used purely because of its status as 'the international language', in other words, just to reach a wider audience, with no recognition of factors other than this focus on a wider readership, for example a desire to contribute to a long-standing tradition of historiographical or poetic writing.[3] The first aim of the present study is therefore to raise awareness of the centrality of the learned language as an instrument of political, diplomatic and military power during the dynastic conflict and to highlight the varied roles that were accorded to Latin discourse at this very crucial juncture in European history. This will not come as a surprise to scholars of Neo-Latin literature, who have long considered the role and function of Latin as a propaganda instrument from the fifteenth to the twentieth century, particularly in times of military conflict in Europe and beyond (Enenkel, Laureys and Pieper 2012 and Waquet 2001).[4] But the range and richness of the Latin material produced by the War of the Spanish Succession are certainly noteworthy, especially when compared to other contemporary conflicts. Though the Thirty Years' War had elicited 'a plethora of [Latin] reactions in the epic and panegyric vein' (Seidel 2015: 453) and Latin would continue to serve a political function at the time of the Great Northern War between 1700 and 1721 (Dahlberg 2016), in the Austrian succession struggle of the 1740s (Geelhaar 2010) and during the Napoleonic wars (Krüssel 2011, 2015 and 2020), the breadth and variety of Latin texts produced during this Spanish hereditary feud remain unparalleled. Ranging from official documents, epic, satirical and panegyric poetry to defamatory pamphlets, coronation and funerary verse and prose, letters, historiographical and juridical tracts, medals as well as permanent and ephemeral architecture, this vast textual corpus has, however, gone almost unnoticed. That said, I do not claim to be the first to have examined Latin texts related to the War of the Spanish Succession. My task has been greatly facilitated by previous research on the subject and I duly acknowledge the debt to my sources throughout this volume. Yet, when attention has been paid to this corpus by literary critics, the analysis has been constrained by geographical boundaries (Coroleu and Paredes 2014), confined to specific case studies (Money 2006 and 2008) or subsumed into more general narratives (Klecker 2008).[5] This study constitutes an attempt to remedy some of these deficiencies by crossing academic boundaries. The aim here is not to examine Latin texts related to the dynastic conflict merely as literary artifacts, but to pay attention to the historical, intellectual and social contexts in which they were produced. In the following pages – above all, in the paragraphs focusing on issues of legitimacy – I have attempted to recognize the significance of the texts surveyed in the realm of historical praxis. The volume also highlights the nexus between eighteenth-century international politics and Latin culture.

The bulk of Latin texts under review in this book could be classified as occasional literature, mostly poetry specifically written for certain social occasions (Römer 1997 and De Beer 2014). Most Neo-Latin occasional poetry – and indeed many of the occasional texts examined in this monograph – is modelled on specific classical examples dealing with broadly similar occasions but we also find pieces which combine imitation of different literary frames, both ancient and modern. Long dismissed and overlooked as formulaic and lacking in originality, occasional poetry and prose have in recent times been recognised as having important literary, social and historical values. Scholars have called for a fuller appreciation of this vast body of literary compositions, 'which formed part of the very fabric of the Neo-Latin world' (De Smet 2014: 2, 1146), and this book would like to serve as a modest contribution to the rehabilitation of the genre. For my examination of this corpus – particularly for the texts discussed in the second and third chapters and in Appendix 3 – I have drawn on the approach favoured by Paul Gwynne and Bernhard Schirg in *The Economics of Poetry* (2018), which highlights the occasional poet's ability to react in a timely and rapid manner to contemporary events. It is to be hoped that the present volume will help rehabilitate a body of texts which, until very recently, has been largely absent from the canon of Neo-Latin studies. One further goal of this volume has been to retrieve the early eighteenth century from the marginal status within the historiography of Neo-Latin literature it has traditionally occupied.[6] Although scholarly interest in Neo-Latin literature has increased exponentially in recent years, there is still a tendency to restrict the study of Neo-Latin writing to works from the fifteenth, sixteenth and seventeenth centuries, certainly for those countries that generated a conspicuous amount of Latin writing at that time, such as Italy, France, and the German-speaking territories. Yet, while the Renaissance and the Baroque as cultural movements produced by far the greatest number of Latin texts, Neo-Latin literature was still being published well beyond the Enlightenment. Stretching the chronological scope of Neo-Latin studies must go hand in hand with geographical expansion. As my investigation demonstrates, in the early decades of the eighteenth century Latin was still a prestige language even in those countries that produced far fewer Latin works, thus confirming Gwynne and Schirg's dictum that 'we no longer talk of the "lost Renaissance of Latin literature", but instead of the "Empire of Latin"' (Gwynne & Schirg 2018: 7). A further conclusion to be drawn from the literary and historical material under review in this volume is that in areas such as eastern Europe, Britain, Scandinavia or the Iberian Peninsula Latin itself came to assume very similar functions to those it possessed in other parts of the continent at the time. My investigation endeavours to show how the dynastic feud at the heart of the War of the Spanish Succession produced impassioned and vital verse and prose in Latin both in central areas and on the periphery of Europe.

A final word on the methodological and structuring principles underlying the study which follows and the contents of the four chapters making up the book.

This volume explores the privileged position of Latin in the political discourse around the War of the Spanish Succession. Though a small amount of the manuscript and printed material discussed in the following pages has been known to scholars, most manuscripts and editions are presented here for the first time. One of the merits of this book is, I believe, to act as a point of departure for future work in the field. For this reason, and for the sake of bibliographic clarity, I have included a list of primary sources and provided full details of copies inspected. Likewise, because so many of my characters are less well-known, I have erred on the side of chronological precision (one may say punctiliousness) and given dates and brief biographical information for historical figures (except when the character is sufficiently famous). For the benefit of a wider academic audience, I have also provided English translations of practically all titles and passages in Latin and in any modern language.

The division of the material presented here into relevant and adequate genres is not an easy task. The boundaries of occasional literature are inevitably porous, and the circumstances for production of such works very often overlap. I have therefore favoured attention to the different settings for the commission, circulation and consumption of the manuscripts and editions under consideration – defining them by their uses as much as by their genres and contexts for production. With its constant recourse to the classical tradition, the Latin literature of the age broadly echoes the ancient world and its authors. The use of Latin by most eighteenth-century authors reviewed in this book is, for the most part, determined by a long-standing tradition of Latin writing. These are, ultimately, men who had been schooled in the reading, interpretation, translation and imitation of the classical and humanist authors considered suitable literary models for their own writings. To the best of my abilities, throughout these pages I have signalled allusions and instances in which a modern Latin writer may mirror an ancient or humanist source. But I have also tried to tread this path with caution, for, as persuasively argued by David Money, 'the issue of possible influences [of ancient and Renaissance texts on a later Neo-Latin writer] is something of a minefield' (1998: 13).

Chapter One explores the strategies developed across the dynastic divide to defend the dignity and legitimacy of Archduke Charles and the Duke of Anjou's rights to the Spanish throne. My investigation shows how, both in the early and final years of the conflict, Latin was employed by writers of encomiastic and vituperative poetry and oratory as well as authors of juridical and historiographical tracts on both sides to extol the glories of the Habsburg or Bourbon claimant and their own time-honoured aristocratic lineages. In Chapter Two I investigate literary recreations of some of the most relevant battles and sieges fought between 1701 and 1712 (to the best of my knowledge, no military episode after the Peace of Utrecht was the subject of a work in Latin verse or prose). This is a large corpus of poetic and prose texts whose generic diversity lends itself to being considered separately from other forms of occasional literature featured elsewhere in this volume (hence the length of the chapter). I study these writings both as an expression of martial triumphalism at the expense of political rivals and for their outstanding aesthetic values. The following chapter looks at the propaganda functions served by Latin writing arising from three interconnected contexts – court, church and academic institutions – during the War of the Spanish Succession. Here I look at the ways in which authors of nuptial, eulogistic and funerary verse and prose skilfully employed devices and motifs from ancient literary traditions for their own pressing political aims. Nowhere is this clearer than in the large corpus of Latin works composed to mark the coming of peace as the conflict was drawing to a close in 1712 and 1713. This chapter reveals how Latin poets and orators from both sides at the time of the Peace of Utrecht were instrumental in the realisation of international political decisions and in the construction of international political alliances. Chapter Four extends this general narrative and explores the unexpected ways in which Latin continued to function as an instrument of political propaganda on both sides of the dynastic feud after the end of the hostilities in the summer of 1715 and beyond, up until the death of Emperor Charles VI in October 1740. In this final chapter I first pay attention to a cluster of Latin texts written by Catalan scholars who settled in Italy and Austria after 1714. In addition, this chapter examines several contemporary examples of Neo-Latin antiquarian tracts in which the echo of the military campaigns from the dynastic conflict is still remarkably resonant.

1

Praise and Blame: Legitimizing the New Kings' Old Dynasties

On 1 October 1700 Archduke Charles of Austria celebrated his fifteenth birthday. To mark the occasion Emperor Leopold I's younger son was presented with a *genethliacon* ('a birthday poem') composed by Franz Ferdinand Scharff.[1] As well as portraying Charles as 'a new Hercules' (l. 7), the text praises his father's military triumphs over the Ottoman empire. The poet refers to Leopold I's victory at the Battle of Gran in Hungary and to the siege of Neuhäusel (Nové Zámky, in current-day Slovakia), both fought 'in the year in which you, Charles, were born', and closes his piece with an allusion to the siege of Pylos in the same year.[2] Continuity with a more distant past is also emphasized through repeated reference to the name of Charles, shared by the young archduke and one of his most illustrious ancestors – the author claims –, Emperor Charles V, thus bringing together the Spanish and Austrian branches of the House of Habsburg. Moreover, the poem prophesizes that Archduke Charles will achieve great deeds against his rivals as he shall 'not have to fear either the colour of the Moor or the radiance of the lilies [the symbol of the Bourbon dynasty]' (*Nec enim Maurorum color nec liliorum candor / tibi metuendus est*, ll. 43–4). Written only four weeks before Charles II of Spain's death and in the midst of hectic diplomatic negotiations between European powers over the Spanish succession, Scharff's encomiastic piece makes subtle connections between Charles's biography and the impending succession conflict. The text includes several references to France and Spain: with aid from St Remigius, the 'apostle of the Franks' whose feast day is celebrated precisely on 1 October, Charles's power shall stretch to the ends of the earth and the young prince 'shall row to the remote shores of the world' (*in dissitas orbis oras / remigaturum*, ll. 32–3). 'Nor', concludes the poet, 'shall the Frenchman hinder you from becoming Galician' (*Et non impediet Gallus / quin fias Galecianus*, ll. 45–6), for Charles shall rule over the land of St James, patron saint of Spain, whose shrine is in the Galician capital, Santiago de Compostela.[3]

Scharff's *genethliacon* is a good example of some of the strategies and literary motifs employed by political propagandists to extol the glories of the Habsburg or Bourbon lineages in the course of the War of the Spanish Succession. Such endeavours often used theological, genealogical and legal argumentation published in juridical and historiographical tracts to counter the claims presented by political opponents. But, as with Scharff's composition, poetry was also chosen as a medium for political propaganda in the feud about the Spanish succession because of its ability to persuade: as noted by Jensen and Corporaal in their examination of political verse during the War of the Austrian Succession, the rhetorical character of poetry 'made it apt to influence the public's opinion by combining rational argumentation with emotional appeal' (2016: 378). During the War of the Spanish Succession a significant body of this type of propagandist literature found its expression in the vernacular and has been duly examined by scholars.[4] But writing in Latin – whether conceptual or descriptive, panegyric or critical – was also published by thinkers, historians, jurists and poets on both sides of the dynastic feud in their attempts to defend the dignity and legitimacy of Archduke Charles's or the Duke of Anjou's rights to the Spanish throne. In this chapter I focus on three different contexts within the dynastic dispute, where Latin writing proved particularly prominent in this respect. In the first section I analyse texts related to Philip's and Charles's proclamations as legitimate kings of Spain in November 1700 and September 1703 respectively. This is followed by an examination of a sample of historical and juridical tracts produced by both sides in the early years of the conflict as each camp's propaganda machine generated more and more material. As will become apparent, several of these works were published in Naples, a contested territory which fell into Austrian hands in 1707. The final section, whose title echoes Virginia León Sanz's seminal biography of Archduke Charles (2003), will concentrate on the years 1711 and 1712, when – following his coronation as Emperor Charles VI – the dynastic rights of the Habsburg claimant to the Spanish throne were defended further in historical tracts on the House of Austria and in several coronation poems and orations on behalf of the new emperor published in Barcelona and Vienna as well as at various German courts.

Royal proclamations in the early years of the conflict

In 1707 the Barcelona-based printers Josep Llopis and Francesc Guasch published two broadsheets in Catalan purporting to describe fortunes told by two Gypsy girls for Philip, duke of Anjou, and Archduke Charles of Austria prior to their departure to take possession of the Spanish territories claimed by their respective dynasties after the death of Charles II.[5] Expressing wishes for a prosperous journey to the departing pretender, or foretelling impending disaster, these popular poetical compositions served a clearly propagandist function in praising the favoured candidate and deriding his political rival. Dressed up as prophecies and overtly satirical in tone, several more accomplished Latin counterparts to these two Catalan pieces of farewell (or *propemptica*, as they were referred to by rhetoricians) were also produced on both sides during the conflict.[6] These valedictory texts and other contemporary examples of Latin celebratory verse and prose written at the time of the proclamations of Philip V and Charles III are the subject of the following two sub-sections.

The proclamation of Philip V

On 16 November 1700 Louis XIV accepted Charles II's will and proclaimed Philip of Anjou king of Spain with the regnal name of Philip V (Figure 1). Accompanied by his two brothers, the dukes of Burgundy and Berry, the new king left Versailles for Spain on 4 December. Passing through Étampes, Poitiers and Mirambeau, he reached Irún, on the Spanish border, on 22 January 1701 and arrived in Madrid on 18 February.[7] The journey was celebrated not only in yearbooks (Torrione 2007: 33–4) but also in Latin verse in some of the towns the royal train visited. We know that at Bordeaux a certain Monsieur Saro composed a Latin poem for the Duke of Anjou (Levantal 1996: 132). Tutors and pupils from several Jesuit colleges en route to Spain also contributed Latin pieces in honour of the new king. At Orleans and Blois the royal guest was greeted by local schoolboys with short collections of occasional verse to mark his stay in both cities between 7 and 9, and 10 and 11 December 1700 respectively.[8] The best examples of celebratory poetry and prose in support of Philip recited in Jesuit refectories and halls are provided, however, by several Parisian colleges. On 31 December Balthasar Gibert (1662–1741), professor of Eloquence at the Collège Mazarin, delivered a speech 'on the transfer of the inheritance of the kingdoms of Spain', which was prefaced by a 60-line Sapphic ode written by his colleague Jean Le Comte, *professor humanarum litterarum*.[9] At the Collège de Louis-le-Grand Father André Le Camus celebrated the union of the two Bourbon crowns in another Latin speech.[10] A booklet entitled 'A congratulation from the Muses at the Royal Collège Louis-le-Grand for Philip V, Catholic king, as he left for Spain' includes pieces by several teachers from the college, among which we find a short *vaticinium* ('a prophecy') in verse and a 48-line iambic ode for Philip 'leaving for Spain' (*in Hispaniam abeunti*) by Professor Jean Commire, SJ (1625–1702).[11] As with many of these pieces of valedictory verse and prose, Commire's poems go beyond the particular episode for which they were composed, namely Philip's departure for Madrid in December 1700, and are primarily designed to endorse Charles II's will and celebrate the accession of the new Spanish monarch. The prophecy foretells 'a sweet and soft yoke' for the Spaniards (*dulce ac molle iugum*, l. 8) but has words of warning for anyone who might oppose Philip's rule. In the ode the new king's rights to the Spanish crown are asserted, first and foremost, on the basis of Charles II's will: 'Declared heir by Charles's final will and testament, you now claim that honour, conferred on you by the law of blood, which your grandfather Louis and your father the Dauphin had promised you long ago' ([*Quod decus*] *avusque Lodoix atque Delphinus pater / olim tibi spondederant: id sanguinis nunc iure delatum obtines, / heres supremis Caroli / scriptus tabellis*, ll. 3–7). Significantly, however, the ascent of the Bourbon dynasty to the Spanish throne is further justified through the adoption of Habsburg Imperial imagery by Philip and the fabrication of a genealogy going back to the so-called Catholic Monarchs, Ferdinand and Isabella, and to their grandson Emperor Charles V (Charles I of Spain):

> *Conscende solium, quo tot et belli artibus*
>   *pacisque studiis incliti*
> *sedere reges: Ferdinandus barbaro*
>   *exuere Granatam iugo*
> *ultrice dextera natus et coniux viro*
>   *suppar virili pectore*
> *Isabella, quique fabulosas Herculis*
>   *ultra ire metas gestiens*
> *signis volucres iunxit Ausonias suis,*
>   *nulli secundus Caesarum*
>
> ll. 15–24

['Ascend the throne on which so many kings renowned in the art of war and the pursuit of peace have sat: Ferdinand, born to free Granada from the barbarian yoke with his avenging hand, and his wife Isabella, almost equal to a man, with a manly spirit, and he who, second to none of the Caesars, whilst longing to go beyond the celebrated columns of Hercules, joined the Ausonian birds to his standards'].[12]

At the Collège de Louis-le-Grand – where, as documented by Compère and Pralon–Julia (1992) in their reconstruction of Latin school exercises around 1720, contemporary events were considered suitable subject matter for verse

Figure 1 *Le Roy accepte le Testament de feu Roy Catholique Charles II et declare Monseigneur le Duc d'Anjou Roy d'Espagne sous le nom de Philipe V à Versailles le XI Novembre MDCC*, 1701, BnF, Estampes, Hennin 6667.

composition – loyalty to crown and country was also expressed through the communally-written *Musae rhetorices*. These poetic anthologies produced by students of the Rhetoric class (with plenty of help from their teachers) provide 'a window into the eighteenth-century Parisian Jesuit schoolroom' (Haskell 2003: 323). Two editions appeared in 1701 alone, and one of these collaborative volumes, *Musae iuveniles rhetorum* ('Youthful muses of the Rhetoric class'), was entirely devoted to celebrating Philip's departure for Spain in Latin (and, in three instances, Greek) verse.[13] The collection is divided into several thematically arranged sections. Some groups of poems praise Louis XIV's perceived virtues: his affection for the Duke of Anjou (pp. 1–18) or his political and diplomatic skills in securing the throne of Spain for his grandson, which should bring peace across Europe (pp. 28–45). Other sections depict the joyful union between the kingdoms of Spain and France, now ruled by the same dynasty (pp. 77–84). Further clusters chronicle the royal journey. In a handful of poems in hexameters, for example, older (*veterani*) and younger (*novi*) boys beg Zephyrus, the gentlest of the winds, to grant the departing king a propitious journey (pp. 19–27). The volume also includes eight pieces making up 'a prophecy by the river Garonne' (*Garumnae vaticinium*, pp. 52–64), which the royal train crossed before entering Aquitaine on its way to Spain. Seven pieces in elegiacs (pp. 84–9) describe an episode on the Spanish border where the new monarch bid his brothers farewell and was symbolically greeted by the Latinity of Hispania – best represented by Seneca, Lucan and Martial (pp. 98–9). The *Musae iuveniles rhetorum* concludes on a self-referential note with a handful of epigrams, iambics and elegiacs in which Mercury is called upon to deliver this broad collection of poetic voices to Madrid and to the wider world (pp. 107–27).

In Madrid, Philip of Anjou was proclaimed King of Spain on 24 November 1700. In the ensuing months, local celebrations were held in many towns across the Spanish empire, which – as convincingly argued by González Cruz (2009b: 198–202) – were utilized by Bourbon propaganda writers to show that political legitimacy had been conferred on Philip V by his own subjects. In this context prophecies and exegetical texts were also employed as a powerful propaganda weapon by supporters of the young king (González Cruz 2002: 107–12 and Bouza 2008: 182–3). As an example, the anonymous author – probably of Catalan origin – of the *Coronatio Philipi [sic] quinti, Hispaniae regis, ab auctore quodam veridico conscripta et in partes digesta* ('The coronation of Philip V, king of Spain, described by a certain truthful author and divided into several parts') chronicled Philip's ascension to the throne of Spain and hailed the new sovereign, comparing him to King David.[14] In accordance with a clause in Charles II's will, in which the new king was called upon to swear to maintain the laws and customs of the territories within his new kingdom, Philip V summoned the Castilian parliament, or *Cortes*, in May 1701 at San Jerónimo el Real in Madrid. In mid-July he convened the Catalan parliament, or *Corts*, and on 3 October he swore to uphold the Catalan Constitutions in a ceremony held in Barcelona. On his way to Catalonia the king had visited Saragossa, where he swore to observe Aragonese privileges and rights on 17 September (Pérez Álvarez 2012: 40–2). The Jesuit College of Saint Vincent Martyr in nearby Huesca marked the occasion with the public recitation and subsequent publication of a *Festiva, gratulatoria proclamatio* by Juan Miguel Estarrués, *magister et doctor Sertorianus ac tanti Collegii semper alumnus et collega* ('Sertorian graduate and doctor, and forever an alumnus and fellow of such a great college').[15] A literary recreation of the festivities held in Saragossa, the speech acclaims Philip as the legitimate successor to the Spanish branch of the Habsburg line (*Venit Philippus ... Venit, vidit, vicit Caesarum Caesar, haud dubie Carolum quintum imagine referens, a secundo vocatus* – 'Philip came ... The Caesar of Caesars came, saw and conquered, bringing back with his image Charles V, summoned by Charles II', sign. A2v). The loyalty sworn by Aragon to the new monarch and the oath the kingdom received from Philip V in return are highlighted through careful choice of vocabulary. Philip 'is fortified with the applause and the solemn promises of the Aragonese people', who show their fidelity and obedience. And 'he stands by the sacred laws of justice [the Latin *Fori* could be interpreted as a reference to the 'Fuero de Jaca', the origin of Aragonese general law]'.[16] The text praises the young king for choosing to visit Saragossa (the speech begins with the sentence *Non venit invite Philippus* – 'Philip did not come unwillingly') and thus helping to dispel rumours about the disquiet his accession to the throne was said to have caused in several territories across Spain (*Venit Philippus, fracta omnino ingrati rumoris cuspide* – 'Philip came, once the sharp edge of ungrateful talk had been blunted', sign. A2v). Estarrués also alludes to Philip's decision to postpone his official entry into Saragossa, opting instead to continue his journey to Catalonia to meet his future wife Maria Luisa Gabriella of Savoy (1688–1714):

> *Venit Philippus; mansit at augustae urbis placidiori limine captus. Ultra protendere nitens, ut Sabaudicae Margaritae augustius ditaretur dotibus, lente carpit iter, quasi indicendi amoris obsessus remora. Hic poeta: 'nec pes ire potest; intra quoque viscera saxum est'*
>
> sign. A3r

['Philip came but remained on the more pleasant threshold of the venerable city. Although keen to proceed further, so that he may with more dignity be enriched by the dowry of Margarite of Savoy [*sic*], he set off slowly, as if beset by some obstacle to proclaiming his love. As the poet says [Ovid, *Metamorphoses* 6.309]: "nor can his foot move; his internal organs too are turned to stone"'].[17]

The reasons for such a postponement were, in fact, far less idyllic. Pérez Álvarez (2012: 40–2) authoritatively argues that the alarming and ill-grounded reports of a possible hostile reception written by the viceroy, the Marqués de Camarasa, dissuaded Philip from staging an official entry into Saragossa. The author concludes his speech by encouraging Philip to return to the city together with his wife (who in fact came to Saragossa herself, unescorted, to open the Aragonese parliament in May 1702).

As with territories elsewhere under Spanish rule, in Sicily and Naples the viceroys followed the existing protocol and Philip V was also proclaimed king shortly after he left Versailles for Spain in December 1700. In Palermo the date chosen for the occasion by the Duke of Veragua was 30 January 1701.[18] The festivities included a grand parade, profuse decoration on the façade of the Jesuit college and the erection in the Piazza Marina of a marble statue sculpted by Giambattista Ragusa bearing four Latin inscriptions. The first text presented Charles II and Philip V as links in the same legendary and genealogical chains, and the Bourbon claimant was once again exalted as the Habsburg king's legitimate heir:

Atlanti Hesperio Gallicanus Hercules iure sufficitur.
    CAROLO II
Hispaniarum rege piissimoque nuper emortuo,
    serenissimus Andegavensis Dux
    Carolo vicinior sanguine
ab eodem regnorum institutus est haeres.
Hinc cum primum rex salutaretur Panormi
    die 30 Ian. 1701
    satis auspicato PHILIPPI V nomine,
    S. P. Q. P.
hoc illi regale simulacrum erexit
Europae quieti et regni huius felicitati
    dicatum

['The French Hercules is rightly chosen to take the place of the Spanish Atlas. After the recent death of Charles II, most devout king of Spain, the most serene Duke of Anjou, closer to Charles by blood, was declared heir by Charles himself. Hence, as soon as he was proclaimed king in Palermo on 30 January 1701 assuming the duly auscpicious name of Philip V, the senate and the people of

Palermo erected for him a royal image, dedicated to peace in Europe and to the happiness of this kingdom']. [19]

In Naples celebrations on 6 January 1701 had been equally lavish, as recorded by several contemporary reports in Italian (Mínguez Cornelles et al. 2014: 126, n. 250 and 130, n. 265). A few months after the proclamation of the new king, however, a group of local noblemen in favour of Archduke Charles attempted to assassinate the viceroy, Luis Francisco de la Cerda y Aragón (1660–1711), ninth duke of Medinaceli, and occupy the Castel Nuovo but the conspiracy was discovered and foiled by the Spanish authorities.[20] Though this anti-Bourbon revolt of September 1701 was not of much consequence, Philip V, encouraged by Louis XIV, decided to visit his Italian possessions to shore up his position and, on 8 April 1702, he set sail for Italy from Barcelona. Eight days later the king landed in Naples, the first Spanish monarch to do so since Charles V in 1536, and on 20 May he made his official entry into the city.[21] Philip's voyage to Naples was commemorated with three medals, on which ancient gods and classical references play a prominent role, emphasizing the beneficial effects the new monarch's arrival may have had on the realm (Sabatier 2007: 77–8). One of these medals represents King Philip V of Spain on the obverse while on the reverse Neptune is featured crowned, standing on a seashell in a calm sea, in front of a distant view of Italy and Sicily, with the legend SIC CVNCTVS PELAGI CECIDIT FRAGOR ('Thus ceased all the tumult of the sea'), reproducing a line from Virgil (*Aeneid* 1.154).

The proclamation of Charles III

Between November 1700 and April 1702, before the war became a serious threat, Philip's proclamation and subsequent departure for Spain, as well as his arrival in Madrid and Naples, were lauded in France, Spain and Italy chiefly as a celebration of the Bourbon dynasty, devoid of any reference to a political or military conflict with a rival pretender to the throne. In contrast, Archduke Charles's declaration as Spanish king at the Favorita, the Imperial summer residence outside Vienna, on 12 September 1703 and his departure for the Spanish battlefield one week later prompted more outspoken responses across the various media used by the Habsburg propaganda machine.[22]

Prepared 'as a reply to the medals which had been struck at Versailles for Philip in 1700' (Sabatier 2007: 75), a Viennese medal minted to mark the occasion of Charles's elevation as king of Spain bears Aeneas's statement to the Sybil in

Virgil's epic, NON INDEBITA POSCO / REGNA MEIS FATIS ('I only ask for the realms due to me by fate', Aen. 6.66–7), thereby presenting his claim as unequivocally legitimate. The medal also features the following inscription, further endorsing the legitimate transfer of power from Leopold and Joseph to Charles: A PATRE ET FRATRE AVGVSTISSIMIS CESSIONE FACTA XII SEPTEMBRIS HISPANIAM PETIT 1703 ('He leaves for Spain, after the concession from his most worthy father and brother on 12 September 1703').

Charles's departure for the Iberian Peninsula was further commemorated in several Latin poems of farewell composed for the occasion. As an example, the chronogrammatic collection *Austriacum vale et Hispanicum ave* ('An Austrian farewell and a Spanish greeting') by Engelbert Bischoff, SJ (1654–1711) includes short auspicious pieces purported to have been written by Charles's parents, his brother and sister-in-law, or to have been contributed by the House of Austria and Mariazell, a Marian shrine of particular significance for the Habsburgs, which Charles had visited following his elevation to the Spanish throne.[23] Several other poems are composed on behalf of the nations which made up the Grand Alliance (England, the United Provinces of the Low Countries and the Holy Roman Empire). Having recently joined the anti-Bourbon coalition, Portugal proudly declares:

> aCCeDo parIter IMperatorI. = 1703
> Ingenitum est Gallo promissis iungere falso,
>   post initam pacem belli animare facem.
> Hinc iustae accedo concluso foedere causae,
>   ut redeant domino debita regna suo
>
> Bischoff 1703: 2

['I also support the emperor (in 1703). The deceitful Frenchman is congenitally bound to make promises, to fan the flames of war after initially suing for peace. Hence, I support this just cause with the signing of a pact, so that the kingdoms due to him may return to their lord'].

The vocabulary employed throughout the volume clearly aims to depict Charles's rights to the Spanish throne as lawful and to present the monarch as the 'true, legitimate and rightful heir' (*verus, legitimus et de iure heres*) to Charles II. The tone is encomiastic but also aggressive. The following riddle (*Votum aenigmaticum*) shows the determination and confidence with which the Habsburg dynasty claims to have entered war with France:

> Dum decimus quartus quintum stabilire laborat,
>   tertius ut regnet, primus utrumque fugat.
>   Oedipus solvit aenigma:

Dum Rex Galliae Ludovicus decimus quartus Ducem Andegavensem Philippum quintum stabilire laborat, ut regnet Carolus tertius augustissimus Leopoldus primus utrumque fugabit

p. 3

['Whilst the fourteenth strives to establish the fifth, the first chases both away so that the third may reign. Oedipus solves the riddle: whilst Louis XIV, king of France, strives to establish the Duke of Anjou as Philip V, the most august Leopold I will chase both away so that Charles III may reign'].

As recorded by contemporary press reports, on 18 September 1703 a farewell ceremony in honour of the newly declared king of Spain was hosted by the university authorities in Vienna.[24] To mark Charles's departure the following day, they brought out two Latin volumes, one comprising the official valedictory oration together with a rather conventional *propempticon* and a congratulatory chronogram, and a second one featuring a collection of poems edited by T. A. Hunoldt.[25] It is the latter on which I would now like to focus my attention.

Prefaced by short preliminary remarks in prose, Hunoldt's volume includes seven pieces in different metres and poetic forms. Charles's departure is immortalized in three of the texts: a Sapphic greeting ode, an *Acroama triumphale ad Hispaniam* ('A triumphant entertainment for Spain') in hexameters built on the biblical verse *Ecce rex tuus venit tibi* ('Behold, thy king cometh unto thee', Matt. 21.5) and a chronogrammatic congratulatory poem based on the words *DIVI, VIDI, VICI, LVXI, DVXI* ('I enriched, I saw, I conquered, I shone, I led'), the letters of which, when added together as Roman numerals, come to 1703. The other four compositions attack the Bourbon claimant: two prophecies predict Philip's imminent fall and in a short invective the Duke of Anjou is compared to the cynical philosopher Zoilus (*c.* 400 – *c.* 320 BCE), as both suffer from bouts of rage (*rabies*). The remaining anti-French piece, written in elegiac distichs and entitled *Epigramma ioco-serium de Philippo quinto biennali Hispanorum rege super puro hoc chronographico: IVI, VICI, DVXI LIXIVIUM* = 1703 ('A humorous-serious epigram on Philip V, two-year king of Spain, based on this pure chronogram: "I advanced, I conquered, I brought lye"'), is doubtless the most ingenious poem included in Hunoldt's collection. Its title seems to indicate that at least some of the satirical content of the poem derives from a contrast with the earlier 1703 chronogram about Charles; whereas the Archduke proudly states: 'I lead'(*duxi*), Philip can only claim: 'I brought soap' (*duxi lixivium*). I reproduce the text here in full:

Quam pulchri gressus plantarum, Galle, tuarum!
    Laetus ut ivisti nunc male pulsus abis.

> *Scilicet ivisti nec iure nec omine fultus;*
>   *hinc summo pulsus iure Philippus abis.*
> *Iure Philippus abis; Carolos haec regna tuentur,*
>   *his iustum caelum iustaque causa favet.*
> *Non bene post Carolum quadrat regnare Philippum,*
>   *Carolus Austriacis ius soliumque dedit.*
> *Vicisti regnum sceleratis fraudibus utens,*
>   *quas duplici poena nunc malecaute luis.*
> *Vicisti gravido nummorum pondere mentes,*
>   *non expugnasti, dum tua fata volunt.*
> *En duplicem poenam: nunc regno pelleris et quos*
>   *lucrabare animos, vota fidemque negant.*
> *Nam male conveniunt nec in una sede morantur,*
>   *Gallus et Hispanus, ceu canis atque felis.*
> *Lixivium regni duxisti, Galle, per oras:*
>   *sed tibi lixivium Carolus acre dabit.*
> *Lixivium dabit, Hispano si cedere regno*
>   *coget et ad propriam turpe redire domum.*
> *Hic te lixivio poteris sine fine lavare;*
>   *Carolus interea rex novus est et erit*
>
>   sign. D2v

['How pretty your footsteps are, Frenchman! You marched in happily, but now you leave badly defeated. It is clear you marched in neither by right nor supported by any good omen. You leave here, Philip, expelled by the highest right; you leave, Philip, rightfully. These kingdoms support those called Charles; rightful heaven and a rightful cause favour them. It is not fitting for Philip to reign after Charles. Charles [II of Spain] gave the Austrians the right and the throne. You conquered the realm by means of wicked deceits which you are now atoning for with a double punishment. You conquered minds with large amounts of money, but as long as the Fates wish it you have not been able to persuade them. Behold the double punishment: you will now be driven out of the realm and the souls you profited from deny you their prayers and their loyalty. For the French and Spanish do not get along well and do not care to live under the same roof, just like cats and dogs do not. You brought lye, Frenchman, into the kingdom, but Charles will give you bitter lye. He will give you lye, if he forces you to withdraw from the kingdom of Spain and to beat a shameful retreat to your own home. There you will be able to wash yourself with lye without end; in the meantime, Charles is and will be the new king'].

The entire epigram depends on stereotypical contrasts between Habsburg probity and Bourbon deceitfulness, a common theme widely used by Allied pamphleteers. The central claim is that whilst Philip should never have lawfully ruled, Charles's rights to the Spanish throne were upheld by his ancestors and, above all, by God. The poem ridicules the Duke of Anjou's alleged heroism, exploiting a play on words on the famous phrase *Veni, vidi, vici* ('I came, I saw, I conquered') attributed to Caesar (Suetonius, *Caes.* 37). As with the Roman general and statesman, Philip triumphed in Spain and conquered the minds of his subjects, though only through fraud and bribery. The author mocks Philip further: on his advance into Spain, he brought *lixivium* ('lye') with him, a word very close in sound to the delicate *lilium* ('lily'), the symbol of the Bourbon dynasty. Lye is used in making soap, so it will help the Frenchman wash himself at home on returning from his shameful (and perhaps fetid) withdrawal.[26] One may conclude that Hunoldt's puns on Philip confirm John Gilmore's dictum that 'a conceit which would soon have been stretched thin over a page or two in prose, manages well enough over a few elegiac couplets' (2008: 109).

After an official reception with Queen Anne at Windsor Castle in England on 9 January 1704, Charles set sail for the Iberian Peninsula and landed in Lisbon on 7 March. As noted by Sabatier (2007: 84), his arrival in the Portuguese capital was commemorated with a medal bearing yet another line from Virgil's *Aeneid*. Here the reference is to Rome's imperial mission, memorably articulated by Aeneas' father Anchises: *PARCERE SVBIECTIS ET DEBELLARE SVPERBOS* ('To spare the humble and to subdue the proud', 6.854). Meanwhile, in Vienna, the end of Charles's voyage and the beginning of military operations in Spain also inspired the collection *Hispania terque quaterque beata in septem Austriacis regibus* ('O thrice, four times happy Spain in seven Austrian kings!'), a biographical synopsis in verse of the six Spanish kings of the House of Austria who reigned before Charles III together with a versified account of his journey to Spain.[27] The book displays all the hallmarks of a *Promotionsschrift*, a congratulatory volume written on the occasion of a student's graduation from a Jesuit university in the German-speaking world (most notably, in Vienna). Distributed among relatives attending the graduation ceremony, some of whom might feature in the *tabula gratulatoria* at the end of the volume, these books in user-friendly octavo or duodecimo format include speeches or poems purported in some cases to have been presented as school exercises by pupils of the Gymnasium's final class of Rhetoric or Poetry.[28] In the last piece for Charles (consisting of 170 lines in irregular metre) events from the ruler's biography – his birth and early life at court, his emotional departure from Vienna following his elevation, his visit to Queen Anne and the joy with which the archduke was greeted on his arrival in Lisbon – are intertwined with proclamations of Charles's legitimacy as Spanish king, praise for the British-Dutch-Habsburg alliance and explicit threats to the usurper Philip, whose treason will be avenged. References to ancient history are not uncommon: towards the end of the poem (l. 160) the Bourbon claimant is dismissively compared to 'the equestrian Sejanus' (20 BCE–31 CE), the prefect of the Praetorian Guard who usurped Tiberius's authority in Rome and was finally executed by the emperor.[29]

Though some of the texts under review in the preceding paragraphs were produced in the classroom and could be regarded as part of the literary training in academic institutions, they are far from devoid of interest. The literary talents they exhibit were deployed to celebrate the Duke of Anjou's and Archduke Charles's proclamations and departures as well as emphasize loyalty to a particular ruler, and thereby to influence public opinion. Latin authors writing in support of Philip V or Charles III presented them as legitimate kings of Spain on the grounds of dynastic inheritance or international endorsement from other European powers. Papal support was, for example, adduced first by Philip and subsequently by Charles as proof of their divine right to rule over the Spanish territories.[30] Portugal's incorporation into the Grand Alliance in May 1703 and involvement in the dynastic war were also defended by António Rodrigues da Costa (1656–1732) in his *Iusta Lusitanorum arma pro vindicanda Hispanorum libertate Gallico dominatu oppressa asserendoque Hispaniae imperio* ('Just arms of the Portuguese to lay legal claim to the freedom of the Spaniards oppressed by French domination and to protect the Spanish empire', Lisbon, 1704), a text dedicated to Charles III which was in turn refuted by pro-Philip propagandists (Cardim 2009: 248). Moreover, the Bourbon propaganda campaign invoked Charles II's will and claimed that the transition of power had been conducted in a peaceful manner.[31] This claim was in turn countered by Allied pamphleteers, who declared Charles II's will invalid and accused Philip of having usurped the Spanish throne.[32] As the following section will show, neither side stood, however, on entirely firm ground and the genealogical, historical and juridical arguments provided by either party could be all too easily refuted by their political rivals.

Questions of legitimacy

Leaving aside the issue of Charles II's will, both lineages involved in the War of the Spanish Succession could claim uninterrupted bloodlines to the last Spanish Habsburg monarch and could therefore defend their own candidate's rights to the Spanish throne (see the genealogical tree in Appendix 1). For those in the Bourbon camp, the Duke of Anjou's claim to the Spanish crown was as a hereditary possession from his grandmother Maria Theresa of Spain (1638–83), the daughter of Philip IV and his first wife, Elisabeth of France (1602–44), who married Louis XIV in 1660. For their part, shortly after Charles II's acceptance of Philip of Anjou as his sole heir, Imperial apologists sought to demonstrate that the succession should have reverted to the surviving and senior branch of the Habsburg family and declared Archduke Charles of Austria a direct descendant of the late monarch. Two juridical treatises published in the Holy Roman Empire in or around 1701 are here worthy of note: the anonymous *Synopsis quorundam iurium* [sic] *Austriacorum in successionem Hispanicam* ('A summary of several Austrian laws on the Spanish succession') and Johannes Friedrich von Seilern's *Ius Austriacum in monarchiam Hispanicam assertum* ('The Austrian legal claim regarding the Spanish monarchy').[33] Seilern builds his defence of Charles's right of succession on the grounds that the archduke's father Emperor Leopold I had married Charles II's older full sister Margaret Theresa of Spain (1651–73). Moreover, to counter the Bourbon claim of legitimacy via Philip's grandmother, he invokes the principle of agnatic seniority, which debars the women of the dynasty and their descendants from the succession, by arguing that 'not long ago French jurists, having endeavoured by means of various assertions to completely exclude all women not only from the throne of France but also from any of its dominions that may have been handed down to the kings of France via the female line, vehemently defended the male succession of the royal family according to the genealogical lines'.[34] With help from a broad range of supporting documents in Latin, French and Spanish appended to the main text, the anonymous author of the *Synopsis* also resorts to genealogical, historical and juridical arguments. He claims that Emperor Leopold takes precedence over Philip because Leopold's sister (and therefore Archduke Charles's aunt) Mariana of Austria (1634–96) had been Charles II's mother:

> *Carolo quinto, seu si mavis, Hispanica in causa primo, post Philippum secundum, tertium et quartum successit Carolus secundus beatissimae memoriae, nuper defunctus. Hic matre Maria Anna gravisus est, iam dicti Ferdinandi tertii filia et Leopoldi sorore, duplicato consanguinitatis vinculo, si et proximum maternum genus et avitam quoque propaginem Austriacam in adiunctis sub n. 3 et n. 4 genealogiis intueamur, cum Caesare Leopoldo colligatus*
>
> sign. A2v

['Charles V – or, if you prefer, in the Spanish reasoning Charles I – and subsequently Philip II, Philip III and Philip IV were succeeded by Charles II of most blessed memory, recently deceased. His mother was Mariana, daughter of the aforementioned Ferdinand III and sister of Leopold. He was connected to Emperor Leopold through a double bond of consanguinity, if we consider both the nearest descendant from his mother and the ancestral Austrian progeny in the appended genealogical tables 3 and 4'].

Furthermore, the anonymous author of the *Synopsis* believes that Philip V's claim to the Spanish crown could also be challenged by invoking other sources. To that effect, the text includes a discussion in intricate detail of several articles from the Treaty of the Pyrenees signed between France and Spain on 7 November 1659 as well as Philip IV's will written six years later (sign. A3r–B1r). Reproduced in an appendix at the end of the text, all these documents are presented to show that Philip's grandmother Maria Theresa of Spain had been forced to renounce her claims to the Spanish throne in perpetuity, thus invalidating the Duke of Anjou's alleged succession rights to the Spanish throne.

The dynastic dispute was also the subject of intense debate in the Spanish possessions in Italy, chiefly in the kingdom of Naples. Although Philip V remained in Naples only until 2 June 1702, promptly moving to northern Italy to monitor the course of military operations against Prince Eugene of Savoy, the new king was careful to forge a personal link between himself and the realm. Indeed, later that year he petitioned Pope Clement XI (r. 1700–21) – albeit unsuccessfully – to have St Januarius, patron saint of Naples, made co-patron of the Spanish monarchy, in a move which 'must be interpreted in the belligerent context of the War of the Spanish Succession and, particularly, as proof of the support of vast territories of the Crown of Aragon to Archduke Charles of Austria' (Suárez Golán 2017: 77). During the early years of Philip's reign, the Neapolitan political and intellectual elites were eager to display their loyalty to the new monarch through a well-orchestrated propaganda campaign, with which they endeavoured to legitimize Philip's ascension to the Spanish throne and thus guarantee political stability at home. Initially, however, there was some dissent. As mentioned earlier, in 1701, shortly after Philip's proclamation, several nobles took part in the so-called Conspiracy of Macchia, a short-lived uprising that aimed to wrest control of the kingdom from the Spanish viceroy. The revolt failed in a matter of days, but the conspirators, from their exile in Vienna, justified their action by citing their fear that Naples would ultimately fall into French hands if Philip were to succeed to the Spanish throne (Robertson 2005: 159). The situation is further complicated because Naples was a feudal possession of the papacy: Philip V could not therefore use the title of king without authorization from Clement XI, so the Spanish monarch turned to leading intellectuals and lawyers for the legal defence of his claims. Accordingly, and coinciding with the beginning of military operations on the Iberian Peninsula in October 1702 and the proclamation of Archduke Charles as Charles III of Spain eleven months later, a cluster of Latin texts across a broad variety of literary genres and forms were published in Naples, through which the Bourbon monarchy strove to uphold Philip's claims to be the true legitimate and incontestable Spanish king.[35]

The controversy over the Spanish succession also involved the learned academy created by Viceroy Medinaceli in 1698 (Stone 1997: 93–109). The viceroy himself commissioned members of his academy to prepare 'vigorous refutations of the traditional claim of the papacy to grant the kingdom by investiture' (Robertson 2005: 158). Though not a formal member of the institution, the jurist Serafino Biscardi (1643–1711) participated in some of the activities undertaken by the academy (Ricuperati 1968). One of the staunchest supporters of Philip's investiture, he contributed an *Epistola pro augusto Hispaniarum monarcha Philippo V* ('A letter on behalf of Philip V, august king of Spain'), in which Philip's right of succession was defended 'under Spanish, Roman, and Neapolitan law, with supporting reference to the authority of Cujas, Hobbes, Grotius, and Pufendorf' (Robertson 2005: 160).[36] Biscardi often lets his sources speak for themselves, quoting them at length. The principal target of the opening sections of his epistle is the aforementioned principle of agnatic seniority: drawing on historical precedents, in the section entitled *In regnis nulla agnationis causa* Biscardi adduces the absence of a rule of female exclusion in Spanish public law (Biscardi 1703: 15–26).[37] He also objects to those who declared that Charles II was of unsound mind and that his decisions at the time of drafting his testament had been influenced by agents on behalf of the French monarch (pp. 58–60). Against the claim that Philip V's grandmother had renounced the Spanish throne for her descendants as part of her marriage contract, he devotes the second part of his work to demonstrate how Maria Theresa's renunciation was void since the large dowry of 500,000 écus d'or, which the Spanish monarchy was due to have rendered in return had never been paid (pp. 68–73).

A legal defence of Philip's claims by Biscardi's fellow Neapolitan Muzio Giuseppe Verderosa in his *Philippi V Catholici regis Neapolis ac totius Hesperiae in imperium de successione* ('On the succession of Catholic king Philip V to the rule of Naples and the whole of Spain') was published in Naples in December 1703, only a few weeks after Charles's proclamation in Vienna. Verderosa's tract is in two parts, with a first section entirely devoted to the succession to Charles II of Spain and a second part in which the controversial issue of Philip V's investiture as king of Naples is examined.[38] In the first section, Verderosa justifies Philip's succession on genealogical and historical grounds. He does not dispute the fact that Margaret Theresa of Spain was Philip IV's daughter but claims that the Spanish infanta was from the king's second marriage, to Mariana of Austria, thus making her the elder full sister – not half-sister – of Charles II. As *Primus rex Christianus et acerrimus defensor fidei* ('Foremost Christian king and most ardent defender of the faith', Verderosa 1703: 67), Philip V was closest to the last Habsburg ruler of Spain and therefore took precedence over Leopold, head of the House of Austria:

> *si idem augustissimus Caesar velit cum rege nostro Philippo concurrere, etiam hic eum antecellit ac vincit, nam, uti ex dicto Delphino ortum habens, licet in quarto reperiatur gradu (iure dictante civili, quod in feudis attenditur) dicto Carolo regi, attamen uti ex linea recta descendens dicti regis Philippi quarti, immo uti ex primogenita descendens, iste erit Hispani imperii successor legitimus; Caesar quippe nullo modo potest concurrrere in illo per lineam dicti regis Philippi quarti*
>
> pp. 55–6

['Should the most august Emperor wish to enter into competition with our king Philip, he will be surpassed and defeated by the latter. Bearing in mind that Philip is the son of the Dauphin, even though – as dictated by civil law, which applies in fiefs – he is fourth in the line of succession to the aforementioned King Charles, he nevertheless descends in direct line from the aforementioned King Philip IV, indeed from the firstborn woman [Maria Theresa of Spain, Charles II's sister], and so shall be the legitimate successor of the Spanish empire: the Emperor cannot in any way enter into competition with him through the genealogical line of the aforementioned Philip IV'].

In the section related to Philip's investiture, Verderosa seeks to tread a careful path: on the one hand, he presents Philip as natural lord of Naples and rejects French claims to the kingdoms of Naples and Sicily, and yet, on the other, he is at great pains not to undermine the French and Spanish alliance which had triggered the dynastic dispute. Philip's investiture as king of Naples is, rather conveniently, granted by the Pope:

> *cum non modo tacite, sed expresse quoque per sanctissimum dominum nostrum Clementem XI Sanctae Romanae Ecclesiae Pontificem maximum praedictus rex noster Philippus fuit cum huius regni diademate investitus, utpote legitimus Neapolitani regni successor ac dominus; quodque hoc ita sit, elucidator; nam mortuo rege Carolo II statimque praedicta sua aequa cognita dispositione, non obiiciente Pontifice, immo acquiescente, fuit investitus per excellentissimum*

> D. Ludovicum de la Zerda y Aragona Ducem Medinae Coeli, tunc dignissimum huius regni proregem, nomine dicti regis Philippi, totius regni sumpta possessione, recepit vassallorum obedientiam, claves aliaque gerens, quae possessionem indicarunt et haec dicitur tacita investitura iam data
>
> pp. 91–2

['For our aforementioned King Philip was crowned with the diadem of this kingdom, not only tacitly but also clearly through our holiest lord Pope Clement XI, Supreme Pontiff of the Holy Roman Church, as legitimate successor and lord of the kingdom of Naples, and that this was the case must now be clarified. After the death of King Charles II, immediately after his aforementioned just disposition was known, without any objections from the Pontiff, rather with his acquiescence, he was crowned through the most excellent Luis de la Cerda y Aragón, Duke of Medinaceli and then worthiest viceroy of this kingdom, in the name of said King Philip. Having taken possession of the entire kingdom, he received the obedience of his subjects, bearing the keys and other objects which declared such possession and so was this tacit investiture said to have been granted'].

As we shall see in the next chapter, during 1704 Philip V's side suffered a succession of military failures, both in Europe and on the Iberian Peninsula. Looking back on the certainties of the past, another Neapolitan scholar, Giovanni Caracciolo (d. 1707), chose to memorialize the early months of Philip's reign in three short epic poems, or epyllia. The proclamation of Philip V at Versailles and the new king's journey to Madrid are described in *De adventu Philippi V Hispaniarum regis inclyti in Matriti regiam* ('The arrival of Philip V, renowned king of Spain, at the royal palace in Madrid').[39] For its part, the central theme of *De adventu Philippi V Hispaniarum regis inclyti in urbem Neapolis* ('The arrival of Philip V, renowned king of Spain, in the city of Naples', sign. B1r–D4v) is Philip's voyage to Italy and his official entry into Naples as king in the spring of 1702. Consisting of 369 hexameters, the poem begins with an account of the circumstances surrounding Charles II's death in November 1700 (ll. 1–22). 'Dear to the late monarch and a relative to him through consanguinity' (l. 6), Philip is proclaimed king in a peaceful manner and without dispute. Yet, 'nations previously hostile to each other by lineage come together in friendship' (l. 19) to form a Grand Alliance opposing Philip's proclamation and war breaks out. The poet provides a clearly partisan report on the devastating progress of war in Europe in the early months of the conflict, for which Emperor Leopold I and the Grand Alliance are to be blamed (ll. 23–90). The action quickly moves to Naples, and the poet describes the lavish ceremonies and festivals with which the capital of the kingdom marked the transition of power from one dynasty to the other, and praises the city for its loyalty to the new monarch, which – and here Caracciolo clearly paraphrases the final lines of Ovid's *Metamorphoses* – 'neither Jupiter's anger, nor the harsh rage of death, nor long age shall consign to oblivion' (*... quam nec Iovis ira nec Orci / immitis rabies nec longa obliteret aetas*, ll. 108–9). Philip's legitimacy is, however, called into question by a group of 'hostile citizens' (l. 160) responsible for the aforementioned unsuccessful Conspiracy of Macchia, described at length by Caracciolo (ll. 91–169).[40] Interweaving history and mythology, the poet goes on to narrate Philip's voyage to Naples, which – though undertaken long after the insurrection had been crushed – is credited with bringing stability to the realm and to the whole of Italy (ll. 170–305). Described as 'the Bourbon hero' (l. 183), Philip is sent by Jupiter (with Louis XIV's approval) 'to free the suffering city from its sorrows, to expel the darkness and bring back the sun' (*aegram moeroribus urbem / solvat et expellat tenebras solemque reducat*, ll. 176–7). The new king is enthusiastically greeted by his subjects, who acclaim him as an ancient warrior and statesman:

> *Venisti tandem, decus immortale tuorum,*
> *illius ingentis Ludovici maxima cura*
> *egregiusque nepos, similem cui nulla tulerunt*
> *saecla virum: mendax Pellaeos Graecia quamvis*
> *iactet Alexandros Phtiosque extollat Achilles:*
> *efferat Augustos quamvis Mavortia tellus*
> *Scipiadas, Fabios et dantes iura Catones.*
> *Macte animi pietate, Deo gratissimus heros*
> *venisti tandem et fessis solatia praebes*
>
> ll. 268–76

['You finally arrived, immortal glory of your family, greatest concern and illustrious nephew of that remarkable Louis; no century has begotten a man similar to you, even if mendacious Greece brags about Alexander, born in Pella, and about Achilles, born in Phtia, even if the land of Mars brings forth Augustus, Scipios, Fabii and the law-giving Catos. Glorified through your pious mind, you finally arrived and you provide solace to the weary'].

The last section of the poem (ll. 306–69) briefly foretells Philip's direct involvement in the upcoming military operations conducted against the forces of the Grand Alliance in northern Italy.[41] Eager to prove his military credentials, Philip is praised for his determination to lead the attack against the enemy despite his young age. Presenting an alternative version of events, Caracciolo describes Philip's deeds in Italy as ultimately resulting in victory and universal peace. As with the Habsburg propaganda we saw earlier, Anchises' prophecy in the *Aeneid* (6.854) is used by the Latin panegyrist to sing of Bourbon domination across Europe:

Qui teneros superans animis ingentibus annos
festinabis ovans dubia in certamina Martis,
hostibus fies constanti pectore notus;
[...]
Magna tibi assurget viridanti Insubria tractu
nimbosumque suum flectet caput Apenninus.
At simul ac Latio immanes eieceris hostes,
iunxeris et concordi Europam foedere pacis.
[...]
parcere subiectis populosque domare superbos.

ll. 312–17, 326–9 and 335

['You who, overcoming your tender years with remarkable resolution, shall hasten exultant to Mars' uncertain battles, shall be known to the enemy for your unwavering spirit; ... Great Insubria will rise up to you with its lush territory and the Apennines will bow their cloud-covered peaks. But at once you will have expelled the fierce enemies from Latium [= region around Rome] and will have joined Europe together in a harmonious alliance of peace ... [your intention will be] to spare the humble and to vanquish the proud'].[42]

As military operations across Europe intensified after 1704, Allied and Bourbon propagandists continued to endorse Charles's or Philip's dynastic claims to the Spanish crown. Within the Neapolitan intellectual community the Spanish Franciscan Benito de Noriega (1650–1708) – bishop of Acerra, near Naples, and confessor to Viceroy Medinaceli – published 'a theological and juridical treatise' (*syntagma theologico-iuridicum*) entitled *Iniustitia belli Austriaci contra Catholicum Hispaniarum regem Philippum V gliscentis* ('Injustice of the spreading war waged by the Austrians against Philip V, Catholic king of Spain').[43] In the text the conflict against Philip is deemed unjust on three grounds: on account of those who have instigated the war (*a parte authoris*), on account of its unjust cause (*a parte iniustae causae*) and on account of its purpose (*ex parte finis*). From the outset Noriega dismisses those who 'claim to liberate Spain from Philip's tyranny' and accused him of having usurped the Spanish throne. Drawing chiefly on Spanish legislation, he furnishes his argument with the same pieces of evidence employed by other pamphleteers in the Bourbon camp. Leopold's war against Louis XIV and Philip V must be regarded as unjust because the emperor failed to announce the beginning of the hostilities (Noriega 1705: 64–71). Noriega also concurs with other Bourbon pamphleteers in their recourse to Philip IV's genealogical line as the sole criterion for determining who should be Charles II's successor:

> *Ex his satis superque claret quomodo sit instituenda collatio inter serenissimum Archiducem Carolum Austriacum, vel eius augustissimum genitorem, et Catholicum regem nostrum Philippum, maioris vel minoris proximitatis ad effectum succedendi in regnis Hispaniae, quae omnia Castellae successioni uniformantur, ex lege nostra saepius laudata. Nempe statuendus est Carolus II dulcissimae memoriae, tamquam limes et punctum centricum, a quo petenda est proximitas vel distantia utriusque cum sit ultimus rex, in cuius iure et mancipio monarchia ultimo fuit: quo statuto videndum quisnam ipsi linea magis appropinquet et cum ipse lineam non produxerit descendentem, quaerenda est eius linea ascendens et inveniemus lineam Philippi IV, in qua ipse reperiebatur tamquam filius eius et quia in eadem linea reperiebatur serenissima infans Maria Theresia tamquam soror; eius soboles in eadem linea est nullusuqe alius superest eiusdem lineae, nec etiam augustissimus Caesar, qui ex Philippo IV non descendit sed ex tertio. Unde planum est quod Catholicus rex Philippus V linea proximior est. Et cum gradus computatio institui debeat inter eos qui sunt in eadem linea, non in diversa; sive Caesar gradu aequalis sit sive non, nihil nostra referre potest, quia gradus proximioritas in eadem linea praefert; in diversa impertinens est et minime attendenda*

pp. 205–6

['From this it is sufficiently and abundantly clear in which way we should establish the contest between the most serene Archduke Charles of Austria, or his most august father, and our Catholic king Philip, concerning their greater or lesser proximity to the succession in the kingdoms of Spain, all of which come together in the succession of Castille, according to our frequently praised law. Indeed, Charles II, of sweetest memory, must be designated as the boundary and the central point from which the proximity or distance of either candidate must be calculated, for Charles is the last king in whose right and ultimate possession the monarchy lay. Once that is established, we must consider who is closest to him in line and, since Charles himself did not produce an heir, his family tree must be examined. And we will come upon Philip IV's branch, in which we find Charles as his son, and because in the same branch we find the most serene infanta Maria Theresa as his sister, and her offspring is in the same branch, and no other person from that branch survives, not even the most august emperor who does not descend from Philip IV, but from Philip III [whose daughter Maria Anna (1606–46) was Leopold I's mother], hence it is plain that our Catholic king Philip is closer in line. And since the calculation of the degree ought to be established among those who are in the same branch and not in a divergent one, whether the emperor is equal in degree or not, there is nothing we can report, because the proximity of the degree takes precedence in the same branch, whereas in the divergent one this is not pertinent and does not apply at all'].

A further point of agreement with other Bourbon propaganda writers is his assertion that Maria Theresa's renunciation of the Spanish crown was void (pp. 269–78). Noriega concludes his tract with an outright condemnation of the armed conflict initiated by the Grand Alliance. Unlike past battles and military campaigns, which were waged to guarantee tranquillity and stability in Europe, the purpose of this war on behalf of Archduke Charles was never to usher in an era of peace and prosperity but to deepen divisions and antagonism among European nations (pp. 356–69).

On the Habsburg side the death of Leopold I in May 1705 led to the publication of further declarations of Archduke Charles's alleged rights to the Spanish throne. This is most apparent in the work of the Portuguese jurist and historian João Álvares da Costa, the author of *Aquila augusta trisulco obarmata fulmine seu Carolus tertius Austriacus rex Hispaniarum assertus* ('The august eagle armed with a three-pronged thunderbolt or the declaration of Austrian Charles III as king of Spain').[44] The tract is divided into three books – 'on the just exclusion of Philip of Bourbon', 'on the just inclusion of Charles of Austria', and 'on the resolution of the objections and on issues which can be challenged' –, and includes a short corollary on the Portuguese contribution to Charles's cause. The genealogical, legal and historical arguments and sources deployed by Álvares da Costa do not diverge to any great extent from those found in the works of other pro-Austrian pamphleteers, but his style and presentation are very different. The narrative contains light-heartened features, such as the 'serious' claim that Charles – like several mythological characters in Antiquity – could reign and take precedence over Philip on account of his handsome and robust appearance (Book 2, Chapter 10). Alongside learned justifications of Charles's legitimate claim to the Spanish crown, Álvares da Costa provides a highly dramatic account of the political machinations as the genealogical crisis unfolds. For example, in the following excerpt from the pages devoted to Charles II's final days, note how the author recreates the feverish atmosphere in the royal chamber prior to the king's rewriting of his will, switching in the final sentence from the past tense to the historic present to heighten the sense of drama:

> *Itaque sine valetudine, sine obedientia et sine fidelitate in subditis, summe conflictatus extremum vitae periculum subivit Carolus; ultimaque debilitate iam*

prostrato nihil praeter admissionem Andegavensis dicebant pauci illum in morbo comitantes, praecludebatur enim aditus omni sceleris Gallici non conscio. Crebro et his suasionibus ingravescebat morbus, sed non ideo minus cessabant suggestiones. Nullus, nisi de gloria Hispaniae eventura ex successione Andegavensis, sicut de destructione ex illius exclusione, sermo erat. Quibus Caesaris oratorem etsi non latentibus, evitare non poterat tantum scelus; roganti quippe ut regem alloqui ei liceret, non iam de negotio tractando tempus esse respondit curio maximus; cum tamen ut de rebus Galliae pertractaretur superesset tempus. Fugatis itaque qui de scelere testificari palam possent, clausis ostiis ipsique reginae non libero facto aditu, regem iam mente et spiritu summe debilem aperte alloquuntur eique dicunt nullam Hispaniae salutem fore nisi in inclusione filii secundogeniti Delphini

Álvares da Costa, 1705, 104–5

['Without good health, with neither obedience from or faith in his subjects, Charles approached the final sickness of his life in great torment. Those few who remained with him in his illness spoke to him, exhausted by his latest infirmity, of nothing else but an audience with the Duke of Anjou for access to the king, who was completely unaware of the French crime, was blocked. His health deteriorated further because of these repeated petitions but not even for this reason did the suggestions cease. There was no talk of anything except the honour which would befall Spain from the succession of the Duke of Anjou, or similarly the destruction if he was excluded. Though these discussions were not kept secret from the emperor's spokesman [the Duke of Moles, Spanish ambassador to Leopold I], he was powerless to stop such a great wrongdoing. When he requested permission to address the king, the highest priest [Cardinal Portocarrero, Archbishop of Toledo and Primate of Spain, 1635–1709] replied that it was not yet time to attend to such business, even though there had been plenty of time to discuss the state of France. After those who could openly testify to the wrongdoing had been dismissed, the doors closed and the queen [Maria Anna of Neuburg, 1667–1740] was barred from free access to the king, [those supporting Philip] openly address the king, greatly weakened in mind and spirit, and tell him that there can be no salvation for Spain except through the inclusion of the second-born son of the Dauphin'].

A new emperor, who could not be king of Spain

The premature death of Joseph I on 17 April 1711 dealt a serious blow to the stability of the government in Vienna. Urged to return home at once, Archduke Charles delayed his planned voyage to Italy. However, on 27 September he set sail from Barcelona for Genoa and on 12 October he was elected Holy Roman Emperor by the prince-electors. After he was officially crowned Charles VI in Frankfurt am Main on 22 December, he finally arrived in Vienna a month later. With war in Spain now confined to Catalonia and peace negotiations well underway, at the crucial time of Charles's election to the Imperial see and subsequent coronation the prospect of his accession to the Spanish throne had almost been abandoned. Yet, the Habsburg propaganda machine regarded the acquisition of the Imperial throne as an excellent opportunity to continue to highlight the rights of the Austrian claimant to the Spanish crown. To this end, a considerable body of Latin works celebrated not only Charles's elevation to the Imperial throne but also the uninterrupted continuity of the lineage at a crucial time when government of the Habsburg lands elsewhere in Europe had to be stabilized. Two texts published in 1711 are worthy of note here: *Corona Austriaca augustissimo Carolo sexto, Romanorum imperatori gloriosissimo ... Europa applaudente ... subiectissime cantata* ('The Austrian crown's most submissive praise for the most august, most glorious Holy Roman Emperor Charles VI whilst Europe applauds'), a poem in 392 hexameters by Johann Wilhelm Petersen (1649–1727) and *De augustae domus Austriacae fatis commentatio historica* ('A historical commentary on the destiny of the august House of Austria'), a scholarly tract written by the professor of Rhetoric and History at the University of Kiel, Johann Burchard May (1652–1726).[45]

Petersen's piece begins with an exhortation from mountains, rivers and other notable geographical features within the Holy Roman Empire to Charles, who is implored '[to] abandon your remote Spanish fatherland and the excessive sun, [for] the divine election of the German people summons you to the highest seat of judgement' (*...patriam relinque remotam / Hesperiam et solem nimium, te electio gentis / Teutonicae in sublime vocat divina tribunal*, ll. 27–9). There follows a brief account of the War of the Spanish Succession (ll. 69–109) in which the poet is particularly concerned with chronicling the clashes in the early stages of the conflict between Austrian troops and the joint forces of France and Elector Maximilian II Emanuel of Bavaria, who is compared to the traitor Sinon in Virgil's *Aeneid* (2.79). The central part of the poem includes a description of the various territories which make up the Empire and of the military deeds of Charles's predecessors on the Imperial throne. At this point Petersen deftly handles the change in regnal numbering from King Charles III of Spain to Charles VI Holy Roman Emperor proclaiming that 'in the kingdom of Spain, Charles, you hear [the praise] as the third but in the Roman [empire] you shall be the sixth as the years increase' (*in regno Hesperiae rex, Carole, tertius audis, /*

Romano sed sextus eris, crescentibus annis, ll. 260–1). Biblical imagery – the sixth day of creation followed by God's day of rest – is employed to convey the tranquillity and peace Charles VI's reign will bring to his territories (ll. 266–70). After declaring himself 'the humblest among a thousand poets' (l. 317) Petersen urges the French 'to surrender to the king of the eagle' (namely, the heraldry of the Habsburgs and Holy Roman Empire, ll. 346–7) and expresses his hope that Charles will shortly be joined by his wife, who, 'having left her grandfather, father and fatherland, crossed the seas without delay to the western Spaniards' (l. 386–7). Published by Ulrich Liebpert, royal printer to Frederick I of Prussia, Petersen's poem constitutes a good example of what Maria Goloubeva has termed 'associated glorification', the process whereby territorial princes in the early modern period indicated their loyalty and respect towards the Holy Roman Emperor by means of laudatory works (2000: 224). Analogous aims seem to have been fulfilled by Johann Burchard May in his painstaking history of the Austrian branch of the House of Habsburg. Drawing on an extensive range of literary and historical sources (above all, on Nicolaus Vernulaeus's *Historia Austriaca* of 1651), May chronicles the lives of the emperors since Rudolf I (1218–91). Though the distant past plays a significant role in May's account, and the bulk of his work is devoted to the early centuries of the lineage, his framing of contemporary rulers and events is also important. Accordingly, the emperors who merit most attention and praise from May are Charles VI, whose legitimacy as king of Spain is again declared (May 1711: 47–50), and his father Leopold, decorated with the laurels of many victories during the War of the Spanish Succession. The author argues that Leopold's endeavours to bring harmony and peace to the Empire and Europe were destroyed by Louis XIV's political and military ambitions. He illustrates the French monarch's thirst for war by recalling his financial and military support for the Hungarian revolt of 1703, which May claims was happily ended by Charles VI with the signing of the Treaty of Szatmár in 1711 (pp. 117–19).[46]

Unsurprisingly, most texts written to solemnize Charles VI's election as Holy Roman Emperor in October 1711, the Imperial coronation two months later and his arrival in Vienna in January of the following year were published chiefly in locations and settings closely related to the new Imperial couple, notably the court of Prince Anton Ulrich of Brunswick-Wolfenbüttel (1633–1714), the current empress's grandfather; Barcelona – where Elisabeth Christine remained until March 1713 –; and Vienna, Charles's final destination. We know of several examples of Latin verse composed at Brunswick, most conspicuously a collection of poems featuring anagrams and chronograms.[47] One of the pieces combines anti-French sentiment with a celebration of the legitimate worldwide power of Charles VI, who 'alone cares for six [nations]' (*Carolus sextus – sex solus curat*):

> *Divide, Galle, tuis, quae sunt tua; quae tua non sunt,*
>   *legitimo domino linquito regna suo.*
> *Hispanos, Indos, Germanos atque Boiemos,*
>   *Pannones, Insubres sit separare nefas.*
> *Sex istis populis CAROLUS bene sufficit unus;*
>   *SEX SOLUS CURAT; cede, PHILIPPE, locum;*
> *seX CaroLo seXto SVA regna tVere IehoVa;*
>   *retIa rVMpe potens qVae strVIt InVIDIa*
>
> [= 1711] p. 2

['Divide among your people, Frenchman, the kingdoms that are yours; the kingdoms that are not yours, leave them to their legitimate lord. Let it be forbidden to separate Spaniards, Indians, Germans and Bohemians, Pannonians (Austro-Hungarians) and Insubrians (Northern Italians). Only Charles provides well for these six peoples; he alone cares for six nations. Relinquish, Philip, your place; protect, Jehova, the six kingdoms of Charles VI and with your might break the traps which Envy created'].

In Helmstedt, in the vicinity of Brunswick, several local professors who – as we will see in Chapter 3 – had contributed panegyric Latin verse and prose on the occasion of Elisabeth Christine's wedding three years previously were again summoned by the university to mark the Imperial coronation. On 20 December, Rector Friedrich August Hackemann addressed his colleagues, fellow citizens and, above all, Prince Anton Ulrich in a Latin leaflet, inviting them to attend the ceremony in which the university was to honour the new emperor 'at 10 o'clock the following day'.[48] This included the delivery of a Latin oration by Justus Christoph Böhmer (1670–1732), professor of Politics at the university.[49] Here the focus is the defence of the Habsburg claim to universal monarchy and to authority 'over the vastest and entire Spanish territories', to which the new emperor continues to be entitled 'by birth right' and because 'his father and his brother transferred and conceded it to him'.[50] Historical parallels are drawn between Charles and his illustrious predecessors in the Imperial line, most notably Charles V. Both emperors were compelled to fight against a formidable French enemy (Philip of Anjou and Francis I) and they both received news of the deaths of their predecessors on the Imperial throne whilst at Barcelona, Charles V after his grandfather Maximilian had passed away in 1519 and Charles VI following the sudden loss of his brother in April 1711:

Eadem illi contingit felicitas, quae ex familia sua uni data est Carolo V, cuius nomen auspicato refert, ut simul Hispaniarum rex sit et imperator Romanorum. Barcino sibi merito gratulatur, quod in ista urbe Carolus V commoraretur, quum litteras nuntiosque de sui in Caesarem electione facta e Germania acciperet: eadem in civitate sextus etiam Carolus fuit, quum illi nuntiaretur electores tantam de ipsius fide et felicitate concepisse spem, ut neminem ad imperii gubernationem, quam ipsum, evehere malint

sign. D1v

['To him (Charles VI) is due the same good fortune, which within his family had only been bestowed upon Charles V, whose name is particularly auspicious, of being king of Spain and Holy Roman Emperor at the same time. Barcelona rightly manifests her joy that Charles V was sojourning in that city when he received a letter with news from Germany of his election as Holy Roman Emperor. And in that same city Charles VI was also present when it was announced that the electors had so much hope in his faith and good fortune that he was their only choice for the government of the Empire'].

Böhmer concludes his oration with an exhortation to 'Queen Elisabeth Christine' to continue the fight on behalf of the pro-Habsburg cause in Spain. As noted above, the queen had remained in Barcelona, still referred to by Böhmer as the seat of the royal court (*sedes regia*, sign. C2v). As the last bastion of pro-Habsburg resistance to Philip, the Catalan capital also plays an important role in a panegyric in prose delivered by Marco Antonio San Marco in 1712.[51] As well as celebrating the Imperial coronation, this speech also praises the political skills and military prowess of Elisabeth Christine, who – shortly before Charles's departure – had been sworn in as Lieutenant and Captain General of Catalonia. In addition, San Marco testifies to the affection the local Barcelona populace had for the new empress (sign. A4v) and praises the courage shown by her troops in central Catalonia. The Battle of Prats de Rei, a confrontation between positions that was fought between September and late December 1711, and the lifting of the siege of Cardona on 22 December 1711 are described at length as episodes of heroic resistance against the Bourbon enemy, at a time when final defeat was, however, almost inevitable (sign. A6v–7v).

As with Philip V's journey to Spain in December 1700 and January of the following year, Charles's return to Vienna after his coronation proved a fitting opportunity for several towns along the Imperial route to display their loyalty to the new sovereign. A medal bearing the Horatian tag *recepto Caesare felix* ('Joyful at Caesar's return', cf. Horace, *Odes*, 4.1.47–8) was struck by the local authorities in Nuremberg to honour Charles's stay in the city between 15 and 18 January 1712, and two days later Regensburg city council also offered the emperor a commemorative poem in Latin.[52] Charles's entry into Vienna on 26 January was marked with a guard of honour, the ringing of bells and a *Te Deum* at St Stephen's Cathedral (Hengerer 2018: 220). As recorded by a contemporary press report, the university also participated in the celebrations and the following day Rector Paul Christoph von Schlittern (d. 1715) pronounced a brief oration in Latin, which was subsequently published with an accompanying German translation.[53] In line with the customary descriptions of Imperial virtues we have found in other works, in the text Charles's piety, justice, beneficence and wisdom are extolled by the four faculties within the University (Theology, Law, Medicine and Philosophy). But Schlittern's was not the only coronation oration pronounced for Charles in an academic setting in early 1712. On 28 January – on the very same day Charlemagne had died in 814, as obliquely proclaimed through the words *quae dies in fastis Carolo festa est* on the title page – members of the Gymnasium Casimirianum in Coburg (Bavaria) heard 'a solemn oration in which Georg Friedrich von Tann manifests his joy to Charles VI, Holy Roman Emperor'.[54] Charles's elevation to the Imperial throne is of course celebrated, but his legitimization as king of Spain still dominates the text. At the outset the orator praises Charles's moral virtues and military valour during the Spanish campaign of 1705 and 1706:

> *Magnitudinis animi et fortitudinis bellicae, quae in laude dignissimo imperatore Carolo V admirabilis fuit, Carolo VI victoriae, Barcinonensis et Caesar-Augustana, iterataque eiectio usurpatoris regni Hispanici ex primariis eius provinciis testes sunt locupletissimae*
>
> sign. B2v

['Charles VI's victories at Barcelona and Saragossa and the repeated expulsion of the usurper of the kingdom of Spain from its most important provinces are the most reliable witnesses of greatness of spirit and of military fortitude, qualities which were admired in the worthiest Emperor Charles V'].

Von Tann goes on to recall the young monarch's heroic defence of Catalonia against Philip's troops:

> *Caroli iuventus senilem probavit prudentiam, quum fidam sibi Cataloniam contra iniustissimum invasorem, qui in possessionem Hispaniae venerat, omnibus Galliae et fraudibus et opibus subnixum, tot iam annos mirifice defendit*
>
> sign. C1r

['Charles's youth showed mature prudence, when for so many years he admirably defended Catalonia, which remained faithful to him, against the most unjust invader, who, relying on all the deceit and power of France, had come to take possession of Spain'].

Throughout the speech Charles's legitimate claims to the Spanish crown are articulated in an unambiguous manner. For Friedrich von Tann these are in fact reinforced both by the acquisition of the Imperial sceptre and the successful (albeit rather short-lived) performance by Charles's army on the Spanish front while events were unfolding in Frankfurt. The date of the Imperial coronation comes to take on a particular significance as the ceremony coincided with the Bourbon defeat at Cardona mentioned above (22 December 1711). Von Tann's oration, pronounced on the eve of the signing of the Peace of Utrecht, which the Imperial party refused to join, is further proof of Charles's determination to uphold his claims as Spanish king, despite the unfavourable course of the war in Spain and Europe's preparations for peace. Hence the continuous references in the speech to the Habsburg pretender's past military prowess and to the recent triumphs won by his troops on the Catalan battlefield:

> *Iamque ad firmius sperandum favor Dei signum extulit auspicatissimum, quum sibi dilectissimum Imperatorem augustum, qua die corona Caroli magni in Germania condecoravit, eadem in disiunctissimis etiam Hispaniae terris victricibus lauris coronavit: ut et in Hispanicis et Germanicis regnis eius imperio subiecti, quotquot in fide manserunt, uno tempore, alteri prospere peractae coronationis, alteri victoriae causa, laetas faustasque ederent acclamationes. Ita Deus Hispaniae gaudia Germaniae gaudiis sociare incipit et hoc exoptato auspicio indicat Germanici solii conscensionem initium fore Hispaniae a Gallica servitute liberandae, sub qua iam per multos annos hunc legitimum regem suum anhelat ac suspirat*
>
> sign. C2v

['And to give greater hope God's favour brought forth a most auspicious sign, when the day He crowned in Germany his dearest august emperor with Charlemagne's crown, that same day He also crowned him in the most distant lands of Spain with the laurels of victory, so that those subject to his rule in the kingdoms of both Spain and Germany, however many remained faithful, whether for the sake of the triumphal celebration of the coronation, or for the sake of the victory, may at the same time utter joyful and propitious acclamations. Thus, God undertakes to unite Spain and Germany in joyous celebration and by means of this highly anticipated sign He is showing that the accession to the

German throne shall be the beginning of Spain's due liberation from French servitude, under which for so many years it has strived for and longed for this legitimate king'].

Later in 1712 the Viennese printer Ignaz Dominik Voigt published a history of the Habsburg dynasty written by the abovementioned Schlittern. Under the title *Divinae providentiae cura singularis in erigenda, conservanda augendaque augustissima domo Habsburgo-Austriaca* ('A particular concern of divine Providence for the building, preserving and strengthening of the most august Austrian House of Habsburg'), the text was issued to commemorate the beginning of Charles's reign after his return to Vienna.[55] Though the title of king of Spain still features in the dedicatory remarks addressed to the new emperor, in Schlittern's tract the ongoing dynastic feud and Charles's claim to be the only legitimate Spanish king go unmentioned, and the author focuses his praise exclusively on the moral and political virtues of the Austrian branch of the House of Habsburg. Rather than dwelling on the past glories of Charles's ancestors who had ruled on the Iberian Peninsula since Philip I of Castile (Philip the Handsome, 1478–1506), Schlittern salutes the new sovereign and welcomes a period of prosperity and peace for his realm. Unlike other transitions of power within the House of Habsburg examined elsewhere in this chapter, in this instance continuity with the Spanish past no longer appears to be of any concern to Schlittern. For his master, however, Spain and the Spanish past never ceased to exert a powerful attraction. Having re-established himself in Austria in 1712, Charles VI continued to lay claim to the crown of Spain, formally until the signing of the Treaty of Vienna in 1725 and informally until his death fifteen years later, as we shall explore elsewhere in this book.

Conclusion

Military operations during the War of the Spanish Succession were accompanied by an ideological feud, in which the Bourbon and Habsburg candidates sought political and dynastic legitimization for their claim to the Spanish throne. Beginning before the outbreak of war, this dispute was conducted in texts in several vernacular languages and in Latin, depending on the genre and target readership. Throughout the conflict Latin theologians, historians, orators and poets operating on either side of the dynastic divide were recruited to serve the interests of pretender, dynasty and country. Scholarly treatises, medals as well as encomiastic and vituperative prose and poetry were produced by both parties in their efforts to create a genealogy that either exalted and legitimized the political *status quo* or sought to overturn it. All these authors had recourse to – at times identical – juridical, historical and theological evidence to confirm or subvert the rights of the Duke of Anjou or Archduke Charles with regard to the succession of Charles II of Spain. The validity or invalidity of the will written by the last Spanish Habsburg in late 1700, the religious virtues and political wisdom of their sovereign or his opponent's lack thereof, the genealogy of their immediate or more distant ancestors (at times, as remote as kings and heroes of classical antiquity) or the military and political endorsements afforded by other European powers, the papacy in particular, were all arguments provided by Latin political propagandists in their defence of their chosen candidate's claim to the Spanish crown. Yet, alongside literary devices and legal and historical evidence, royal legitimacy was granted, first and foremost, through victories on the battlefield once hostilities began in February 1701. Latin writers of the age were well aware that military glory could help advance – and ultimately determine – the cause of their favoured candidate within the dynastic dispute, and they duly assisted by singing of the deeds of their heroes in verse and prose, as the following chapter will illustrate.

2

'Bellonae et Martis genitus': Mapping the Spanish Conflict in Latin Verse and Prose (1701–1712)

As was often the case with many early modern conflicts, during the War of the Spanish Succession representations of contemporary military episodes played a central propagandistic role. For both sides of the dynastic divide, the most important war-related representations were victory celebrations in the form of a *Te Deum laudamus* ('We praise Thee, O God', González Cruz 2002: 209–12). Waged as much on the printed page as on the battlefield, the War of the Spanish Succession also gave rise to an astonishing variety of Latin writing across the continent – in print and in manuscript, in verse or in prose, on both the pro-Habsburg and pro-Bourbon sides – celebrating recent military successes. Following Clément Oury's detailed chronology (2020: 481–5), in this chapter I chart the progress of war in Europe between 1701 and 1712 by discussing literary recreations of some of the key battles fought during the conflict. It should be noted that, though examples of battle accounts in *cento*, elegiac, emblematic and epic verse as well as in epistolography and oratory abound across the dynastic divide, the body of texts composed on the Allied (pro-Habsburg) side outnumbers the Bourbon-related output. In what follows each section includes a brief historical introduction prior to the discussion of the texts under review.

Initial encounters in Italy

The ascent of Philip, duke of Anjou, to the Spanish throne as Philip V after the death of Charles II in November 1700 was soon greeted with distrust and apprehension in most European states. On 7 September 1701 England, the United Provinces of the Low Countries and the Holy Roman Empire signed the Treaty of

The Hague and reconstituted the 1689 anti-French Grand Alliance. In May 1702 this coalition declared war on the Bourbons of France and Spain, and a hostile visual and literary campaign ensued (Figure 2). Fighting had, however, begun the previous year. Following the occupation of Milan and Mantua by French troops in February 1701, an Imperial army under the command of Prince Eugene of Savoy (1663–1736) moved into northern Italy, recaptured both cities and on 9 July defeated Marshal Nicolas Catinat (1637–1712) at Carpi. The man appointed by Louis XIV to replace Catinat, the Duke of Villeroy (1644–1730), could not prevent a further defeat at Chiari on 1 September. The poor start to the 1701 campaign for the French continued into 1702 which was also fraught with difficulties. It began at Cremona, where on the night of 31 January / 1 February Eugene of Savoy was granted access to the city through a contact he had on the inside, a priest named Cuzzoli, who admitted a party of Imperial grenadiers and fusiliers by means of a hidden culvert. With Villeroy 'still in bed' they took the French by surprise and the marshal was captured in his quarters (Oury 2020: 89–90). With daylight and a French relief unit arriving, Prince Eugene was forced to withdraw. A month later,

Figure 2 Title page etching for a tract entitled *Europe Nooit voor Een* ('Europe never for one', Amsterdam, 1702); in the centre, a lioness (Britain) and a fox (the Netherlands) clipping the claws of the French tiger while two other lions approach from the right. The inscription on the monument reads: *Sic pax cum tigribus esto* ('How to make peace with tigers'). Reproduced in Cilleßen 1997: 351.

the Duke of Vendôme (Louis Joseph de Bourbon, 1654–1712) took command of the French forces and was substantially reinforced, with around 80,000 men at his disposal. Aware of the strategic influence Italy could have on the progress of the war, after sojourning at Naples, Liguria and Piedmont, on 1 July Philip V joined Vendôme and participated in his triumphant advance. On 26 July an Imperial cavalry detachment under General Annibale Visconti (1660–1747) was defeated at the Battle of Santa Vittoria, near Modena, and, on 15 August, Philip and Marshal Vendôme took on Eugene and other Imperial field marshals at the Battle of Luzzara, with both sides claiming victory. Despite the inconclusive outcome of the battle, the Italian theatre remained quiet in 1703, and over the next two years Vendôme gradually conquered most of Lombardy.

In the initial months of the War of the Spanish Succession the Viennese Jesuits promoted the heroic image of Leopold I and his two sons Joseph and Charles in *Achilles Germanicus* ('The German Achilles'), a play in which a parallel is drawn 'between Emperor Leopold I and Otto I (912–73), the conqueror of the Vandals' (Goloubeva 2000: 152). At about the same time Eugene of Savoy's early campaign in Italy was also celebrated by Imperial propagandists in Latin prose and verse. As noted by Hengerer (2018: 217), the Prince of Savoy made sure that his achievements were solemnly recognized because of his critics and enemies at court. In 1702 the Jesuit and professor of Rhetoric Franz Staindl edited in Graz a collection of five eulogizing speeches entitled *Annus primus belli Italici serenissimo Eugenio Caesarearum in Italia copiarum supremo duce ter secundus Suada panegyrica celebratus* ('A celebration in panegyrics by the goddess of persuasion of 1702, first year of the Italian war with most serene Eugene as supreme leader of the troops in Italy and three times favourable').[1] The five speeches included in this *Promotionsschrift* focus on the campaign waged by Prince Eugene in northern Italy. After a preliminary panegyric, orations two to five are each devoted to a key military episode coinciding with one of the four seasons. The last text – *Hyems laurearum fertilis* ('Winter fertile in triumphs') – praises Eugene for his decision to conduct military operations in late winter and describes the fighting at Cremona and Marshal Villeroy's captivity on 1 February. Throughout the speech, in which the author continuously makes direct appeals to his immediate audience's emotions (*Sic actum est, auditores!*, 'That's what happened, listeners', p. 106), a careful balance has to be struck since the initially successful siege of Cremona ended in Eugene's retreat. The orator concentrates therefore on the Prince's magnanimity towards Villeroy drawing a parallel between that and Charles V's treatment of Francis I of France, captured and imprisoned at the Battle of Pavia in 1525 (pp. 108–9).

Eugene's raid on Cremona also elicited more humorous responses in a bilingual (Latin and German) collection of eight emblems exalting the achievements of the Imperial commanders during the Italian campaign, the *Elogia heroum Caesareorum in Italia* ('On the Imperial heroes in Italy', Vienna, 1702, copy at ÖNB, 303026-B. Adl. 3). Each emblem consists of a dedication, an illustration, a motto and an epigram. The two concluding pieces praise, respectively, Eugene and Imperial Marshal Guido Wald Rüdiger, count of Starhemberg (1657–1737), and refer to Villeroy, now by the fortunes of war a prisoner of the victorious Prince Eugene. The penultimate emblem, *Ex villa regia flecto meo Domino coronam* ('From my royal palace I bow the crown to my Lord'), exploits a pun on the name of the vanquished general (*villa regia*, a royal palace, being a literal Latin translation of 'Villeroy'). Even if they were not explicitly told, readers of the final emblem, *Dolus, an virtus, quis in hoste requirat?*, were expected to recognize its origins in Coroebus' words from Virgil's *Aeneid*: 'Who shall ask of an enemy whether he succeeded by guile or by valour?' (2.390). This passage describes an episode during the sack of Troy in which Coroebus convinced some of his fellow soldiers, including Aeneas, to dress in enemy armour to disguise themselves. Dedicated to Starhemberg and other Imperial commanders, 'who robbed the French at Cremona' (*Gallos Cremonae intercipientibus*), emblem eight pictures a fox approaching a chicken coop at dawn, the door ajar, as the inattentive and sleepy birds are about to come out (Figure 3). The emblem's overriding theme is the combination of dexterity and fortitude – personified by Pallas, goddess of war and wisdom – as a key to military success. For all the bravery shown by Hercules whilst fighting the Nemean lion, he proved himself inferior to Starhemberg and his companions, who, like the fox, displayed both valour and cunning (or was it rather deceit?) and caught the Gauls off guard. As with other anti-Bourbon epigrammatists and visual artists, the author of the Latin text puns on the word *Gallus* ('Frenchman') – *gallus* ('cockerel'). He also exploits the various meanings of *acies* ('a sharp edge of a sword', 'mental acuity' and 'the front of an army') and the verb *exacuere* ('to make pointed' and 'to incite'):

Ingenii ferrique acies ubi ringitur, ultro
in falcem veniunt palmae: dea Martia, Pallas,
utramque exacuit. Victoria nobilis illa est,
quam parit ingenii suffultus robore mucro.
Non raro Alcidi melius vulpina quadrare
pelle leonina visa est: quis in hoste requirat,
an dolus, an virtus? Dolus hic virtute iuvatur,
haec ars cristatos capiendi est optima Gallos

['When the edge of the mind and the sword are riled, victories are spontaneously reduced to a hook.² Pallas, goddess of warfare, sharpened both. That is a noble victory, attained by the sword and supported by strength of mind. Not rarely did the skin of a fox appear to be more fitting for Hercules than that of a lion. Who shall ask of an enemy whether he succeeded by guile or by valour? Here guile is assisted by valour, this is the best way to catch crested cockerels', p. 10].³

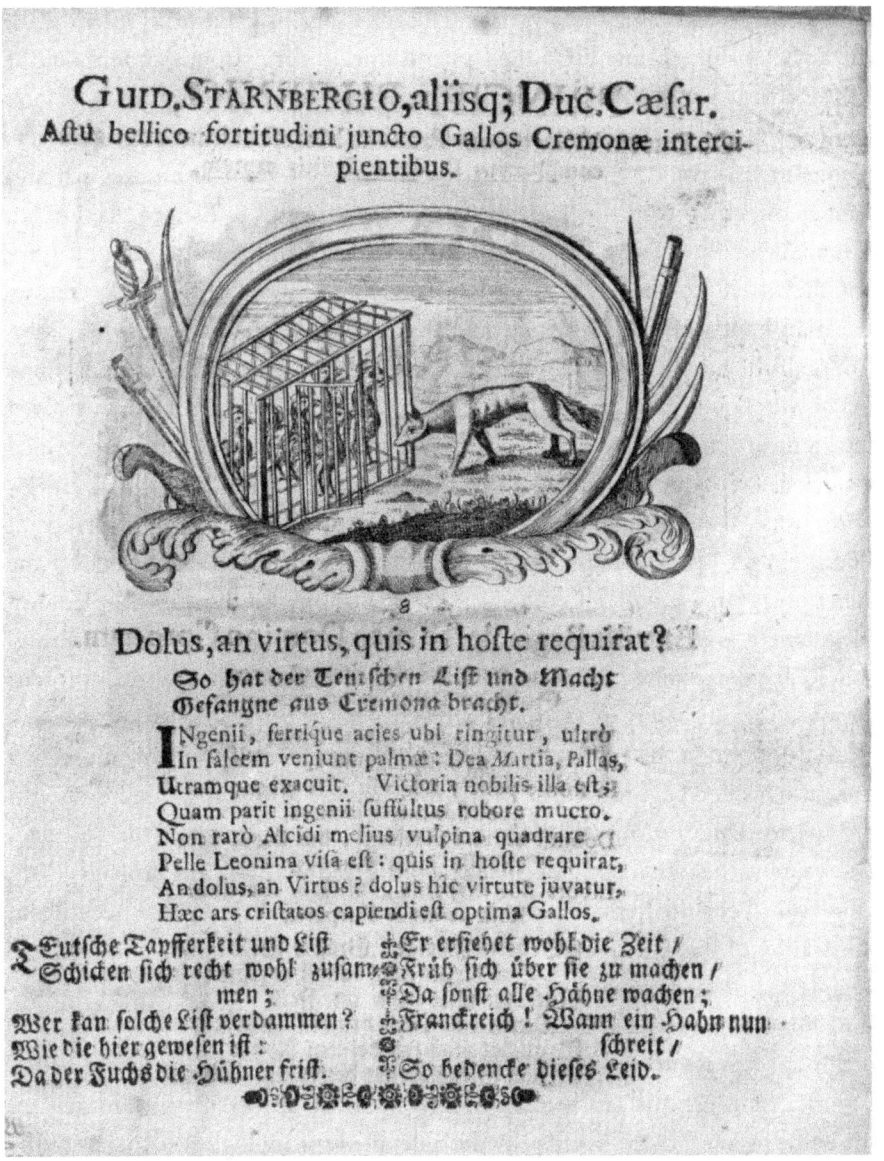

Figure 3 *Elogia heroum Caesareorum in Italia*, Vienna, 1702, p. 10; ÖNB, 303026-B. Adl. 3.

Elsewhere in Europe between 1702 and 1704

War was also waged elsewhere in Europe. On the Iberian Peninsula, an Anglo-Dutch fleet defeated the French on the bay of Vigo on 23 October 1702, a victory which helped persuade the Portuguese King, Peter II (1648–1706), to abandon his earlier treaty with France and join the Allied side.[4] The first objective for the Grand Alliance in the Low Countries was to secure the Dutch frontiers, threatened by the joint forces of France, Bavaria and Joseph Clemens of Bavaria (1671–1723), ruler of Liège and Cologne. On the Upper Rhine, Imperial troops under Louis of Baden (1655–1707) and Archduke Joseph (the future emperor, Joseph I) took Landau on 9 September 1702. Throughout 1703, French victories at Friedlingen, Blenheim (Höchstädt) and Speyerbach with the capture of Kehl, Breisach and Landau directly threatened Vienna.[5] That year the troops of Elector Maximilian II Emanuel of Bavaria (1662–1726) and the Duke of Vendôme also invaded Tyrol but they were compelled to withdraw shortly afterwards.[6] In 1704, Franco-Bavarian forces continued their advance. To relieve the pressure, on 19 May John Churchill, first duke of Marlborough (1650–1722), marched up the Rhine, joined forces with Louis of Baden and Prince Eugene, and defeated the Bourbon army at the Battle of Schellenberg, near Donauwörth on the Danube, on 2 July. The Allied victory at the Battle of Blenheim on 13 August, where Marshal Tallard (1652–1728) was taken prisoner, forced Bavaria out of the war and the Treaty of Ilbersheim of 7 November placed it under Austrian rule. Three weeks later the Allies recaptured Landau. Given the state of Europe shortly after the Battle of Blenheim, it is not surprising that an anonymous Latin poet (possibly a Dane) should have exclaimed in despair: 'O Europe, loosen your hair, expose your sorrow and your pain, and weep, you who have never been sadder'.[7]

At this point in the conflict both sides wished to flex their military muscle on the Latin printed page as well.[8] This was especially so for Philip as, in the autumn of 1704, the Duke of Anjou could only exhibit a draw on his scorecard, at Luzzara two years earlier. This circumstance was exploited by Bourbon propagandists, who were keen to herald Luzzara as a victory for their side. An excellent illustration of this is provided by the aforementioned Giovanni Caracciolo (see Chapter 1) in his *Philippo V Hispaniarum regi invictissimo epinicium* ('Victory song for most undefeated Philip V, king of Spain'), an account in 818 hexameters of Philip's voyage to Italy and subsequent campaign in northern Italy in the summer of 1702. The last section of the poem (ll. 637–818) concentrates on the battle of Luzzara itself and provides a detailed chronological sequence of the encounter.[9] It begins with the military operations of early August, when a detachment under Vendôme besieges Luzzara; Prince Eugene responds by abandoning his blockade of Mantua and marching on the besieged town (ll. 637–52). The action quickly moves to the morning and early afternoon of 15 August, as Eugene orders a general assault (ll. 653–84). After the Irish units (*miles Hibernus*) assisting Eugene are repulsed by the French and victory appears to be within reach, Caracciolo portrays Philip in prayer:

> *Tunc pius ad caelum palmas cum voce Philippus*
> *extollens ait: 'O rerum inviolata potestas,*[10]
> *omnipotens genitor, sancto qui numine torques*
> *cuncta tuo terrasque regis, moderaris et astra;*
> *tu qui unus secreta hominum sensusque latentes*
> *scrutaris, quantum Germano sanguine nollem*
> *foedari quamque invitus contendere cogar,*
> *aspice et aetheream, iuste si sumpsimus arma,*
> *affer opem auxiliumque mihi'*

ll. 685–93

['Then pious Philip, lifting his hands to heaven, exclaims: "Oh, unchallenged power over the universe, almighty Father, you who direct everything with your blessed spirit, who rule the earth and govern the stars, you who alone explore the secrets of mankind and their hidden meanings, behold how greatly I wish not to be defiled with German blood and how unwillingly I shall be forced to fight; but if we take up arms justly, grant me your divine might and assistance"'].

Caracciolo describes the bloody struggle that ensues, in which Charles de Lorraine, prince of Commercy (b. 1661), and several senior Imperial commanders are killed (ll. 733–83). The Bourbon army is credited with the final victory as it managed to hold its lines until darkness brought an end to the fighting around midnight (ll. 784–810). The poet expands his focus, however, beyond the immediate military action to legitimize the Bourbon claimant's rise to power, as well as his mission and purpose. This is achieved through a series of devices. In Philip's prayer assistance is also sought from the late Charles II of Spain, for 'it was you who, aside from all others, ordered me on your deathbed to protect the sceptre of noble Spain and to receive by succession such great kingdoms' (ll. 699–701).[11] Moreover, the poem concludes (ll. 811–18) with a prophecy and praise for the victorious king, *Borbonius heros*, whose empire – as in Virgil's vision of Augustan rule – will extend 'beyond the lands of the Garamantes and Indians, beyond the passing of the year and the passage of the sun'.[12]

The Allies also found an original way to promote their cause and celebrate their own military successes in Europe. In May 1705 the University of Vienna issued a new *Promotionsschrift*, under the title *Affectus Musarum Viennensium* ('Passions of Viennese Muses'; ÖNB, 296336-A. Adl.5). Publication of the text was partly to mark the accession of Joseph I to the throne that same month. Indeed, part three of the volume (sign. B4v–C2v) consists of votive poems on behalf of the new emperor, and his brother Charles, at the time involved in military operations in Spain. Of more interest to our enquiry here are the first two sections of the booklet. The first section (sign. A1r–A6v) contains six poems in elegiacs that constitute a kind of Marian calendar: each one celebrates an Allied victory across the continent between 1702 and 1704 that (roughly) coincides with one of the Virgin's feast days. It is significant that the Allied triumphs here, though achieved against a fellow Christian monarch, whose grandfather – as with all French kings – was accorded the title *Rex Christianissimus* ('Most Christian King'), are commended as proof of Habsburg piety and lauded as victories over heretics.[13] The first poem recreates Villeroy's captivity at Cremona and is framed by the Feast of the Purification (2 February); poems two and five celebrate the Feast of the Assumption (15 August), around the time of Luzzara (as with pro-Bourbon propaganda, presented here as a victory) and Blenheim; the third piece bears the title *In Festo Annuntiationis Beatae Virginis, fugatis ab Austria hostibus gloriose Iaurinum miles Caesareus advenit MDCCIV* ('On the Feast of the Annunciation of the Virgin [25 March] of 1704, the Imperial army gloriously reached Győr [in western Hungary] having driven the enemy from Austria'); the date of the following poem is 2 July, to coincide with Schellenberg and the Feast of the Visitation (celebrated on that day until 1969); and the last poem describes the capture of Landau on 9 September (the day following the Feast of the Nativity of the Virgin) and the recapture of the city on 28 November, one week after the Feast of the Presentation of the Virgin (21 November).

For its part, section two (sign. A7r–B4r) is made up of eight fictive letters, which 'give us an insight into contemporary political events almost from a "private" point of view' (Klecker 2008: 70). The choice of genre is hardly surprising: the first form of Latin prose composition practised in schools and universities was the letter; and fictive letters proved extremely popular in the eighteenth century, having been used as propaganda tools since the Thirty Years War (Dahlberg 2014: 48).[14] Peppered with classical allusions (just as contemporary school exercises were), the texts reflect on the favourable course of the war. The author of letter four, for example, writing from Lisbon to a friend in Vienna, compares the seizure of Gibraltar in the summer of 1704 to the siege of Saguntum during the Second Punic War (sign. B1v). In the final exchange between two correspondents, one in Innsbruck and the other in Vienna, the hero of the day is, of course, Eugene, who embodies all the qualities of a perfect general as described by Cicero (in his *Pro lege Manilia*, 28) and by Justus Lipsius:

> *Multa vos de bello auditis; nos multa videmus, tulimus etiam libenter omnia et fide constanti in Augustam domum. Annus iam quintus est, et turmae, aut cohortes?, exercitus integri commeaverunt. Novisti ab Italia et Bavaria impetum hostem fecisse, sed novisti virtutem ac constantiam civium, et qui Alpinus Hercules cum duobus certaverit. Dum haec scribo, copiosus iterum et florens omnino in Italiam miles delabitur. Aliquid ibi Deum agere velle confidimus: quantum ducem huic bello destinat! qui heri ad nos. Habet Eugenius, quae Cicero in summo imperatore: 'scientiam rei militaris, virtutem, auctoritatem, felicitatem'. Malles cum Lipsio quinto addere 'providentiam'? Adde*

sign. B3v

['You hear many things about the war; we [in Innsbruck] see many things and have endured everything willingly and with constant faith in the august house (= House of Habsburg). It is already the fifth year [of war] and troops (or cohorts?), entire armies have come and gone. You know that the enemy attacked from Italy and Bavaria, but you also know the valour and steadfastness of our citizens, and the man who has fought with both these qualities like an Alpine Hercules. As I write this, a vast and outstanding army descends again on Italy. We trust we will achieve something there, God willing: what a great commander He has appointed for this war, as I recently heard. Eugene has what Cicero wishes of the best commander: "Knowledge of warfare, valour, prestige, and good fortune". Would you like to add "prudence" from Lipsius' fifth book? Go ahead'].[15]

We are starting to see commonalities here. The writers on both sides of the dynastic divide employ a variety of literary genres and forms – poetry, in hexameters or elegiacs, and prose – but both, unsurprisingly, claim to have God on their side, for example depicting Philip as piously at prayer, or connecting Allied success with the Virgin's feast days, and, by extension, her patronage. Classical references or comparisons also abound, regardless of the genre or the allegiance, used to bolster the profiles of the corresponding pretenders to the throne and military commanders. And, as we shall see, authors continue to utilize these methods from the propaganda playbook as the war wears on.

The Peninsular front: Barcelona twice besieged (1705–1706)

In Catalonia the succession to Charles II in November 1700 went ahead with apparent normality and the new king summoned the *Cort General* (parliament) and swore to uphold the Constitutions. Over the following years there were several conflicts between the Catalan institutions and Philip V due to the crown's increasing authoritarianism. The arrival of Archduke Charles boosted the hopes of the pro-Habsburg cause, or *vigatà* party, which were, however, dashed by the unsuccessful Allied landing in Barcelona on 28 May 1704. The disappointment of this military defeat was, nevertheless, mitigated three months later by the seizure of Gibraltar and the victory of the Allied fleet at the naval Battle of Malaga. The failure of the 1704 landing confirmed the need for more adequate Allied support in Europe. To that end, the Pact of Genoa (20 June 1705) was signed by Catalan exiles on behalf of the resistance and by England. The agreement facilitated a new landing near Barcelona, on 22 August, of Allied troops bringing Charles III with them. On 14 September 1705, the fortress of Montjuïc overlooking the city was seized by Charles's army at the command of Charles Mordaunt, third earl of Peterborough (1658–1735), who, on 9 October, forced the Bourbon viceroy, Francisco Antonio Fernández de Velasco (1646–1716), to capitulate.[16] The capture of Barcelona paved the way for Charles's official and solemn entry into the city on 7 November. Shortly after his acclamation as King Charles III of Spain, the monarch summoned the Catalan parliament and swore to uphold Catalan privileges and rights. It did not take long for Philip V to fight back. Advancing through Catalonia in March 1706, he soon reached the outskirts of Barcelona and on 3 April began his attack on the capital. Philip's chief target was the seizure of the fortress of Montjuïc, which would guarantee easy access to the city walls and thus make the fall of Barcelona almost inevitable. He continued to press forward, keeping the Allies on the back foot, to such an extent that Charles III considered fleeing the city. Despite the obvious danger, Charles decided to remain in Barcelona. This became, therefore, the only occasion when the two claimants to the throne almost came face-to-face with each other. Eventually the arrival of a large Anglo-Dutch fleet forced the assailants to lift their siege and withdraw in haste on 12 May, coinciding with a solar eclipse.

Divine intervention

As we saw in the *Affectus Musarum*, in pro-Habsburg propagandistic literature, the military campaign against the Bourbon pretender – despite his status as 'most Christian king' – is often depicted as being a fight on behalf of the true faith, and Charles is commonly described as *Rex Catholicus*, a title awarded by the pope to Spanish sovereigns. For example, we find Christian imagery effectively deployed by the author of the earliest Latin text to feature the military episode of 1705 described above, which survives in an anonymous two-page broadsheet entitled *Elegiaca narratio auspicatae obsidionis cum deditione excellentissimae civitatis Barcinonensis totiusque Principatus Cathaloniae* ('An account in elegiacs of the auspicious siege together with the surrender of the most excellent city of Barcelona and the entire Principality of Catalonia').[17] Written by a 'trustworthy and most loyal follower of His Royal Highness Charles III of Spain', the poem (66 lines in total) was printed in Barcelona in 1705, most likely to coincide with Charles's official entry into the city in November of that year. The text recounts the key moments of the battle: the king's arrival on the Catalan coast in late August (l. 2); the successful attack on Montjuïc by the garrison led by Prince George of Hesse-Darmstadt, who was however killed during the military operation;[18] the bombing of the city from the Allied camp (ll. 27–8); Viceroy Fernández de Velasco's capitulation and the ensuing peace negotiations (ll. 31–4), as well as the popular revolt and looting in Barcelona following rumours that the Bourbon officials who had surrendered intended to take their prisoners off with them (ll. 41–2). After the Bourbon retreat 'Spain herself is saved by the combined love of the alliance' (*Servat Iberum ipsum foedere iunctus amor*, l. 40). This account is then followed by a eulogy of Charles, whom Barcelona welcomes as the new king with utmost fervour and gratitude (ll. 46–56), and an appreciative acknowledgment of the military support provided during the siege by British and Dutch troops (ll. 57–64). Individual praise of Charles III, Prince George of Hesse-Darmstadt (b. 1669), the Earl of Peterborough and Queen Anne of England, reigning monarch since 1702 who 'shall be a mother to Spaniards, a valiant lady' (*Anna haec Hispanis mater erit; domina / belligera*, ll. 58–9), is reinforced by the harmony prevailing within the coalition of forces fighting against the Bourbon claimant. The poet concludes his account expressing the hope that 'God may bless you, Charles, with descendants forever more and that Barcelona may never be without them' (*Omnipotens utinam faciat te prole perennem, / Carole, ne careat Barcino prole tua*, ll. 65–6).

Throughout his text the poet employs Christian imagery and references which clearly serve a political purpose. The assault on the fortress of Montjuïc took place on 14 September, the Feast of the Exaltation of the Holy Cross (*Tempore, quo colitur sancta exaltatio ligni, / mons Iovis irruitur, caetera cuncta runt*, ll. 9–10). As mankind was delivered from sin by the death of Christ on the Cross and his subsequent ascension from the Mount of Olives, Spain's own redemption began on the Mount of Judea (the Catalan 'Montjuïc' translating to 'Jewish Mountain'): *Iudae in monte fuit celebrata redemptio tota, / ad montem Iudae nascitur Hesperica* (ll. 13–14). The battle of Montjuïc witnessed a further exaltation, that of Prince George of Hesse-Darmstadt, whose achievements on the battlefield are now surpassed by the glory he shall attain in heaven (*Dum moritur ne maior erit, cum vivus agebat? / Profecto vivus maximus esse nequit*, ll. 25–6).

'After the capture of the Mount of Jupiter' (*Monte Iovis capto...*, l. 15) peace negotiations were initiated by the defeated Fernández de Velasco on behalf of Philip.[19] They are known to have started on 4 October, the Feast of Saint Francis of Assissi (*Enituit tandem festum, quo Assissius almus / incolitur, cum Dux* [Fernández de Velasco or Philip of Anjou] *tentat inire quiem*, ll. 31–2). We are, however, advised by the author of the poem not to draw any parallels between Francisco Fernández de Velasco and Saint Francis. Instead, he is at pains to point out that the virtues of the saint as a messenger of peace are in complete contrast to the Viceroy's behaviour during his tenure in Catalonia. Moreover, the excesses committed by Fernández de Velasco after the outbreak of the War of the Spanish Succession – most contemporary sources agree on the ruthless manner in which he suppressed all opposition against the Bourbon government (Torras i Ribé 1999: 74) – are sharply contrasted with the heroic and magnanimous behaviour shown by the Allied generals during the siege.[20] Significantly, Velasco's rule is compared to that of an oriental prince (*dynastes*) and his ferocity to that of the Arcadian King Lycaon, who was turned into a wolf by Jupiter for having defiled his altar with human sacrifices (Ovid, *Met.* 1.163–239):

> *Dum rexit pavidus, voluit praecepta capessi,*
>   *quae primum rumpens terque quaterque fugit.*
> *Destruxit dominans urbem feritate Lycaon*
>
>   ll. 37–9

['Whilst he ruled fearfully, he wished that the laws, which – once violated – he avoided time and again, should be obeyed. Like Lycaon, he dominated and destroyed the city with ferocity'].[21]

Just as Jupiter took revenge on Lycaon and St Francis tamed the wolf at Gubbio – one of the legends linked with the life of the saint –, Fernández de Velasco was also vanquished by 'warlike, invincible, combative, pious and peace-bringing Charles' (*armipotens, invictus, belligerator, pius, placidus*, l. 51), victorious at the battle of Montjuïc.

Religious propaganda also features prominently in Latin texts related to the siege of Barcelona of 1706. Shortly after hostilities had come to an end Charles decided to mint a medal depicting the king in profile on one side and, on the other, the city of Barcelona in the midst of a solar eclipse together with the words

O nimium dilecte Deo, tibi militat aether ('O most beloved of God, heaven is fighting for you'), a Latin device which – in several different versions – recurs in texts in praise of the Habsburg pretender.[22] In the weeks immediately following Philip V's withdrawal several religious festivities were held in Barcelona.[23] Two days after the end of the siege a service of thanksgiving took place at the church of Santa Maria del Mar. In addition, in a letter of 12 June 1706, Charles ordered the city councillors to erect a pyramid-shaped statue with an image of Mary and other figures related to the Immaculate Conception in front of the side entrance of Santa Maria del Mar.[24] Provisionally built in wood, the monument was inaugurated in a solemn ceremony eight days later, during which – as was customary – popular poems in the vernacular praising the Virgin Mary (*Goigs* in Catalan) were sung.[25] The statue also bore the following Latin dedicatory inscription, seemingly conceived by Charles himself:

> *Carolus tertius, Hispaniarum monarcha, cum Virginem immaculate conceptam sui regnorumque suorum patronam delegerit eique sacrum ex aere et lapide monumentum in hac urbe Gotholoniae primate spoponderit, quam Deiparae patrocinium, ipsomet intus obsesso defendit, Duce Andegavense eiusque exercitu profligato, ne promissus clementissimae matri cultus retardaretur, suppositum hoc altare et simulacrum in futuri operis signum, se, clero, senatu populoque praesentibus, solemniter consecrari iussit anno Salutis MDCCVI, die XX mensis Iunii*

['Charles III, king of Spain, chose the Immaculate Virgin as his patron and patron of his kingdoms and solemnly promised a sacred monument in bronze and stone in this principal city of Catalonia, which, whilst he was being ambushed inside, was defended under the protection of the Mother of God. Once the Duke of Anjou and his army had been overthrown, and to ensure the worship promised to the most clement Mother might not be delayed, he himself, in the presence of the clergy, the senate and the people [of Barcelona], ordered that this altar and this image be solemnly consecrated as a sign of the future work. On 20 June in the year 1706 of Our Salvation'].

In the instructions addressed to the local authorities on how to mark the liberation of Barcelona, Charles also pledged to honour Our Lady of Montserrat, a Marian title associated with the statue of the Mother of God venerated at the Benedictine monastery of Montserrat near Barcelona (Mollfulleda 2007: 111). The king was a devout follower of the cult of Our Lady of Montserrat, who had also been worshipped by Benedictine monks in Vienna since the early seventeenth century (Albareda 1924: 39). En route to Madrid, Charles fulfilled his vow during a visit to the abbey from 24 to 27 June 1706, when he offered his sword at the Virgin's altar as a token of gratitude for Her protection during the siege of Barcelona. At the ceremony the following dedication document – dating to 1706, as inferred from the Roman numerals on three of its lines – is described in a contemporary account of Charles's visit to the abbey as also having been deposited in a side chapel shortly before the king's departure:

> Ad aram Virginis
> quae sacris in paginis nigra dicitur sed formosa,
> quae mater est eius,
> per quem reges regnant,
> humillime provolutus in genua,
> in perpetuam memoriam Austriacae devotionis,
> DeVoto anIMo ConseCro,
> et depono
> gladium, lateri meo detractum,
> ut
> pro me, ita exarmato,
> fortioribus armis caelum militet,
> sub auspiciis
> magnae huius coelorum reginae,
> quam eligo ac confirmo
> In beLLo DVCeM exercitus,
> In paCe CVstoDeM
> regnorum,
> ac advocatam ad Deum pro me maximo peccatorum,
> Montserrati VII Cal Iulii
> eiusdem Virginis Mariae coeli
> terraeque dominae
> infimus clientum servusque perpetuus Carolus[26]

['Most humbly genuflected before the altar of the Virgin, who in the Holy Scriptures is described as black yet beautiful and is the mother of He through whom kings rule, in permanent remembrance of Austrian devotion, I, Charles, the humblest client and eternal servant of the Virgin Mary, Lady of Heaven and Earth, with devotion, dedicate and place my sword, removed from my side, so that with stronger weapons heaven may wage war on my behalf; so disarmed, under the auspices of this great Queen of Heaven, I choose and confirm Her as my army's guide in battle, as my kingdom's protector in peace, and as an advocate for me, the greatest of sinners. Before God, at Montserrat on 25 June'].

According to Voltes Bou (1963: 133), Charles's decision to offer his sword to the Virgin and to present the dedication document was prompted by news of the Allied victory at Ramillies on 23 May 1706, which may have reached the monarch whilst still in Montserrat. Meticulously studied by Matsche (1981: 176–7), who has identified the biblical sources of some of the lines, the document elicited in turn an extended version, also in Latin – previously unnoticed by scholars – entitled *Anathema serenissimi Caroli tertii regis Catholici in Monte serrato ad Beatae Virginis aram ab eodem affixum, nunc paraphrasi elegiaca plenius explicatum* ('An offering from the most serene Catholic King Charles III placed by himself on the altar of the Blessed Virgin at Montserrat, now more fully illustrated in a version in elegiac distichs'). Lacking details of the year and place of publication, the only copy of the poem known to exist is held in Vienna (ÖNB, 307648-A), where the text may have been printed sometime after 1706. The text of the document which Charles is said to have placed on the altar precedes the extended version, which runs to 332 lines.

Anathema serenissimi Caroli tertii constitutes an exaltation of the tenets of the Counter-Reformation, which the Habsburg dynasty firmly defended (Coreth 1982). Unsurprisingly, in the poem Charles is compared to Ignatius of Loyola (1491–1556), who hung his sword and dagger at the Virgin's altar in Montserrat during an overnight vigil at the shrine in 1522 (ll. 311–14). Charles, the putative author of the text, begins his prayer by expressing his devotion to the Mother of God. In so doing he claims to be 'walking in my ancestors' footsteps' (*Certe ego si quoties stirpis vestigia nostrae / persequor et patres, nomina magna, meos*, ll. 45–6), in particular those of his great-grandfather Ferdinand II (1578–1637), on whose initiative the aforementioned Viennese monastery of Montserrat had been founded in 1636, and of his grandfather Ferdinand III (1608–57) and father Leopold I, who had several statues erected in Mary's honour in Vienna and made regular pilgrimages to Mariazell, Altötting and Mariahilf ob Passau, well-known centres of Marian devotion in Austria and Bavaria (ll. 65–72).[27] Like his forebears, Charles wishes to express his gratitude to the Mother of God and promises to erect a column to the Virgin in Barcelona (l. 114). He pledges to continue the fight against his enemies with Mary's assistance, unlike the generals in the fables of ancient poets who were aided by pagan goddesses.[28] In the central section of the poem (ll. 167–275) the young king begs the Virgin, whom he addresses as the highest warrior queen, to grant his troops victory. Significantly, Charles's military endeavours are here compared to those undertaken by illustrious and pious commanders from the past who defeated heathen rulers: Narses, whose devotion to the Virgin Mary helped him overcome the Ostrogothic king Totila in 549; Emperor John II Komnenos (1118–43), victorious against the Serbs; and Don Juan de Austria (1547–78), half-brother of Philip II of Spain and best known for his naval victory at Lepanto in 1571.

Queen Anne, a mighty ally in Catalonia

As well as divine intervention and favour, military support from other members of the Grand Alliance was also acknowledged by Latin writers of the age as having played a crucial role in victories over the Bourbon army in 1705 and 1706. As noted above, in the *Elegiaca narratio auspicatae obsidionis* Queen Anne is lauded for sending her troops to Charles's aid during the siege of Barcelona in September 1705.[29] Similarly, the anonymous author of *Anathema serenissimi Caroli tertii* praises the valour exhibited by her people and the fleet she sent in support of Charles's war effort in the spring of 1706 (l. 141). Another poet who portrayed the English monarch directing her lines of battle during the siege of 1706 was Basilius Affatighi. A Florentine Dominican, he penned a series of seven short poems in elegiacs dating from July 1706 and dedicated to Queen Anne (University of Nottingham Library, MS. Pw V676).[30] All the pieces within this small collection are prefaced by a title or heading summarizing the contents of each text. In the first three compositions [*Barcino ab obsidione liberatur* – 'Barcelona is freed from siege'; *Anna Anglorum regnatrix cum Anna Samuelis matre confertur* – 'Anne, Queen of England, is compared to Anna, mother of Samuel'; and *Eadem Anna Amazonibus praefertur* – 'The same Anne is exalted over the Amazons'] Anne is compared to courageous women in classical and biblical antiquity, whose bravery, however, she surpasses. In *Barcino ab obsidione liberatur* the comparison is with Judith, who, as the Assyrian general Holofernes was poised to destroy the city of Bethulia, entered his tent. She then beheaded the drunk Holofernes, thus preventing the final assault on her home city (Jdt. 8.7). Anne – as a second Judith – is credited with the final defeat of the French at Barcelona:

> *Qualiter Assyrias vicit Bethulia turmas,*
>   *insidiata sibi Barcino castra terit.*
> *Gloria cui tanti debetur summa triumphi?*
>   *Utrobique suum foemina iactat opus.*
> *Quae tulit ambarum potiores foemina palmas?*
>   *Victrix prima manu, mente secunda fuit.*
> *Prima soporati tantum caput abstulit hostis;*
>   *agmina quae vigilant mille secunda necat*

['Just as Bethulia defeated the Assyrian troops, Barcelona crushed the ambushing camp. To whom should the glory be owed for such a mighty triumph? In both cases a woman boasts of her own deed. Which woman carried the most important victory? The former vanquished with her hand, the latter with her mind; the former only beheaded her inebriated enemy, the latter killed a thousand vigilant troops'].

For its part, poem 4, *Ipsa Regnatrix pro Carolo tertio Hispaniarum Rege multas instruit militum acies* ('The queen herself draws up her troops' battle lines for King Charles III of Spain') refers specifically to Anne's intervention during the siege of Barcelona of 1706 by praising the crucial assistance provided to Charles by her fleet.[31] The fearlessness of Anne's troops at Barcelona is also extolled in poem 5, *In quemdam, qui aequo animo insignes ferre non valens Anglorum victorias, eas daemonis blaterat potestate peractas* ('Against someone who, unable to calmly accept the remarkable English victories, bleated about those deeds under the influence of the devil'), this time in response to any critics who may belittle the military achievements of the English army. Anne's triumphant campaigns are indeed celebrated by her compatriots, as described in poem 6, entitled *De triumphalibus Anglorum festis* ('On the triumphal festivities of the English') and across the world, as in poem 7, *Rudis horum carminum effictor vellet, sed non potest tantae regnatricis interesse victoriis* ('The humble writer of these songs would like to, but is unable to, take part in the victories of a such a queen').

Queen Anne also features in another Latin poem on the siege of Barcelona of 1706, entitled *Carolo III Austriaco, Hispaniarum atque Indiarum regi, regnorum avitorum vindici ac assertori, terra marique triumphanti, sacrum* ('A poem for the Austrian Charles III, king of Spain and the Indies, avenger and protector of the kingdoms of his ancestors, triumphant on land and at sea'). Totalling 109 hexameters and two elegiac couplets, the text was written by poet laureate Jakob Haake (J. I. Haakius de Bopfing, fl. 1699) and is dated 1 June 1706, only a few weeks after the end of the siege of Barcelona.[32] Queen Anne's name is celebrated in the final section of the poem, where the author invites Philip V to bow to Charles, 'the just heir, for whom Anne is fighting, for whom Dutch and English winds come, sworn to obey, at the call of the trumpet' (*Et cede haeredi iusto, cui militat Anna, / cui Batavi ac Angli veniunt in classica venti*, ll. 108–9). Haake's concluding words are an adaptation of Claudian's famous verses from his panegyric on the third consulship of the Emperor Honorius in which the pagan eulogist commemorates Theodosius' victory over the usurper Eugenius (394 CE), and credits the god Aeolus with dispatching wind favourable to Theodosius' cause.[33] Like Claudian, Haake describes how a sudden miraculous wind – here personified in the arrival of the Anglo-Dutch fleet – reversed the outcome of the battle and helped defeat the usurper Philip.

In Haake's poem the description of the siege of Barcelona of May 1706 is the last in a long series of military episodes revolving around Charles III. These begin in Vienna, shortly after the proclamation of Charles as the new king in September 1703. After the customary praise of the monarch (ll. 1–16), in which he is compared favourably with several heroes from antiquity, the author reflects on the deplorable state of Spain, engulfed in internal war (ll. 17–29). Haake then introduces a Spanish ambassador who pays a visit to the new king at the Imperial court and begs him to cross the seas to Spain, like Moses crossing the Red Sea, to free the country from the French (ll. 30–44). Charles's departure from Vienna and subsequent offensive on the Iberian Peninsula following his arrival in Lisbon are prophesied in detail by Nemesis (ll. 45–109). In her speech, the goddess of justice alludes to the seizure of Gibraltar by Allied troops (ll. 64–6) and to contemporary uprisings in Naples and Sicily against Bourbon rule (ll. 86–7). The main focuses of Nemesis' account, however, are the two successful sieges of Barcelona of 1705 and 1706. The 1705 siege results not only in the liberation of the city but also in the taking of most of Catalonia, which – like Achates, Aeneas' armour-bearer (*Aen.* 1.120, 174) – will remain ever loyal:

> *Tenditur ulterius, bona sors fit sola viarum*
> *arbitra duxque simul, socia dum Barcino classis*
> *vi petitur ruptisque seris tibi, Carole, iurat*
> *atque tui ingressu mox felix cingula laxat.*
> *Iamque tibi Catalonus ager quasi fidus Achates*
> *clamat ovans: 'Vindex vivat! Mea vincla revinxit*
> *Carolus, ut liceat manumisso plaudere; servus*
> *ante fui Gallo, canitur modo faustior ode'*

ll. 67–74

['The contest continues, and good fortune becomes both the only witness and guide to the roads, whilst Barcelona is attacked by the allied strength of a fleet and, once the defences are breached, it takes its oath to you, Charles, and, upon your entrance, it soon happily unlooses its belt. Like faithful Achates, the Catalan territory already proclaims exultant: "Long live the liberator! Charles released me from my chains to allow the emancipated to applaud; before I was a slave to France, now a more favourable song is being sung"'].

The siege of May 1706 – during which 'Gallic weapons fall under fearful shadows' (*Gallica dumque cadunt horrendas arma sub umbras*, l. 95) in a reference to the solar eclipse – paves the way for Charles's military expedition to Madrid. Once the enemy has retreated, the king is encouraged by Nemesis to march on the capital: 'Charles! Now that the enemy has been overcome, at last proceed to cherish your city of Madrid with its royal seat' (*Carole, perge tuam fusis hostibus urbem / denique Madritum regali sede fovere!*, ll. 99–100).

In June 1706, with the war on Spanish soil turning in Charles's favour if only for a few months, we can detect a note of triumphalism at the expense of Philip and his allies. We see this in the way Haake's poem combines celebratory verse with a more satirical account of the action. For example, following the first siege of Barcelona the entire principality stinks as the fleeing French soil themselves in terror (*Fit via vi, Gallus trepidis procul avolat alis, / cuius adhuc pavido Catalonia stercore foetet*, ll. 81–2). In the midst of all the hostilities, the sun is ashamed to rise at the sight of the filthy and deplorable flight of the French (*nempe die, solem qua solis ferre pudebat / ac spectare fugae foedos tristesque labores*, ll. 95–7). At the end of the poem – by means of wordplay on the etymology of the Bourbon's name Philip ('fond of horses') – Haake advises the Duke of Anjou to flee Spain on his own fleet-footed pack horse (*Sed tu tolle, Philippe, citum fugiture caballum*, l. 107). The Bourbon pretender and his allies are further derided in the two elegiac couplets appended to the poem, after the author's name. Here the invective is directed against Louis XIV and the Bavarian elector Maximilian Emanuel who was forced to seek refuge in Versailles following French defeat at the Battle of Ramillies. In the first couplet (*Dicitur Emmanuel comedens cum melle butyrum, / ut reprobare malum norit, amare bonum*) Maximilian Emanuel is compared to Immanuel, who 'shall eat curds and honey when he knows how to refuse the evil and choose the good' (Isa. 7.15); the second couplet addresses the French king and accuses Louis of 'bewitching and playing tricks on your supporters by mixing poison with honey' (*Miscuit incantans Ludovicus melle venenum, / ludis amatores sic, Ludovice, tuos!*). In Haake's piece, burlesque verses against the Bourbon pretender are found alongside an exaltation of Charles and his dynasty. The Latin mottos adopted by Charles and by his brother Emperor Joseph I (*Virtute patrum* and *Amore et timore* respectively) are skilfully inserted into the poem (ll. 22, 53 and 57).[34] Echoing Virgil's description of Aeneas, 'father of the Roman nation' (*Romanae stirpis origo*, Aen. 12.166), and his son Ascanius, 'the other hope for Rome's great future' (*magnae spes altera Romae*, Aen. 12.168), Nemesis celebrates Charles as 'the other hope for the Austrian nation' (*spes altera stirpis / Austriacae*, ll. 50–1). Throughout the poem, Haake is at pains to present Charles, whose dynastic rights to the Spanish throne had been upheld by his father in 1703, as a defender of the genealogical line and the political *status quo*, which Philip V's ascension to the Spanish throne had abruptly interrupted.

In these pro-Habsburg texts focused on the campaign in and around Barcelona, we see the continued use of Christian imagery, with a particular focus on the advocacy of the Virgin, as well as more references to classical and historical figures. The writers here, however, are not confining themselves to praising Charles, his commanders and his key ally, Queen Anne; they are also employing other propagandistic techniques – humour, mockery and invective – to attack the Bourbon camp.

Madrid and beyond

With Philip seeking refuge in France, the successful defence of Barcelona in the spring of 1706 had important consequences for Charles, who decided to march on Madrid. He left Barcelona on 23 June and, after completing a three-day sojourn in Montserrat to pay his respects and leave his sword, he resumed his journey. Charles's initial intention was to travel to Madrid via Valencia, but once the royal train had visited the monastery of Santa Maria de Poblet in southern Catalonia on 5 July, it progressed towards Lleida and Saragossa, where Charles had been proclaimed king on 29 June, three days earlier than he was in Madrid (2 July). However, hostility towards his troops prevented Charles from entering the Spanish capital in person. Threatened by a regrouped and stronger Bourbon army, he was forced to withdraw from Saragossa to Valencia, which his army had controlled since December 1705, and where he remained until 4 March 1707, only a few weeks before the disastrous defeat at Almansa (25 April) which changed the course of the war on Spanish soil (Albareda 2010: 129–91).

The end of the siege of Barcelona in the spring of 1706 opened Spain up to the Allied armies. This favourable backdrop provided several contemporary Latin poets with an excellent opportunity to signal their alliance with Charles's political faction. Praise of the House of Habsburg, – 'under which the entire world extends from sunrise to the western waves' (ll. 55–6) – is, for example, central to the poem *Carolus III invictissimus Hispaniarum rex* ('Charles III, most invincible king of Spain'), which is reproduced in Appendix 3. Running to 70 lines, this epyllion has been preserved in a single copy held in the library of Montserrat (Res. 4° 1/32). The library catalogue tentatively gives Barcelona and 1705 as the place and date of publication but the text must have been written to coincide with Charles's visit to Saragossa between 15 and 24 July 1706, when he was sworn in as king of Aragon (Pérez Álvarez 2012: 111–28). Proof of this is provided in the opening line, 'The presence of the king brings light to Caesar's Augustan [city]' (*Caesaris Augustam lustrat praesentia regis*), which includes an oblique reference to the Latin name of Saragossa in Roman times (*Caesaraugusta*).

We shall return to the supposed location of the poem shortly. First, let us focus on the last section of the piece, in which the author declares himself unworthy of describing the deeds of his mighty prince. Such an endeavour – he claims – cannot be undertaken by a petty prophet; rather, Charles requires the pen of a distinguished poet (*non est exigui de tanto principe vatis / scribere; magnificum desiderat ille poetam*, ll. 63–4). On closer examination, the modesty topos used by our poet proves rather misplaced, for the skilful versifier required for the task turns out to be not a single contemporary poet, but a coterie of earlier Latin poets whose works help the author assemble his own composition. To begin with, the concluding verses in which our poet expresses concern about his ability to deal adequately with the subject (ll. 61–6) reproduce verbatim six lines (2 + 4) from *Ligurinus*, an epic about Emperor Frederick I Barbarossa written by the German Cistercian Gunther of Pairis (c. 1150 – c. 1220). As shown in more detail in Appendix 3, literal quotations from Gunther of Pairis's text are reused throughout our poem. In fact, the author overtly acknowledges his indebtedness to *Ligurinus* and quotes in full two lines from book five (223–4) of Gunther of Pairis's epic on the title page (Figure 4).

Nonetheless, *Ligurinus* is not the only voice which can be heard beneath the 1706 Latin poem under review. Lines 3 to 5 and 11 to 33, which include a catalogue of Charles's princely virtues, reproduce almost in its entirety a substantial passage (ll. 69–94) from a piece in praise of Francesco Maria II della Rovere, duke of Urbino (1549–1631), penned by Livio Vitale Orosio (Livius Vitalis Orosius, fl. 1583), professor of Eloquence at Pesaro.[35] Both Vitale Orosio and the author of the anonymous poem of 1706 begin their panegyrics by echoing Virgil's encomium of Augustus (*Hic est, hic vir. . .*; *Aen.* 6.791) and simply replacing the name *Augustus Caesar* for *Franciscus* or *Carolus*. In the following lines, both authors praise the beauty, intelligence, righteousness, inquisitiveness and piety of their dedicatees. Occasionally, the attributes of the Duke of Urbino are adapted to Charles's world: whereas Francesco is carried by a two-coloured Calabrian horse which is compared to Pegasus and 'champs the yellow gold under its teeth' (ll. 87–8), the Spanish king is described as mounting a handsome pinto horse from Andalusia (ll. 26–7), the author of the poem on Charles no doubt reflecting Spain's reputation in antiquity for breeding fast horses (Darder Lissón 1996: 78). Furthermore, this characterization of Francesco and Charles riding is in turn modelled on representations of ancient

✠
CAROLVS III.
INVICTISSIMVS HISPANIARVM
REX.

Principis adventus velut nova Solis imago,
Cœperat optata radios effundere pacis.
Gunther. *Imperatori Friderico* I.
in Ligurino, lib. 5.

Et vt divvs Gregorivs Magnvs,
Phocæ Imperatori Avgvsto:

Sic Omnes
AVGVSTISSIMO PRINCIPI NOSTRO
CAROLO,
EXVLTANTES DICIMVS.

LORIA IN EXCELSIS DEO, qui iuxta quod scriptum est, mutat tempora, & transfert Regna, & qui hoc cunctis innotuit, quod per Prophetam suum loqui dignatus est dicens, Quia dominatur Excelsus in Regno hominum, & cui voluerit, ipse dat illud. In Omnipotentis quippè Dei incomprehensibili dispensatione alternatim vitæ mortalis sunt moderamina, & aliquandò cùm iniustorum multorũ peccata ferienda sunt, vnus erigitur, per cuius duritiam tribulationis iugo subiectorum colla deprimantur: quod in nostra diutius afflictione probavimus.

Ali-

Figure 4 *Carolus III invictissimus Hispaniarum rex*, s.l., s.d. (but surely 1706), title page, reproduced by kind permission of the Biblioteca de l'Abadia de Montserrat, Res. 4° 1/32.

heroes on horseback: underlying the depiction of the two rulers are Virgil's equestrian portraits of Priam's son Polites (*quem Thracius albis / portat equus bicolor maculis*, 'he rode on a Thracian horse with white markings', Aen. 5.565-6) and of Turnus (*maculis quem Thracius albis / portat equus*, 'the Thracian horse he rode had white markings', Aen. 9.49–50), as well as a reference to the horses chosen by Latinus for Aeneas' men (*fulvum mandunt sub dentibus aurum*, 'red-gold the bits they champed in their mouths', Aen. 7.279).

Intertextual echoes abound in the second section of the poem too (ll. 34–70). Here the author first addresses the sites recently liberated by Charles: Tarragona and Barcelona, whose description is drawn directly from Ausonius (*Epistles*, 24.89), the kingdom of Valencia, and finally Saragossa, on the river Ebro. After a spell under Bourbon rule, this city is saluted as the last location to have been freed by Charles's troops in the spring of 1706:

> *Quis decor imperii tanto sub principe surget?*
> *Iam nunc testantur post tot discrimina belli*
> *Tarraco et ostrifero superaddita Barcino ponto*
> *sicque Valentinus sospes, sic liber Hiberus,*
> *cum pius Augustam restaurat nomine Caesar*
>
> ll. 34–9

['What beauty will emerge under such a mighty prince? Now, after so many turning points in the war, bear witness Tarragona and Barcelona, built above the oyster-bearing sea, and thus fortunate Valencia and free Ebro, as devout Caesar restores the Augustan [city] with his name'].

The poem goes on to recreate Charles's arrival in the city. The following passage captures – in poetic language – the fervour with which the king is welcomed by his new subjects and provides the gist of his speech when sworn in as king of Aragon:

> *quae agnoscit dominum supplex regemque fatetur.*
> *Qui tunc ad cunctos sedato pectore fatur:*
> *'Quod nos in vestras bellum convertimus oras;*
> *nil mirum: clamant causae sub iudice iusto;*
> *non fuit hoc animo neque enim mihi quaero triumphos,*
> *antiquas repeto sedes et avita tueri*
> *regia iura volo: procedam Marte benigno'.*
> *Obtulit et princeps hostes auferre tyrannos,*
> *ulcisci scelerum noxas, punire nocentes,*
> *oppressos relevare manu, fraenare superbos*
>
> ll. 40–9

['Suppliant, Saragossa recognizes its master and acknowledges its king. He speaks to all of them with an untroubled heart: "We have turned this war around in your regions; good reasons under a fair judge proclaim that there is nothing extraordinary in this. This was not my intention, nor do I seek triumphs for myself. I reclaim ancient territories, and I wish to uphold the royal oaths of my ancestors: I shall proceed with Mars on my side." And indeed the prince offered to destroy the tyrant enemy, avenge the crimes of the wicked, punish wrongdoers, restore the oppressed by force and restrain the proud'].[36]

A brief analysis of these lines will help us to understand how the author operates. Making the subject of the sentence explicit (*quae*), the first line (l. 40) reproduces *Ligurinus* VI.388. The phrase *sedato pectore fatur* in the next line (l. 41) is the combination of two hemistichs from Virgil's *Aeneid* (*sedato pectore Turnus* – 'Turnus (speaks) with an untroubled heart', 9.740, and *inimico pectore fatur* – 'he speaks with a hostile heart', 10.556), introducing speeches by Turnus and Aeneas. Lines 42 and 43 appear to be original but the following three lines draw on a passage from the *Austrias* (1516) by Riccardo Bartolini, which celebrates Emperor Maximilian I (Book 6.535–7). After a further original line (l. 47) the last two verses reuse material once again from *Ligurinus* (III.92–3).

Analysis of *Carolus III invictissimus Hispaniarum rex* reveals that the poet constructed his verse by reusing lines from a variety of literary authorities. In the light of the author's extensive borrowing (only twenty of seventy lines appear to be original), it is tempting to dismiss his intentions and composition as insincere and mechanical. Yet, it is also possible to applaud the poet for his ability to adapt his epic models – whether classical, medieval, or early modern – to the present situation: the author may have had to complete his text at short notice to coincide with the royal visit to Saragossa in July 1706. Weaving together quotations from previous texts may have seemed the best solution in response to such a tight deadline. In so doing, he also showed his poetical skills.

After the 'ephemeral' proclamation of Charles as king of Spain in Madrid in the summer of 1706, the Allies chose to focus their efforts on the Balearic campaign. On 19 September Ibiza fell, followed by Majorca eight days later. On 4 October Charles was proclaimed king of Spain in Ibiza and Majorca (Albareda 2010: 126–7). The pro-Habsburg revolt that took place in Minorca on 11 October was, however, crushed three months later and the island remained in Bourbon hands until September 1708. The conquest of strategically important Majorca was praised by local writers, who had to put pen to paper promptly if they wished to seize the moment and ensure their texts were relevant to the contemporary readership. A twelve-page broadsheet, signed by Tomàs Barceló (d. 1723) on 7

October 1706, including prose texts and verse in Catalan, Spanish and Latin in praise of Charles III, came off the press of the Dominican convent in Majorca under the title *Pindáricas flores* ('Pindaric flowers', BC, 7-I-18/8). Barceló's choice of date for the publication of his volume – just a few days after Majorca had been restored to the Allies – was no coincidence, for 7 October is the Feast of Our Lady of the Rosary, a feast day instituted by the Catholic Church in thanksgiving for another naval victory, against the Turkish armada at the Battle of Lepanto on 7 October 1571. The title 'Pindaric flowers' adumbrates the mixture of classical and Christian imagery employed by Barceló, who is identified in a manuscript note as professor of Rhetoric at the local faculty and *praedicator continuus Sanctissimi Rosarii* ('regular preacher of the Confraternity of Our Lady of the Rosary [in Majorca]'). The subject matter of Barceló's texts is modelled on Pindar's victory odes, whilst the flowers are the garland of roses given to Mary, a common visual representation of the rosary in art. One of the six short Latin pieces included in the compilation gives a taste of Barceló's skill and eclectic literary sources. Here the poet plays on the various meanings of the Latin word *palma*: the palm of the hand, a palm tree and a badge of victory (and, still more generally, victory), but also the name of the city of Majorca (Palma de Mallorca), recently liberated by Charles:

> *Dum palmam, Carole, ascendis, meditare triumphos;*
>   *hostibus hinc domitis, regna parabis ovans.*
> *I decus, i, nostrum: palmaribus utere fatis;*
>   *stemma triumphantis se tibi palma dedit*

> ['Whilst you, Charles, climb the palm, reflect upon your victories; the enemy has been tamed: triumphant, you shall acquire your realms. Go now, glory of our race: enjoy an excellent fate; the palm has rendered itself to you as the garland of the vanquisher', p. 3].

The first couplet conceals a reference to the Song of Solomon (Cant. 7.9), in which the bridegroom declares: 'I will climb the palm-tree; I will take hold of its fruit' (*Ascendam in palmam et apprehendam fructus eius*). The source of the second couplet is the final line of Deiphobus' farewell address to Aeneas in Virgil's *Aeneid*: 'Go now, glory of our race: enjoy a better fate' (*I decus, i, nostrum; melioribus utere fatis*, 6.546).

The use of source texts here – quoted verbatim in *Carolus III invictissimus* or more subtly referenced in the *Pindáricas flores* – raises some interesting questions. To what extent was the contemporary readership aware or appreciative of these intertextual echoes? Did the need for writers to respond rapidly to events on the ground influence their use or choice of source material? Whatever the case, it is evident just from both poets' skill in handling their source material, not to mention their use of other poetic devices, that they had clear literary pretentions.

On European soil

The successful sieges of Barcelona and Majorca in May and September 1706 coincided with important victories by Charles's commanders elsewhere on the continent. After the Battle of Ramillies in May 1706, town after town in Flanders proclaimed Charles as their sovereign; just over three months later, on 7 September, Turin succumbed to the troops led by Prince Eugene of Savoy and by November most of Piedmont had been liberated from the French, and the war in Italy was over. As with the military victories on the Spanish front discussed in the previous sections, the Allied triumphs of 1706 in Flanders and northern Italy were commemorated by several Latin writers across Europe (Deneire 2006). Upon Eugene's return to Vienna from Turin, accounts in Latin of his earlier military exploits in Italy were reprinted, to the glory of the victorious prince: a clear indication that there was an enthusiastic readership for this material.[37] Last but not least, Allied victories in northern and southern Europe were represented in *Theatrum bellicum* ('A military spectacle'), a series of nine plates brought out in 1707 in a lavish bilingual (Latin and Dutch) edition by the Amsterdam publisher Peter Schenk (1660–1718).[38]

The successes of Charles's armies in Catalonia, Belgium and Piedmont also inspired the poet laureate Erhard Reusch (1678–1740) to turn to prose to celebrate these campaigns in an *Oratio solennis* delivered in February 1707 in Altdorf, where he held the chair of Rhetoric.[39] The speech celebrates the achievements of the Duke of Marlborough and of Prince Eugene at Ramillies and Turin respectively, but the most extensive passage within Reusch's work (eight pages in total) is devoted to the siege of Barcelona, which follows the narrative we have encountered in other accounts of the episode. Though Reusch at times names some of the commanders who participated in the siege and gives exact numbers of the forces involved in the battle, he is not overtly preoccupied with providing an accurate and full description of the events he is recounting. Absent from the battlefield, Reusch must have consulted some of the *relationes*, the official – and clearly partisan – reports printed in several languages immediately after the fighting, which may have supplied him with precise information about the siege.⁴⁰ Among other sources available to him was the *Relation und Continuation Diarii Ihrer Königl. Majest. in Spanien Karl des Dritten vom 29 Mertz biß 15 May 1706* ('An Account with its Continuation of the Diary of his Majesty Charles III in Spain from 29 March to 15 May 1706').⁴¹ This extensive report describes the prelude to the siege, the siege itself in some detail, and its outcome. It also contains specific information about the disposition and composition of the forces employed by both camps. Though chiefly concerned with charting the daily progress of military operations, the text occasionally presents vivid accounts of certain episodes and gives an insight into the behaviour of the protagonists, above all Charles. The entry for 6 April describes, for example, how 'today His Catholic Majesty rode once again through the city, accompanied by the customary cortège of Catalan noblemen, and summoned his people to fight with courage and valour' (p. 5). When encouraged by his subjects on 22 April to seek refuge outside Barcelona, the king addresses the crowd in a paternal fashion and pledges to remain in the city and continue the fight (p. 10).

It is, of course, impossible to say for certain whether Reusch consulted the *Relation und Continuation* but – like the official reporter – he must have recognized the dramatic potential afforded by some of the events which took place in Barcelona in the spring of 1706. Several episodes within the siege are recounted in the first person plural, as if Reusch himself had witnessed the events, and his audience is repeatedly directed to what is purported to be happening on the battlefield. Throughout the speech read at Altdorf, Reusch strives to implant images in the minds of his listeners by means of a series of rhetorical devices. He devotes considerable space to the description of the solar eclipse coinciding with the arrival of the Allied fleet, which is interpreted by Reusch as an ominous sign of the Sun King's twilight.⁴² Charles's determination in leading his troops – claims the author – must be considered all the more extraordinary given the sovereign's age: 'we never knew the prince as a child, never as a youngster, always as a king' (*quem [principem] nunquam puerum fuisse, nunquam adolescentem, semper regem comperimus*, Reusch 1707: 7). In addition, comparisons with figures from antiquity also help animate the narrative. The courage exhibited by local women surpasses that of the Amazons; Queen Anne is commended as a second Semiramis, the celebrated queen of Assyria, and a second Tomyris, a Scythian queen who defeated and killed the elder Cyrus; and Charles is favourably compared to Codrus, whose death ensured the safety of Athens against the Dorians.⁴³ Reusch notes that Charles showed the same valour as Codrus but, unlike the Athenian king, he saved

Barcelona without having to sacrifice his life. By contrasting the wickedness of the Bourbon troops with the fearlessness shown by all civilians, 'the highest, middle and lowest; the sacred, the profane; men, women, the very old and peace-loving children' (*Maximi, medioxumi, infimi; sacri, profani; viri, foeminae; senes decrepiti, imbelles pueri*, p. 7), Reusch condemns the French soldiers, referred to as 'those sly foreigners' (*callidi isti hospites*, p. 6), and ridicules the enemy for the manner in which it was obliged to abandon the siege: 'Here you would have witnessed a Troy outside Troy' (*Troiam hic vidisses extra Troiam*, p. 11).

The sense of drama in the *Oratio solennis* is heightened primarily through the introduction of passionate speeches with which Reusch tries to move his audience by blurring truth and fiction. When news of the imminent siege reaches the Allied camp, the crowd promises to defend the city at all cost: '"To arms, to arms! they shout"' ('*Ad arma, ad arma!, clamitant*', p. 7). Charles's commanders react to his decision to remain inside the walls with an anxious plea about his wellbeing:

'*Quid, quod Deus avertat!, si in obsidione perires? Quid, si armati muros parum firmos expugnarent? Quid, si ad deditionem te compellerent? Pauci utique forent, qui virtutem tuam laudarent; multi, qui vitio darent; hostes, qui per regna, per urbes urbiumque plateas, per oppida, vicos, pagos te in triumpho ducentes tibi insultarent; at quid hostium insultatione gravius? Amici et foederati, quos simul tecum in servitutem coniiceres; cives, quos mactandos victori adduceres*'

p. 8

['"What if, God forbid, you died in the siege? What if soldiers broke through a weakness in the walls? What if they forced you to surrender? There would be few who would praise your valour; many who would put it down to an error; your enemies, carrying you in triumph through cities, down broad city streets, through towns, through the country, would insult you. But what is more severe than the enemy's insult? Friends and allies, whom you would throw into servitude; citizens, whom you would lead to be punished by the victor"'].

Allied assistance – as argued by Charles's officials – cannot be guaranteed ('*Classis auxilia incerta sunt; procul enim abest et pericula nostra ignorat; nec aliunde auxilium exspectandum*', '"Help from the fleet is uncertain; it is some way off and unaware of the danger we are facing; nor is assistance expected from other quarters"') and the king's presence in Barcelona will not '"avoid the injustice"' (p. 8). For his sake and that of his friends and subjects, Charles is therefore encouraged to flee, recruit further troops, and break the siege ('*Exi itaque ex urbe, militem conscribe eumque ad solvendam obsidionem adduc; et tibi et amicis et civibus consules quam rectissime*', '"Leave the city, raise an army and lead it to break the siege; thus you look after yourself, your friends and subjects most properly"', p. 8). His lapidary answer puts an end to the matter: '"What are you afraid of?" he says. "Charles is here!"' (*'Quid trepidatis?', inquit. 'Carolus adest!'*, p. 9). Reusch then turns to his audience and rhetorically invites them to decide whether it was Charles's valour and God's assistance or the weapons of civilians and the military that defended Barcelona (*Iudicate, quaeso, auditores, annon Caroli virtus, divini numinis praesidio nixa, magis defenderit Barcinonem quam civium militumque arma?*, 'I beseech you, my audience, to judge whether Charles's courage, bolstered by divine support, was a greater defence for Barcelona than the arms of its citizens and soldiers', p. 9).

Almansa and Toulon

On the Spanish mainland the tide of events was not so favourable to the Allies. By November 1706, Philip controlled the Crown of Castile, Murcia and parts of the kingdom of Valencia. The campaign to recover the city of Valencia was led by James Fitzjames (1670–1734), first duke of Berwick, who was in command of the Bourbon forces in the Peninsula. On 25 April 1707 he was challenged by British and Portuguese troops outside the town of Almansa, near Albacete. The battle was a total defeat for the Allies and Charles was subsequently 'compelled to rely solely on the resources of his Catalan supporters' (Kamen 1969: 19). Bourbon success at Almansa was followed by the siege of Toulon later that year, when a combined Savoyard and Imperial field army supported by a British naval force was defeated by the French.

After Almansa and Toulon the moral initiative was swiftly regained by pro-Bourbon propagandists, who seized the opportunity provided by both military victories with alacrity.[44] Once again we see that authors are quick to react to events on the ground and to incorporate references to or descriptions of recent events, favourable to their side, into their writings. In the summer of 1707, the French Jesuit Noël-Étienne Sanadon (1676–1733) composed an Alcaic ode (see Appendix 2.3), not ostensibly to celebrate Almansa and Toulon, but rather to commemorate the imminent birth of Prince Louis (the future Louis I of Spain, d. 1724), Philip's heir, who was born on 25 August 1707, four days after the siege of Toulon formally ended.[45] There is much of interest in this ode. In the first three stanzas Sanadon addresses the king and expresses his hope that Fortune, however haughty, will guide Philip's efforts and will not remove his crown: the monarch should, therefore, have no fear even if the alliance of the Dutch, the

British, the emperor and the Duchy of Savoy strives to wage a hateful war (ll. 9–12).[46] The glory and valour of the Bourbon dynasty, handed down from generation to generation, will help him overcome the enemy (ll. 13–16). Philip's claims to the Spanish crown will be forever affirmed not only by the birth of young Prince Louis (ll. 17–24) but also by Berwick's victory at Almansa, 'filled with the blood of our enemies' (*hostili ebria sanguine*, l. 25). In stanza eight Victor Amadeus II, Duke of Savoy (1666–1732) is described as 'the fiery Allobrogian' (*fervidus Allobrox*, l. 29) in a subtle allusion to the Allobroges, a warlike Gallic people in what is current-day Savoy, who first swore loyalty to Rome and subsequently rebelled but were finally subjugated in 121 BCE. As with his remote ancestors, Victor Amadeus is depicted as deceitful: he was initially loyal to the Bourbon cause but switched sides, joining the Grand Alliance in November 1703 (Symcox 1983: 108–10).[47] This classical reference enables Sanadon to give a contemporary twist to an episode in 'French' history:

> *Atque pudendae fervidus Allobrox*
> *purgare cladis dedecus adparat,*
> *Telonis obsessas ahenis*
> *fulminibus iaculatus arces,*
> *frustra*
>
> ll. 29–33

['And yet the fiery Allobrogian prepares to atone for a shameful defeat [Almansa], assailing the besieged fortress of Toulon with thunderbolts of bronze, to no avail'].

The last four stanzas (ll. 33–48) constitute a rebuke of Prince Eugene's tactics, which forced him to lift the siege. The prince is compared to a voracious lion chased away by dogs and shepherds (*fugax princeps*) and forced into hiding 'under high forests' (*sub altis sylvis*, perhaps a reference to his flight across the Alps in early September). This was not Sanadon's only Latin poem reflecting on military and courtly events of 1707. Shortly after the royal birth, he composed two further odes and an elegy for the occasion, in which the war also features.[48] In the latter (*Ludovico Asturum principi recens nato munera*, 'Gifts for Louis, the new-born prince of Asturias [the title given to the heir to the Spanish throne]'), the dates of the Battle of Almansa and of Prince Louis's birthday are granted an almost transcendental significance as they coincide with key events within French history, namely the dates of birth and death of Louis IX, commonly known as Saint Louis (25 April 1214–25 August 1270).[49]

That the military balance, at least on the Peninsula, had swung in Philip's favour was sensed by many in the Allied camp. Writing to Gisbert Cuper (1644–

1716), a diplomat and antiquarian based in Deventer, from Florence on 15 November 1707, Sir Henry Newton (1651–1715), Queen Anne's envoy to Genoa and Tuscany, bemoaned the outcome of Toulon.[50] In his letter Newton also deplored the state of 'whatever is left of Charles's Spain, which can barely draw breath', and concluded: 'One would almost have to despair of Catalonia, were this afflicted province not to be aided by the auxiliary troops of the Imperial army from Italy'.[51] By contrast, optimism prevailed among Philip's supporters, who sensed that, while Almansa and Toulon may not have won the war, they could nevertheless have lasting consequences. Only a few weeks after Newton's letter, in a speech given at the Parisian Collège Louis-le-Grand under the title *Res prosperas hostibus minus gloriae, quam adversas Gallis peperisse*, the Jesuit and professor of Eloquence Gabriel François Le Jay rejoiced that the past year of his life had been made memorable by French victories in Europe.[52] By means of the paradox in the title ('Less glory has been attained by our enemies in prosperity than by the French in adversity'), Le Jay demonstrates that all the advantages gained by the Allies in the war's early campaigns have proved in vain. As with Cannae and other defeats, from which ancient Rome emerged fortified, French troops have overcome the initial setbacks, and Archduke Charles is hopelessly constrained by the boundaries of a single province ([*Discat*] *hostis spe frustratus sua ... iam conclusus intra breves unius provinciae angustias*, p. 496). Victory at Almansa has left Valencia and Aragon open for 'the legitimate prince' (*Nam quid Valentiae, quid Arragoniae regnum dicam ad obsequium legitimi principis revocatum?*, p. 501). Aware that his expectant audience credits Berwick and Philippe II, duke of Orleans (1674–1723), with the military success of the past campaign, Le Jay then duly launches into a eulogy of their heroes (pp. 501–2).[53] The speech concludes on an ironic note: 'Let us, my audience, count it among our adversities if our enemies have presumed to attack France's intact borders.'[54] This sentiment is confirmed by the siege of Toulon, where Allied defeat ended hopes of attacking France through its vulnerable southern border.

Remembering past glories

With the occupation of the whole of the kingdom of Valencia, the kingdom of Aragon and the western regions of Catalonia, it was looking increasingly unlikely that Philip V would be excluded from the Spanish succession. At a crucial juncture during the Catalan campaign, after the surrender of Lleida (November 1707) and Tortosa (July 1708), the Allied propaganda machine needed a boost.

Long after the end of the battle the courage displayed by Charles during the 1706 siege of Barcelona was still a source of great pride for the Habsburg side, and this seems to have been understood by those responsible for the poem *Barcino a Carolo III, Hispaniarum rege, feliciter propugnata anno 1706* ('Barcelona auspiciously defended by Charles III, king of Spain, in the year 1706').[55] Printed at Barcelona by Rafael Figueró, this anonymous piece in 653 hexameters divided into two cantos chronicles in heroic style the key events of the siege. The first canto – 349 lines in total – begins with a programmatic declaration on the part of the poet and an invocation to the Muses.[56] After the introductory verses, the author praises the determination with which Charles and his generals pledge to defend the city on the arrival of the Bourbon army (ll. 16–72). The city's defence falls mostly to the urban militia, supported by civilians from other localities at the command of Viceroy Leo Uhlefeld (ll. 73–89). He refuses to accept the surrender terms proposed by a French emissary (ll. 90–110), a decision which triggers Philip's offensive against Montjuïc (ll. 111–232). Following a temporary truce to bury the dead, the Bourbon army attacks Barcelona from both land and sea, but Allied ships successfully break through the enemy's lines and reach the city harbour (ll. 233–83). The poet then extols the fierce resistance of the Barcelona populace and the courage shown by several Allied generals (ll. 284–331), among them Prince Henry of Hesse-Darmstadt (1674–1741), brother of the deceased Prince George and 'son of Bellona and Mars' (*Bellonae et Martis genitus*, l. 335). The fall of the city seems inevitable (ll. 332–44) but the canto concludes on a hopeful note with the announcement of the imminent arrival of the Anglo-Dutch fleet:

I decus, i clarum belli, pete sidera fama,
praebeat emeritos orbis tibi totus honores.
Anglica quid Tethys simul et quid Belgica virtus
nunc egere, canam; Pindi date carmina divae,
altius ut resonet plectrum. Sed Musa quiescit

ll. 345–9

['Go now, illustrious glory of our war, go, seek the stars through fame and let the entire world render you the honours you deserve. I shall now sing of the combined deeds of the English Tethys and Belgian valour; allow my song, goddesses of Pindus, so that my lyre may resound louder. But now the Muse is silent'].

Comprising 304 lines, the second canto commences with a description of the coming of spring featuring Zephyrus, Neptune, the Nereids and Eulàlia, patron saint of Barcelona (ll. 1–14). At the behest of the divine council, Proteus causes great havoc in the Bourbon camp by exploding an arsenal (ll. 15–87). Tethys instructs Aeolus to blow a wind favourable to Charles (ll. 88–120). After disembarking without opposition, British and Dutch soldiers destroy the last vestiges of Bourbon resistance with the aid of Jupiter (ll. 121–86). A solar eclipse appears to herald the defeat of the French army, which retreats in disorder (ll. 187–236). The last section of the poem includes a catalogue of the Allied heroes who fought in the siege (ll. 237–74) as well as verses in honour of Emperor Joseph I and of Charles's wife Elisabeth Christine of Brunswick-Wolfenbüttel (ll. 275–304).

Throughout the text the author shows himself well acquainted with the conventions of the epic genre. Alongside allusions to the king's father, the late Emperor Leopold I, and to his brother Emperor Joseph, Charles's name occurs twenty times, always printed in capital letters. Exaltation of political rulers, catalogues of warriors, elaborate descriptions of weapons and warfare and the use of prophecies and classical mythology to frame the narrative of the battle are all deftly employed by the poet. In addition, from the outset, intertextual echoes from Virgil and Ovid can be heard throughout the text.[57] The poem on the 1706 siege of Barcelona, however, goes beyond an accomplished reworking of its illustrious classical models. Although *Barcino a Carolo III propugnata* may have been written for the most part shortly after the end of the siege, several references to later events at the end of the second canto seem to indicate that the piece was completed as late as the summer of 1707. In the last section of the text the author alludes to John V of Portugal's betrothal to Archduchess Maria Anna of Austria, '[which] will add bonds of blood to the treaty of friendship [a reference to the first treaty of Methuen of 16 May 1703, whereby Peter II of Portugal had joined the allied cause]' (*[Lusitanus] foederi amicitiae rex vincula sanguinis addet*, l. 259), the marriage contract being signed in late June 1707 (see following chapter). By means of an anagram, he describes Elisabeth Christine – whose betrothal to Charles was not announced to the people of Barcelona until 18 August 1707 – as a new goddess of the rainbow, 'who shall restore peace and prosperous times and shall make you, Charles, the father of a beautiful child'.[58]

Further internal evidence seems to confirm that the poem must have been published at a much later stage, certainly not before 23 April 1708, the date of the wedding by proxy of Charles III and Elisabeth Christine, who is referred to as *regina* in two of the four epigrams included between and after the two cantos. The first of these (f. 16) describes the queen's arrival in Milan on 31 May en route to Barcelona, where the ratification of the royal wedding took place on 1 August. The sumptuous ball held at the Palau de la Generalitat in Barcelona during the marriage celebrations is the subject of the second epigram (f. 27). The wedding of Charles and Elisabeth Christine was an important event and no doubt a highlight of life at court.[59] However, the contrast between the austere conditions of war and the luxury and refinement of the court became more pronounced, and relations between the monarch and the local institutions were often strained (Torras i Ribé 1999: 217–61). Printed by Figueró, the man responsible for the publication of all documents related to the royal household since Charles III's arrival in Barcelona (Camprubí 2018), *Barcino a Carolo III propugnata* served a clear political function by looking back at the certainties of 1706 and commemorating – albeit rather late in the day – one of the last victories of the Allied troops against the Bourbon enemy on the Peninsula during this dynastic conflict. It is also a clear indication of just how important the sieges of Barcelona had been to the Habsburg cause in the war that two years on they were still a favoured narrative for Charles's supporters. And this in turn is also a clear sign of how the tide had turned in Philip's favour in the war on the Peninsula.

Oudenarde and Malplaquet

Despite the setbacks suffered at Almansa and Toulon, Allied troops proved to be almost invincible on all the other fronts in Europe. After a prolonged lull in 1707 and the French gains of early 1708, victory over the Bourbon army at Oudenarde in July that year was followed by the surrender of Lille in December. These military successes were also widely celebrated by Latin writers engaged by the pro-Habsburg side. David Money (1998: 133–4 and 328–30; and 2008) has examined the poetic responses to the Battles of Oudenarde and Lille, some of which were included in the university collections of commemorative poetry produced by Oxford and Cambridge to lament the death of Queen Anne's husband, Prince George of Denmark, in October 1708. Academic institutions elsewhere in Europe also issued anthologies of Latin panegyric verse expressing pride in the Allied military achievements since the outbreak of the war.[60] Poems of this kind are, for example, to be found in another *Promotionsschrift*, the *Laureae novi saeculi a Marte Austriaco hoc in bello relatae* ('An account of the victories obtained by the Austrian Mars of the new century in the course of this war', Vienna, 1708).[61] Though most likely penned by Professor Anton Khogler (SJ), the nine pieces in *Laureae novi saeculi* are 'authored' by the Viennese Parnassus, a name concealing the class of Poetry (Dörrie 1968: 417), who also signs the prefatory remarks addressed to the recently graduated cohort in Arts,

Letters and Philosophy. As with many of these *Promotionsschrift* volumes, the annotated poems included in this collection – all rich in allusions to classical literature and history – are thematically arranged, and the compositions included here greet Allied victories (or valiant efforts by Allied commanders) in Europe between 1704 and 1706. The order of the military episodes described is not, however, chronological but hierarchical, arranged in descending order according to the rank of the commander: Emperor Joseph (victorious at Landau in 1704), King Charles III (Barcelona, 1706), Prince Eugene of Savoy and the Duke of Marlborough (Battle of Blenheim, 1704, and Turin, 1706), Prince George of Hesse-Darmstadt (Barcelona, 1705), Colonel Baron Christian Ernst von Fresen (who heroically defended the fortress of Verrua between October 1704 and April 1705), and Count Wirich Philipp von Daun (Turin, 1706). Whereas the penultimate poem celebrates the combined deeds of the Imperial troops during the Italian campaign of 1706, the collection closes on a mournful note, lamenting the death of Joseph, duke of Lorraine, killed at the Battle of Cassano in August 1705.

Though there were important Allied victories at Oudenarde and Lille in 1708, France's northern frontiers remained largely intact, and her army was far from being fully defeated despite being exposed to one of the coldest winters ever witnessed in Europe (Oury 2020: 89–92). In June 1709 an Allied offensive led by Marlborough and Prince Eugene in Flanders was launched against the fortresses of Tournai (which fell after an unusually long siege of almost seventy days), Ypres, and Mons. Under new orders from Louis XIV, Marshal Claude Louis Hector de Villars (1653–1734) moved to prevent the fall of Mons at all costs. After several complicated manoeuvres, on 11 September 1709 the two armies faced each other across the gap of Malplaquet, southwest of Mons. Although it was a Grand Alliance success by the norms of warfare of the era, the number of casualties was very high (25,000 on the Allied side compared to the French losses of 12,000), and it led to a reversal of fortunes, with the dismissal of the Duke of Marlborough, and a newly confident French king resolving to continue to fight (MacDowall 2020). 'A bloody battle fought over an insignificant strategic objective' (Johnstone 2018: 108), Malplaquet represented Marlborough's nadir as a general. Historians of eighteenth-century warfare also agree on Eugene's secondary role on the battlefield, where he appears to have been underused despite his impressive military credentials (Johnstone 2018: 110). This is not, however, reflected in the portrayal of the Prince of Savoy in contemporary visual or literary accounts of the battle from Allied quarters, which describe his performance as well as the overall military operations at Malplaquet in most

Figure 5 *The Battle of Malplaquet*, oil on plaster, by Louis Laguerre (1663–1721) and assistants, c. 1713–14, reproduced by kind permission of the Royal Collection Trust / © His Majesty King Charles III 2023.

favourable terms.[62] Understandably, these reports omit any reference to the high number of casualties or to the Allies' tactical errors during the battle. 'The House of the king of France is for the most part ruined', bragged the authors of the *Lettre de messieurs les deputez à leurs hautes puissances escrite de l'armee devant Mons, le 14. Septembre 1709* ('Letter from the deputies to their commanders written from the army before Mons, 14 September 1709', ÖNB, 71813-B), whilst commending Eugene's 'unparalleled bravery' (p. 3). Similarly, in his *Lettre à leurs hautes puissances, de l'armee a la chapelle de Montplaquet le 11. Septembre 1709* ('Letter to their commanders, from the army at the chapel of Montplaquet, 11 September 1709', ÖNB, 71837-B), Count Claude Frédéric t'Serclaes de Tilly (1648–1723), one of the Allied generals present at the battle, praised the courage shown by Eugene's forces. The prince's heroic leadership at Malplaquet is also the theme of a 44-line *Ode Sapphica serenissimo Eugenio sacra* ('Sacred Sapphic ode to the most serene Eugene') published by the Viennese University printer Christoph Lercher and signed by a *W.E.G. Presbyter* (see Appendix 2.4).[63] The only copy known to exist (ÖNB, 307098-B) is not dated but the poem must have been written (and most likely printed) in 1709 for this is the year given by the Roman numerals M, D, C, L, X, X, X, X, X, V, I, I, I, I appearing in capital letters in each stanza. Throughout the poem, courage is seen as Eugene's foremost quality. Even though other virtues are mentioned, viz. his steadfastness and skill in directing the lines of battle (as depicted in stanza 10), fortitude is always the most highly esteemed and the prince is described as 'brave' on several occasions (*fortis heros*, l. 1; *Eugeni fortis*, l. 7; *tua ferre facta / fortius acta*, ll. 19–20), and he is twice compared to Hercules (ll. 27 and 37). The description of his weapons in stanza 9 also helps to convey his military prowess. After his victory (*cape iure vivas / Martis olivas*, '[Eugene,] take rightfully the fresh olives of Mars', ll. 3–4), Eugene will achieve renown and glory: the poet's heart, full of divine inspiration (*Cor sacra plenum fluat Hippocrene*, 'Let my heart overflow full of the sacred Hippocrene [fountain associated with the Muses]', l. 9), will celebrate the hero's deeds, which will obtain worldwide fame (stanza 2). Countries and people – above all those fighting alongside the Prince of Savoy – will hear of and admire him:

> *Concinunt Anglus, Batavus decores,*
> *debitos laeti resonant honores:*
> *quisque victrici tua gesta lauro*
>   *inserit auro.*
> *Auget applausus Italus per Alpes*
> *et per excelsae iuga magna Calpes*
> *fervet Hispanus tua ferre facta*
>   *fortius acta*
>
>   ll. 13–20, stanzas 4 and 5

['The English and the Dutch celebrate your grace in a song; they rejoice in singing of your well-deserved honours: each inscribes your deeds in gold on the victory laurel. Italians make their applause sound through the Alps and Spaniards eagerly tell of your most heroic actions throughout the high summits of lofty Calpe (one of the pillars of Hercules, now the Rock of Gibraltar)'].

In the following three stanzas (6, 7 and 8) Eugene's princely virtues are sharply contrasted with Gallic rage, cruelty and deceitfulness (*Quas per astutas tenuere fraudes* [*Galli*], l. 21). It is the French army which has poured 'hurtful blood' (*nocuo cruore*, l. 26) into the river Scheldt, in whose vicinity Malplaquet lies. And, yet, 'our Hercules plucked the lilies' (the symbol of the House of Bourbon) and, 'Prince Eugene, your hand crushed the French, often raging with blind fury'

(*Hercules noster . . . lillia pellit*, ll. 27-8, and *Saepe quas* [*Gallicas gentes*] *coeca rabie furentes, / Eugeni princeps!, tua dextra fregit*, ll. 30-1).

Just as Charles's role in the siege of Barcelona continued to provide propaganda material long after the Habsburg's campaign had faltered on the Peninsula, so Prince Eugene continued to be the key commander on the Allied side, consistently praised for his personal and leadership qualities, even when his performance on the battlefield, as at Malplaquet, did not live up to his previous record.

A crucial year: 1710

Within a year the war scenario had changed profoundly. For the forces of the Grand Alliance failure in northern France and Flanders was repeated in Spain. Though the Allies' counter-offensive, led by General James Stanhope (1673–1721) and Marshal Starhemberg (1657–1737), managed to reach Madrid in late September 1710 after victories at Almenar (Lleida) and Saragossa earlier that summer, they were compelled to retreat from the Spanish capital, and British and Austrian troops surrendered at the Battle of Brihuega on 9 December, and the Battle of Villaviciosa the next day. Two days later Saragossa fell again to Philip V. Military reputations come and go, and, at Brihuega and Villaviciosa, Marshal Vendôme exacted some revenge for his defeat at Oudenarde.[64] At the same time another French army under the command of the Duke of Noailles (Adrien Maurice de Noailles, 1678–1766) invaded northern Catalonia. With the intention of smoothing the way to Barcelona, he decided to besiege Girona at the end of 1710, and the city fell to Bourbon troops on 25 January the following year.

In the early weeks of 1711 Italian and French printers chose to mark the victories at Brihuega, Villaviciosa and Girona with laudatory Latin verse.[65] At the behest of the Senate of Palermo, where the Hispanophile, land-owning upper class had remained loyal to Philip V, Antonio Epiro published *Le simpatie dell'allegrezza tra Palermo e la Castiglia* ('Festivities conveying the joyfulness between Palermo and Castile').[66] The volume is an account by Pietro Vitale (1656–1728) of the ceremonies held in the city to commemorate Philip's military triumphs on Spanish soil, and was dedicated to the viceroy of Sicily, Carlos Felipe Antonio Spínola y Colonna (1665–1721), who had been largely responsible for ensuring the island remained in Bourbon hands after the Allied invasion of the kingdom of Naples in 1707. *Le simpatie dell'allegrezza* features abundant miscellaneous material in both Italian and Latin, from recreations of the ecclesiastical and civic processions which took place in the city (Chapters 5 and

10), to descriptions of the ornaments displayed for the occasion on local churches, palaces and private houses (Chapters 4, 6, 7, 8 and 9). In the volume epigrams and inscriptions in Latin (some of them on the temporary arches erected at major city intersections and squares) are presented side by side with sonnets and other poetic compositions in the vernacular.[67] The latter are mostly in praise of Philip V and the Virgin, whose assistance at Brihuega on 9 December – the day after the Feast of the Immaculate Conception – was deemed as crucial to the battle's outcome. As an example, the monarch's birthday (on 19 December, an auspicious date resulting from adding the dates of the two battles fought days earlier) is given added lustre by *La gara planetaria* ('The planetary contest'), a dialogue featuring the sun, Jupiter, Venus and Mars (pp. 10–16). Some of the solemn processions held during the ceremonies were accompanied by music, as shown by a further text in Italian, *Le acclamationi festive del fedelissimo Palermo da cantarsi sotto le machine erette nel passeggio de la cavalcata* ('The festive acclamations of most faithful Palermo, to be sung underneath the machines erected along the route of the procession', pp. 37–40), in which mythological characters (a choir of Sicilian nymphs, Orpheus, Mars and Fortune), a group of soldiers and the city of Palermo praise the victorious king. Underlying this seemingly light-hearted composition is a vehement political diatribe against the enemy. Having tamed the Allies with his lyre, Orpheus mocks 'the Dutch bear and the English lion, the Insubrian serpent [a reference to the symbol of Milan], and the Catalan dragon' (*l'orsa Batava, e l'Anglican leone, / il serpe Insubro, e il Catalan dracone*), which run away in fear at the sight of Philip and his army (p. 39).

The local Jesuit college in Palermo also joined in the celebrations and decided to commemorate the military triumphs in Spain by commissioning a temporary construction on the building's façade, made of wood and painted plaster on cloth. The work displayed an image of the king with the inscription *Regnorum votis Philippo V Hispaniarum regi ac liberatori invictissimo Panormitanum Collegium gratulatur* ('The [Jesuit] College of Palermo congratulates Philip V, king of Spain and most invincible liberator, with the solemn promises of his kingdoms'), and a series of fourteen boards (*tabelloni*), each of them bearing a Latin inscription and representing the fourteen territories of Spain, including Sicily (pp. 59–66). In the Latin texts accompanying the ensemble pride of place is given to New Castile, where Madrid is located; Navarre, incorporated into the Spanish Crown as late as the early sixteenth century, closes the list. The eleventh position is occupied by Catalonia, the only region in 1711 still resistant to the Bourbon yoke, which however promises to repent and strives to free itself from 'the two-headed monster' (an allusion to the Habsburgian eagle). Only then – concludes the text – will the principality be able to appreciate the delicacy of the Bourbon lily:

> *Cataluania. Liceat et mihi gratulari, quando amicus orbis tuis, Philippe, fruitur triumphis. Nonne triumphos comitantur devicti hostes? A monstro bicipite merito ad Lilia me praeripiam. Exanguis si qua vita fugit, suavissimo florum odore redibit. Iuverit aliquando error, qui meliora concinnat obsequia ... I ergo victor, rediturus triumphator. Devicta te victorem Catalaunia sequetur*

> ['Catalonia. Let me also congratulate you, Philip, as the well-disposed world rejoices in your triumphs. Is it not the case that defeated enemies share in the triumphs? I will deservedly snatch myself away from the two-headed monster to the lilies. If it departs bloodless from this life, it will return with the most agreeable scent of flowers. The mistake which brings about better gifts will have done good one day ... Go, therefore, you victor, to come back as one who celebrates a triumph. Defeated, Catalonia will follow you as victorious', p. 64].

Catalonia – and, above all, its capital Barcelona – is also urged to abandon Charles's hopeless cause in a collection of Jesuit Latin verse exalting Philip's military victories on Spanish soil, which was published in Paris in March 1711.[68] As with its Viennese counterpart examined in the previous section, the volume is firmly placed in an academic setting, that of the Collège Louis-le-Grand, where the pieces may have been recited. The six opening compositions – penned by the aforementioned Noël-Étienne Sanadon as well as Jacques Loungueval (1680–1735), Pierre D'Orival, Robert Rauld and Nicolas Chatillon – praise the virtues and military skills of the Bourbon commanders present at Brihuega and Villaviciosa, contrasting them with the cowardice, arrogance and strategic shortcomings of their opponents. Again, references to ancient history feature in almost every line. In Rauld's *Imago prudentiae militaris* ('Portrait of military prudence') Vendôme outdoes the Roman generals Marcus Claudius Marcellus and Gaius Claudius Nero in his achievements, and his defeat at Saragossa in August 1710 and victories over the Allies at Brihuega and Villaviciosa four months later are compared to the Roman defeat at the Battle of Cannae, and subsequent successes at the Battles of Nola and Metaurus respectively during the Punic Wars (ll. 49–60 [p. 17]). In all the poems the subject of derision is 'fierce Starhemberg' (*ferox Starembergus*, l. 26 [p. 4]), commander-in-chief Guido Starhemberg, portrayed as a second Hannibal by Rauld (l. 61 [p. 4]). After the Imperial marshal is constrained to flee by Philip's army, Loungueval asks 'where are the threats and the insolent haughtiness of the enemy now?' (ll. 54–5 [p. 9]).

In an allusion to Horace (*Od.* 4.2.36), Starhemberg's troops are compared by Sanadon to those of 'the frightful Sicambri' (1. 46 [p. 5]), a German tribe who defeated a Roman army in 16 BCE but sued for peace when they heard Augustus himself was marching against them. The parallels between ancient Rome and contemporary Europe are made clear.

A second group of poems – consisting of two odes by Thomas Maria des Antons and Nicolas Louis Ingoult (1689–1754) and two epigrams by D'Orival – chronicle Adrien Maurice de Noailles's campaign in northern Catalonia at the end of 1710.[69] His victory at Girona is compared by D'Orival to the success obtained in 1694 by his father Anne Jules de Noailles (1650–1708), who had taken possession of the city during the Nine Years' War (p. 25). In des Antons's *De Gerunda ab illustrissimo Duce Noallio expugnata* ('The storming of Girona by the most illustrious Duke of Noailles') the duke is praised for his tactical nous and determination in beginning offensive actions in winter, a decision which took the Allies by surprise:

> *Bruma et rigente docilis algorem pati*
> *[...]*
> *mora nulla: caepto Dux praeit Noallius*
> *[...]*
> *Quamquam soluta fluvius exundat nive,*
>   *tota et Pyrene liquitur,*
> *undisque late castra perfusis natant*
>   *et sequitur eluviem fames,*
> *non ardor unda Martius deferbuit*
>   *aut frangitur penuria.*
> *Obdurat ipso miles invictus malo,*
>   *tolerantiaque nobilis*
>
> ll. 7, 11 and 20–7 [p. 23]

['Well schooled by frozen winter to endure the cold ... the Duke of Noailles advances without delay ... Though the river overflows from snowmelt, the entire Pyrenees melt away, the camp swims in floodwater, and the flooding is followed by hunger, his Martial ardour is not dampened nor is it subdued by scarcity of food. Unvanquished by such severe conditions, the soldier holds out, renowned for his endurance'].

Once victory has been achieved, the fall of Girona into the hands of the Bourbon army is celebrated all over Spain (*Sic est: triumphis littus Hesperium sonat, / laudes Philippo concinnens*, ll. 29–30). The loud applause even reaches Barcelona, the last bastion of Habsburg resistance, which 'envies perhaps the fate of allied Girona ... and desires ardently to break the chains of slavery willingly assumed long ago' (ll. 33–5). The poet addresses the Catalan capital, assuring its inhabitants that, as with the people of Girona and Lleida in the past, they shall not be overtaken by threats and revenge but by kindness, peace and tenderness, and their crimes shall be forgotten.[70] Des Antons concludes his poem, however, on an admonitory note: 'should you refuse the mild yoke of your commander and, deranged, reject your master, after sword and fire, after your houses have been burned by the flame and your towers have been levelled with the ground, you shall regret, Barcelona, having atoned for your admitted crime with too late repentance' (ll. 47–52).[71]

The final poem in the collection, Ingoult's *Ad Barcinonem, ut Philippo victori se dedat* ('To Barcelona, that it may surrender to triumphant Philip', pp. 26–8), expands on this point for forty-four lines.[72] The ode begins with a description of the military operations allegedly about to be launched against Barcelona (ll. 1–4) and with an invitation to the city to acknowledge the new monarch and renounce its allegiance to the Habsburgs: 'Recognize your king, perfidious Barcelona. Why do you now favour the trembling eagles? You shall cause ruin, and shall tumble to the ground, totally unprotected, under their clipped wings' (ll. 5–8).[73] Ingoult's piece then concentrates on the Duke of Vendôme, to whom – as it had happened in 1697 – Barcelona shall surrender (ll. 13–16). The following four stanzas (ll. 17–32) celebrate Vendôme's past military campaigns in northern Italy, best represented by his successful siege of the fortress of Verrua in 1704–5.[74] In the concluding lines (ll. 33–44) Barcelona is threatened with retaliation if the city should fail to accept its new master.

Among Philip's ranks, final victory (at least, on Spanish soil) must have appeared within reach after the fall of Girona. This may explain why Ingoult's triumphalist poem presents the offensive against Barcelona as imminent and almost certain to succeed. We know, however, that agreement within the Bourbon camp as to how best to proceed was far from unanimous as the Allies had successfully established a new line of defence connecting Cardona, Manresa and Igualada in central Catalonia, which would protect Barcelona until the end of the war. Whereas Marshal Vendôme favoured an expeditious attack on the Catalan capital, Noailles – only obliquely mentioned by Ingoult (ll. 11–12) – regarded such a move as premature (Oury 2020: 352). In the end, Vendôme did not advance until August 1711. His attempt to cross the enemy's lines culminated weeks later in the Battle of Prats de Rei and the subsequent siege of Cardona, two Allied victories that forced Philip's troops to withdraw to Lleida in late December.

It would take the Bourbon army over nineteen months to reach the walls of Barcelona. By that time, Marshal Vendôme had long passed away.

The road to peace

Between the autumn of 1710 and the summer of 1712 several political developments determined the course of the war. In November 1710 a new parliament was elected in Great Britain with a Tory majority in the House of Commons. The new government was keen to sue for peace in return for trading concessions in Spanish America, a plan which was also seconded by Philip V. The death of Emperor Joseph I in April 1711 and the election of Archduke Charles as Charles VI six months later provided the Tory government and Queen Anne with new arguments for signing a peace agreement with Louis XIV as the union of Spain with Austria was as unwelcome as one with France. Negotiations between England and France led to the signing of the Preliminary Articles of London on 11 October 1711. These included French acceptance of the Act of Settlement (whereby the crown could only be passed down to non-Catholic heirs) and a guarantee that the French and Spanish crowns would remain separate, a condition which was fulfilled when Philip renounced his claim to the French throne on 5 November 1712. Earlier that year peace negotiations had opened in Utrecht, which would eventually produce a treaty in April 1713. While the talks were ongoing both sides continued to fight, hoping to improve their negotiating position, but Henry St John (1678–1751), the Tory leader, issued the now notorious 'restraining orders' to Marlborough's replacement, James Butler, second duke of Ormonde (1665–1745), instructing him to avoid serious military engagements against the French army whilst peace negotiations were underway. Still enjoying a numerical advantage despite the British withdrawal, the Allied commander in Flanders, Prince Eugene of Savoy, 'resolved to breach the last fortress line guarding France' (Lynn 1999: 352). Though Eugene captured the fortress of Le Quesnoy on 8 June 1712 and besieged Landrecies nine days later, he was, against all expectations, outmanoeuvred and defeated by Marshal Villars at Denain on 24 July. Wishing to exploit his victory, Villars forced Eugene to abandon the siege of Landrecies, recaptured Le Quesnoy and took Bouchain in October, thus effectively ending the war in Flanders.

As noted by Lynn (1999: 354), contemporary French sources testify to the enthusiastic public display with which victories at Denain and Bouchain were greeted throughout the kingdom. In Paris Villars's heroic deeds were also celebrated in Latin by Sanadon in a 122-line poem recited on 25 October and printed by

Jacques Collombat only eight days later under the title *Villartio, liberata Victoria, castigata Fortuna, ode* ('An Ode to Marshal Villars celebrating the liberation of Victory and the punishment of Fortune').⁷⁵ The piece describes a contest between Victory and Fortune. Having guided Louis XIV's past stalwarts (for example, Turenne, Catinat and Luxembourg) in successful campaigns along the Rhine and in Italy (ll. 1–27), the goddess Victory now finds herself at the mercy of Fortune.⁷⁶ Disguised as Valour, Fortune tricks Victory into lending her support to France's enemies (ll. 28–46). Obliging Victory then flatters Prince Eugene of Savoy, who directs his forces against Landrecies, the last *pré carré* fortress between the Imperial army and Paris ([*Landrecium*] *tutelam imperii ultimam*, l. 55).⁷⁷ Aware of the fate awaiting France if she continues to assist the enemy, the goddess laments her decision and stands firm at the river Scheldt (ll. 56–72). After coming to her rescue Marshal Villars charges against Eugene and takes Denain (ll. 73–85). Victory describes the bloody fighting, with hundreds of men falling under heavy fire, leading to the seizure of Le Quesnoy and Douai and, ultimately, to victory at Bouchain (ll. 86–113). Upon witnessing Villars's triumph, Fortune throws herself at his feet, and both divinities pledge everlasting loyalty to the French (ll. 114–22).

In his poem Sanadon wishes to stress Villars's courage and resolution: a general who thought 'hiding behind fortress walls was enfeebling and demoralizing' (Sterling 2009: 191), when he heard Victory's lament, he rushed unwearied (*impiger*, l. 74) to her assistance and went on the offensive, even if victory came at a high price: 'Wherever Villars attacks, Libitina [goddess of corpses] bears down on the enemy's troops with her unpitied hand'.⁷⁸ Sanadon's piece concentrates, of course, on Villars but there is a further interesting element in the ode. When Eugene decides to strike, 'Anne – wishing to insert the olive wreaths of peace between the laurel-haired garlands – opposes his foolish plans to no avail'.⁷⁹ Though disguised in poetic language, this is a powerful political statement: Sanadon is commending Queen Anne for having undertaken direct peace talks with the French to extricate her country from the war. It is also worth noting that the monarch is described by the poet as she 'who tempers the British sea [*Britannicum mare*] with gravity' (ll. 49–50), doubtless referring to Anne's new title of Queen of Great Britain since the Act of Union in 1707. The thorny issue concerning Anne's rights to the throne as sanctioned by the Act of Settlement (one of the preliminaries of the peace signed in October 1711) must not have escaped Sanadon's notice. With the end of hostilities between France and Britain, Sanadon's moderate attitude to Queen Anne in a poem whose principal subject is, after all, 'Villars's successful campaign of 1712' (as the title of Caux de Montlebert's French translation boldly states) is indicative of a new sentiment within Philip's ranks. In the build-up to the negotiations which would culminate at Utrecht, peace had to be 'made' and an ode praising Anne's conciliatory terms, if only in passing, was a step in the right direction.

To sum up

This investigation of literary recreations in Latin verse and prose of the most relevant battles and sieges fought in the War of the Spanish Succession has helped to highlight the astonishing range of texts commemorating Habsburg or Bourbon successes during the conflict as well as the variety of propagandistic techniques employed by both sides. One of the aims of the study of Latin representations and celebrations of Allied or Bourbon victories has been to foreground the outstanding literary values of the texts under review and their authors' highly refined verse and prose skills, based primarily on the imitation and emulation of models and figures from classical and biblical antiquity. This corpus did not emerge, however, in a Latin vacuum. Most themes and motifs also featured in more popular forms of propagandistic discourse (literary or visual) which found their expression in the vernacular, and practitioners of Latin war poetry and prose were often forced to draw on their vernacular counterparts, particularly when they had to compensate for lack of information about their subject.

Though the quantitative difference between the Habsburg and Bourbon material diminished as the war progressed, particularly after 1710 when French pamphleteers increased their effective propaganda campaign against their military rivals, the Philip-related output is outnumbered by the large body of texts composed on the Allied side on behalf of Charles.[80] Quite why this is so is unclear. Several poems and orations discussed in the preceding pages were the work of poet laureates or individuals with strong political connections, or were published by royal printers, and it is tempting to speculate whether the authors were working on their own initiative or whether their works were commissioned by a dedicatee. For some of the texts – especially those that have survived in only one copy – it is not possible to estimate the extent of their readership and circulation, even though there is some evidence of keen book consumption. Some questions can, therefore, only be tentatively answered. As the next chapter will show, in the course of the war the Latin tongue continued to be employed as a powerful medium of expression for propaganda even when writers were not describing battles and sieges but were instead focusing their artistic endeavours on more harmonious, transcendental or peaceful matters.

3

Latin Writing between Court, Church and Academia during the War of the Spanish Succession

Sometimes intimately connected, royal and princely courts, the church and institutions of learning were the setting for a variety of social and ceremonial events that prompted the production of Latin works in the early modern period. The range of suitable occasions is reflected in the diversity of literary forms composed, both in prose and verse. The purpose of this chapter is to focus on three types of celebratory literature arising from these contexts during the War of the Spanish Succession. These texts showcase their writers' erudition and literary skills, and the propagandist and political functions these works served in the course of the military conflict fought between Archduke Charles of Austria and Philip, duke of Anjou. In the following pages, I first analyse three *epithalamia* composed to celebrate two royal marriages within the House of Habsburg that took place during the war. The second cluster of texts is made up of funerary poetry and oratory produced on the death of Joseph I in April 1711, an event which speeded peace negotiations and sealed the Bourbon victory in Spain. The final and more extensive part of this chapter will focus on the large corpus of Latin texts written by Allied and French pamphleteers commemorating the signing in 1713 of the Peace of Utrecht, which marked the end of the War of the Spanish Succession, even though fighting continued in some areas until July 1715.

Tu felix Austria nube: Nuptial poetry in the midst of war

In 1708 two royal weddings were held by proxy at the Imperial court in Vienna. On 23 April Princess Elisabeth Christine of Brunswick-Wolfenbüttel, who had converted to Catholicism eleven months earlier, married Charles III, at the time fighting in Spain for his claim to the Spanish throne; on 9 July Charles's sister Archduchess Maria Anna of Austria (1683–1754) married John V of Portugal (1689–1750).[1] Shortly after their marriage ceremonies the newlywed queens left for the Iberian Peninsula to join their spouses in Barcelona and Lisbon, where both weddings were ratified on 1 August and 27 October respectively.[2] The University of Vienna marked the royal weddings and the queens' departures with occasional writing in Latin by Rector Anton Joseph von Öttl (1671–1723).[3] For both celebrations Öttl composed chronogrammatic arrangements and valedictory speeches – not dissimilar to some of the texts examined at the beginning of Chapter 1 – to which poetical compositions were appended. Contemporary accounts of the university receptions report that Öttl delivered an abridged version of his speeches in German, which were subsequently expanded upon and published in Latin.[4] It is at this stage that the poems must have been incorporated into the volumes. Beyond the topical praise of the new monarchs – whose beauty and fortitude are compared to those of Helen of Troy, Lavinia and other ancient heroines – the orations read in Vienna constitute a powerful ideological statement in support of Habsburgian matrimonial policy, best epitomized by the famous saying *Bella gerant alii, tu felix Austria nube* ('Let others wage war; you, happy Austria, marry!').[5] In the first volume, *Festiva acclamatio*, focused on Elisabeth Christine's marriage, Öttl celebrates the royal wedding and proclaims Elisabeth Christine's new husband the natural descendant of Charles II, the last Habsburg ruler of the Spanish Empire (sign. B1v). In the second, *Syncharisticon amoris*, dedicated to Maria Anna, her lineage is traced back to Philip the Handsome, son of Holy Roman Emperor Maximilian I (1459–1519) and the first Habsburg – as king of Castile for a brief time in 1506 – who reigned in the Old and New Worlds.[6] Through Maria Anna's marriage to John V, Habsburg rule – albeit indirectly – will be enhanced and will reach the four known continents:

> *Tibi coelum Brasilos, tibi Afros, tibi Indos populos, tibi per omnem solem et Oceanum protensas terras subiicit, ut illis cum serenissimo ac potentissimo sponso tuo vicaria coeli potestate imperes*
>
> sign. E1v

['For you heaven subjected the peoples of Brazil, for you the peoples of Africa, for you the peoples of India, for you the lands stretching from east to west, so that you may rule over them alongside your most serene and mighty spouse by heaven's delegated command'].[7]

Moreover, 'from this double Austrian marriage the world awaits – expectant not without hope, indeed not without prophetic divine will – its prosperity and happiness' (*orbis expectat attentus non sine spe, immo non sine praesago numine, ex gemino hoc Austriaco connubio salutem suam et gaudia*, sign. H1v). Elisabeth Christine's and Maria Anna's marriages should therefore strengthen the cohesion of the Allied coalition and help determine the outcome of the War of the Spanish Succession in favour of the Habsburg claimant.[8] Fittingly, Öttl concludes his speech by quoting – as a chronogram for the date of composition of his speech (1708) – a line from Virgil's *Eclogues* announcing the coming of a Golden Age, the last age of the Cumaean prophecy (4.7): *progenIes CoeLo DeMIttItVr aLto*.[9]

In addition to the speeches, the volumes published include an *Epithalamium sponsis serenissimis* ('A nuptial song for the most serene spouses') for Maria Anna, an Alcaic ode totalling 136 lines appended to *Syncharisticon amoris*, and an *Idyllion nuptiale* ('A nuptial idyl') for Elisabeth Christine consisting of 350 hexameters included in *Festiva acclamatio*. It is unclear whether they are the work of Öttl himself or collective pieces written by the Class of Poetry at the University of Vienna, but they make a fascinating pair. They clearly outdo their prose counterparts in their adaptation of classical (and non-classical) motifs to contemporary circumstances. This is in part thanks to the venerable tradition of Latin marriage verse running from antiquity to the Renaissance, in which both compositions are firmly embedded (Serrano Cueto 2019). Echoes of Catullus 62 can be heard, for example, in the poem in honour of Maria Anna and John of Portugal, which describes a *deductio*, the bride's journey from her (father's) abode to the home of the groom. Reversing the story of Ulysses – the mythical founder of Lisbon – here it is the wife who travels to her husband. 'Austria's dazzling treasure' (l. 65), Maria Anna is said to surpass the riches found by the Portuguese in Africa and Asia (ll. 69–72). When the queen lands in Lisbon, she is portrayed as 'more beautiful than the daughter of the swan' (*Cycnique nata pulchrior advenit*, l. 102), in a reference to Helen of Troy. The poet describes the fervour with which the city salutes its new sovereign:

> *Tagraee vertex urbsque beatior*
> *cunctis Ulyssis, per reliquas caput*
> *attolle florescens amore;*
> *cui veterem nova sors coronat.*
> *Fulvas arenas nunc gravior Tagus*
> *volvet: sereno Iupiter aethere*
> *effundet auratos in orbem,*
> *divitias superum, liquores*
>
> ll. 117–24

['Summit of Tagrus and you, most joyful city of Ulysses, raise your head above others, blossoming with love; for you a new fortune crowns the old one. The most venerable Tajo will now churn up its gold-coloured sands: from serene heaven Jupiter will pour forth into the world golden liquids, riches of the gods'].[10]

Following this description of Lisbon's ecstatic reception of the new queen, the Portuguese king is urged to 'fill your heart with love and unite it with the beloved bond of marriage'.[11] Such festive and amorous themes are, however, also used by the poet to convey a political message. With this new union, a Golden Age will ensue, and the piece concludes with the hope that the royal marriage will strengthen the Allied cause and bring peace and joy to the world:

Felix beatis plaudito nuptiis
orbis; ligatur foedus amoribus
novis et haec numquam saluti
vincula desidiosa nostrae

ll. 129–32

['Blessed world, applaud this joyful wedding; let the alliance be bound together by new love and may these bonds never diminish our prosperity'].

Uniting the strains of nuptial and pastoral poetry, the *Idyllion nuptiale*, written for Elisabeth Christine's wedding, features two exchanges between two sets of shepherds, whose names are reminiscent of those found in Virgil's *Eclogues*. Set in Charles's newly-adopted country, the first dialogue, between Aepolus and Moeris (ll. 1–227), tells the story of the lovers of the *Peña de los Enamorados* ('The lovers' rock'), a hill near the city of Antequera in Andalusia. The mountain was named after a legend from the local oral tradition, in which a Christian prisoner and a Moorish princess, the daughter of the king of Granada, threw themselves from the rock while being pursued by the woman's father and his men.[12] As noted by Klecker and Römer (1994: 189), from line 228 to the end of the poem Öttl's *epithalamium* takes a different, and rather surprising, direction, one that has more to do with the eighteenth-century dedicatees of the piece than with late-medieval Spain. In this section, a second pair of shepherds, Maja and Daphnis (who, in fact, personify the spirits of the rock), tell the story of Charles's and Elisabeth Christine's love. At the outset, Maja addresses 'the nymphs of the river Genil' (l. 236), and provides a description of various wonders of nature, which reflect the divine order and the love shared by the royal couple (*et superi redeunt, Carolo quoque sponsa sequitur* – 'The gods return, the bride also accompanies Charles', l. 252). She then goes on to reference the original tale, proclaiming that 'the new flame of the lovers' rock moves stones and my rock lives with a new spirit' (... *novus ardor rupis amantium / saxa movet vivitque novo mea numine rupes*, ll. 256–7). Preparations for the wedding are accordingly made by the gods. Venus leads Elisabeth Christine's cortège which is received by the nymphs inhabiting several rivers in Spain:

> Alma Venus, tandem Paphiis iuga iunge columbis;[13]
> iam toto properant occurrere nunina regno
> Baetides et nymphae simul, aurea turba, Tagoeae
> et quas clausit Anas reserant sua limina divae,
> immemor et chalybis, nympharum dura Salonis
> turba, legit flores, operam nec sudat in enses
> Sucronisque chori veniunt et Iberides omnes
>
> ll. 309–15

['Nourishing Venus, tie at last these bonds with Paphian turtle doves; the spirits of the Guadalquivir together with the nymphs of the Tajo, a golden throng, are already rushing out to greet the entire realm. The goddesses confined to the Guadiana are opening their gates; and, forgetful of the sword, the vigorous band of nymphs of the Jalón is collecting flowers and has no thought for wars. And the choirs of the Júcar and all the nymphs of the Ebro join in'].

Echoing the beginning of Virgil's second *Eclogue*, the poem closes with the royal marriage (*Carolus rex ardet Elisam ... in Iberis Austria nubit* – 'King Charles burns with love for Elisabeth ... Austria marries among the Spaniards', ll. 337–8).[14] The moral of the story is clear: unlike the heroes from the original legend – whose sorrowful denouement was caused by the different faiths they professed – Charles and Elisabeth Christine's felicitous union is sanctioned by Man and, above all, by God. The crucial issue of the Princess of Brunswick-Wolfenbüttel's conversion to Catholicism (key to Habsburgian political interests in Europe) had clearly not gone unnoticed by Öttl, a member of the Jesuit order.

The wedding of Charles and Elisabeth Christine in August 1708 also piqued the interest of Latin poets with links to the princess's Brunswick court. They saw the union as an opportunity to praise the dynasty to which the young queen belonged. Of all the works written in this respect, the one with the most literary merit is *Epithalamium potentissimi Hispaniarum regis Catholici Caroli III et serenissimae principis Brunsuico-Luneburgicae Elisabethae Christinae augusto connubio* ('A nuptial song for the august matrimony of the mightiest Catholic king of Spain Charles III and most serene Elisabeth Christine, princess of Brunswick-Lüneberg') by the German jurist and university professor Johann

Werlhof (1660–1711), published in 1708 in Helmstedt, in the vicinity of Brunswick.[15] It is a poem of 1,011 hexameters, prefaced by eleven elegiac distichs dedicated to Anton Ulrich (1633–1714), prince of Brunswick-Wolfenbüttel and Elisabeth Christine's grandfather. The *epithalamium* opens with some preliminary verses (ll. 1–16), in which Werlhof provides a general outline of the work and lays out his literary credentials. Thereafter his account of the conflict begins (ll. 17–85). The narrative is interrupted by the intervention of Venus, the goddess of Love, who draws attention to a number of historic marriages between a member of the Habsburg dynasty and a foreign princess, who, in some cases, was also called Elisabeth (ll. 86–135). This is then followed by Jupiter's response (ll. 136–240): he praises the decision by England and Savoy to join the Austrian side in the conflict. Inspired by Jupiter's words, Venus then travels to Schloss Salzdahlum, Elisabeth Christine's ancestral home near Wolfenbüttel. She considers the artistic treasures housed in the palace and the refined atmosphere of the princess's court an ideal setting for the education of the future queen, whose physical beauty is also worthy of the goddess's praise (ll. 241–324).

The action then moves to two different locations simultaneously, the Iberian Peninsula and the central European front, to resume the account of the military episodes in the conflict (ll. 225–397). Meanwhile, Venus tasks Mercury, the messenger of the gods, with ensuring the safe passage of a portrait of Elisabeth Christine to Charles, an errand that Mercury fulfils without delay (ll. 397–426).[16] Seduced by the beauty of the young princess, the king immediately falls chastely in love with her, but must nevertheless remain in the theatre of war to counter the threat of the Bourbon armies which are regrouping and, during the spring of 1706, launching an attempt to take the city of Barcelona. After days of fighting, with neither side prevailing, the French troops are finally forced to abandon their siege of the city and withdraw, retreating in total disorder (ll. 450–70). Having secured victories in both the Iberian Peninsula and Belgium, Charles strikes up a conversation with Mercury who tells him of Venus's plans. In response to her petitions, Jupiter has brought the painter Peter Paul Rubens (1577–1640) back from the land of the dead and has charged him with painting a work, *rara arte Rubeni* (l. 472), a portrait of Charles, to ignite the flame of love in the princess (ll. 471–551). The painting would have to be similar to the canvases of one of Charles's ancestors, Albert VII, archduke of Austria (1559–1621), and his wife Isabella Clara Eugenia (1566–1633), painted by Rubens himself in around 1615 (and currently housed in the National Gallery in London). All Venus's wishes are fulfilled, the divinely-commissioned portrait of Charles is completed, and Cupid is called upon to transport it to the palace at Salzdahlum, where it has the intended effect:

Elisabeth Christine falls in love. Nevertheless, hostilities on Italian soil – described in ll. 552–640 – prevent the engaged couple from actually meeting in person. Venus appears once again, and orders Elisabeth Christine to depart for Vienna. After bidding her family farewell, the princess travels to the capital accompanied by a sumptuous entourage. On her arrival, she is fêted by the entire Imperial court (ll. 641–77). Preparations are finalized for her onward journey to the Iberian Peninsula, but further military actions once again delay the young lovers' planned meeting: the poet celebrates the incorporation of the kingdom of Naples into the Imperial fold in 1707, but also makes mention of the Austrian side's first military setbacks in Spain (ll. 678–724). Venus interrupts the narrative again, this time in a dream in which she provides an exhaustive genealogy of Elisabeth Christine's family and enumerates the glorious achievements of her dynasty (ll. 725–921). After this protracted dream episode, Charles asks Jupiter to arrange for his fiancée to meet him in Barcelona. Elisabeth Christine arrives in the city, where the wedding is finally celebrated (ll. 922–72). After describing the latest military incursions, Werlhof concludes his *epithalamium* by expressing his very best wishes for the future happiness of the newlyweds (ll. 973–1011).

Dressed up as an epyllion (a short epic poem), Werlhof's text interweaves the military narrative of the War of the Spanish Succession with an account of the love affair between the two royal protagonists. This in turn is set within a mythological frame reminiscent of classical epics in which Jupiter and Venus both feature, alongside Mercury and Cupid. In truth, it is these four gods – and not the lovers, who remain silent for almost the entirety of the text – who are the real protagonists of the poem. In his *epithalamium*, Werlhof demonstrates his familiarity with the epic genre: an invocation to the Muses, lists of warriors, the use of prophecies, dreams and mythological elements to frame the narrative, lengthy battle descriptions, together with a multitude of intertextual elements which refer back, more often than not, to the *Aeneid*.[17] In fact, the clearest source of inspiration is the famous Book Four of Virgil's epic, the one that covers the love affair between Dido and Aeneas. Just like Dido (and Werlhof obviously knows that Virgil also called his heroine Elissa in *Aen.* 4.335), Elisabeth Christine falls in love, but in her case felicitously, thanks to Jupiter's and Venus's plotting. It is the will of Jupiter, the father of the gods, that determines the course of the narrative and that guides Charles towards his amorous destiny, despite the military adversities suffered by the Imperial side along the way. As in the case of Dido and Aeneas, Fame disseminates the news of Elisabeth Christine's and Charles's love for each other. However, in contrast with Dido, whose heart burned with excessive love, in this narrative our monarch promises the god a chaste marriage bed and a sacred Hymen:

> *'Iupiter altitonans, cui vincla iugalia curae*
> *sunt nostra et casti thalami qui vota secundas,*
> *sint toti Hesperiae totique salutiferi orbi,*
> *auspiciis quos pango tuis, hi sacri Hymenaei:*
> *nostra erit Austriaci Caroli Brunsvigica Elisa,*
> *nostra erit Hesperiae rectoris regia coniux:*
> *spondeo per sacras summe hoc tibi, Iupiter, aras'*
>
> ll. 941–7

['Jupiter thundering from on high, guardian of our bonds of marriage, you who second the vows of this chaste bridal bed, let these sacred Hymens which I set under your auspices bring health to the whole of Spain and the entire world: our Elisa of Brunswick will be of Austrian Charles, our royal spouse will be of the ruler of Spain: this I promise you, highest Jupiter, by this sacred altar'].

In the title, Werlhof calls his poem an *epithalamium*, a term which since the late Hellenistic period had ceased to be used to denote its original lyric form but referred instead to the genre of wedding song (Muth 1954). It is a work which is closely aligned with the courtly panegyric, which should come as no surprise given that Werlhof was one of the palace counsellors to Anton Ulrich of Brunswick. His praise, nevertheless, is not limited to the happy couple but extends to their respective dynastic lines, especially Elisabeth Christine's. The poem as a whole shows us how the glorification of Elisabeth Christine's bloodline, underlined by the unusually high occurrence of the name of Elisa throughout the work, is enhanced by the epic literary setting. Unsurprisingly, the most extensive section within the poem – a long speech pronounced by Venus (ll. 725–921) – celebrates the history of the House of Welf (the *gens Guelpha*, from which Prince Anton Ulrich of Brunswick is descended) and in particular its cadet branches, from the twelfth century right up to the age of Elisabeth Christine. This is how the poet describes the early days of the dynasty, in the time of Alberto Azzo II of Este (996–1079):

> *Stemmate iam veteri maiorum explenduit Azo,*
> *magnus in Ausoniis celebratus marchio terris,*
> *Guelphae et Atestinae ille domus communis origo;*
> *prima cui Conigunda uxor, sata semine Guelphum*
> *(semine quod vel Caesareo confuderat olim*
> *Iuditha et claris dederat quod regibus ortum)*
> *antiquum Guelphique soror Carinthii et haeres*

per quartum Guelphum alma novos atque inclita mater
Guelphiadas sevit

ll. 752–62

['Through the already ancient stock of his forefathers Azzo shone forth, a distinguished margrave celebrated in Italian lands, common origin of the Houses of Welf and Este; his first wife was Kunigunde of Altdorf, sprung from the seed of the old House of Welf (for Judith of Bavaria had indeed once joined with Caesarean stock and produced famous kings). She was the sister of, and heiress to, Welf III, duke of Carinthia. A nurturing and renowned mother, through Welf IV she begat new offspring of Welf'].[18]

After covering these early-medieval origins, the poet then has Venus continue chronologically through the family tree. Here is the description of the origin of the Palatinate (Pfalz) and Bavarian branches within the House of Wittelsbach, also related to the House of Welf (Hartmann and Schnith 1996: 417):

Faustior Henricus, natu qui maior Othone,
connubio Palatinae, de fratre creatae
Fridrici primi Augusti, natam inde per Agnem,
illustri nuptam Ludovici filio Othoni
Boiorum Ducis, eximiae praelustria gentis
stemmata prosevit . . .

ll. 822–7

['More fortunate was Henry (of Brunswick), who – older than Otto – brought forth the magnificent stock of distinguished offspring through his marriage to (Agnes) Pfalz, stepsister of Frederick I Barbarossa, and thereafter through their daughter Agnes (of Brunswick), married to illustrious Otto (II Wittelsbach), son of Louis I Duke of Bavaria'].

And this is how George I – the first monarch of Great Britain from the House of Hanover, a cadet branch of the House of Brunswick-Lüneburg – is prophesized to ascend the British throne in 1714:

Et venient anni, vastum quis temperet ipsum
gens Guelpha Oceanum frustraque fremente Sicambro
imperio aequoreos iusto regat illa Britannos

ll. 904–6

['Years will come, in which the House of Welf may rule the vast Ocean itself and it may govern with fair command the sea-girt Britons, whilst the Sicambri [= Germans] complain in vain'].[19]

Consequently, as well as extolling the House of Austria and Archduke Charles, Werlhof's wedding song is seeking, above all, favour and support from the family of his patron. It is worth remembering that throughout the eighteenth century Brunswick was not only a discrete territory with its own political identity; in addition, thanks to the pervasive influence of Enlightenment thinking and philosophy, the duchy became a cultural powerhouse. By way of example, Prince Anton Ulrich was renowned for his literary talents (Dünnhaupt 1990). Indeed, two of his novels in German – one, *Aramena*, on a mythological subject, and the other, *Octavia*, set in ancient Rome – were singled out for particular praise from Werlhof (ll. 289–91). Despite its eminently literary tone, as one would expect in a poetic work, Werlhof's *epithalamium* is remarkable for the abundance of historical content. Perhaps in an effort to delegitimize the alliance between Spain and France centred on Philip of Anjou, Werlhof dedicates several lines of his wedding song to describing two Franco-Spanish wars, namely the one between Charles I of Spain and Francis I of France in the first half of the sixteenth century, and the one between Philip IV of Spain and Louis XIV of France which was finally resolved following the signing of the Treaty of the Pyrenees in 1659. The poet exhibits his wide-ranging knowledge not only of the origins of the Habsburg dynasty and Elisabeth Christine's family but also of the key episodes of the War of the Spanish Succession, especially the military encounters on Italian soil. Werlhof's research for this may well have included reading the relevant chronicles for the period, and it is likely that he was inspired by Erhard Reusch's *Oratio solennis* or one or two of the Latin texts mentioned in Chapter 2.

The coincidence of two royal weddings on the Imperial side presented Latin propagandists with a golden opportunity. By their very nature, weddings are a positive and uplifting occasion, especially so in times of war. The classical parallels authors draw on – both in content and style – elevate their subjects. Furthermore, any royal marriage necessarily focuses attention on the joining of two dynastic lines: writers skilfully exploited this to further legitimize Charles's claim to the Spanish throne, and to emphasize the suitability of his recently-converted spouse.

An untimely death

On 17 April 1711, Joseph I died aged only 32 of smallpox in Vienna. As had been the case with his father Leopold I six years earlier, funerary orations for the emperor were pronounced across Europe, chiefly in various locations across the

Holy Roman Empire and in Rome.[20] The Imperial court also organized obsequies in which temporary structures (*castra doloris* – 'castles of grief') sheltering the catafalque or bier were erected.[21] One such structure was built in St Stephen's Cathedral in Vienna for the funeral services held between 30 July and 2 August (Brix 1973: 262, no. 35). As described in *Memoria posthuma Iosephi primi*, several inscriptions on the monument praised Joseph's bravery by commemorating individual victories achieved by this 'Austrian Mars' during the War of the Spanish Succession (sign. C1r).[22] A further structure, designed by Johann Bernhard Fischer von Erlach (1656–1723) for the University of Vienna, – consisting of a pyramid, an urn and four statues, all of them covered with inscriptions – was set up again in St Stephen's Cathedral between 31 August and 2 September (Popelka 1970 and Brix 1973: 261–2, no. 34). The programme of services and other such events and the exact wording of the funerary inscriptions are recorded in *Theatrum gloriae Iosephi primi* ('A spectacle for the glory of Joseph I'), a volume which also includes the university's official oration, delivered by the Jesuit Albrecht Purgstall (1671–1744).[23] While several sections from the inscriptions in praise of Joseph carved on the pyramid reproduce *verbatim* short passages from classical eulogies of Roman emperors by Pliny the Younger, Cassius Dio and Claudius Mamertinus, each of the four statues representing the faculties within the university celebrates Imperial virtues: piety (Theology), justice (Law), generosity (Medicine) and wisdom (Philosophy).[24] For example, the inscription for the Faculty of Law, addressing Europe, bemoans Joseph's premature death for, 'had such a just Caesar lived longer, you would have expected tranquillity to reign in the empire as long as he was holding the scales'.[25] For its part, the inscription for the Faculty of Medicine extols the emperor's munificence in sparing his subjects prolonged sorrow with his sudden death:

Ad statuam Facultatis medicae.
Complorate, populi!
Pretium orbis sublatum est,
Caesar liberalissimus, eheu!
Mors intravit per fenestras tot,
quot variolae apertae in corpore
principis aegrotantis.
Tam munificus Iosephus fuerat,
ut largitionibus sustulerit
omnem moram supplicum, immo et spem
exspes semper ipse,

dum ex collatis nihil in eum redundaverit,
nisi plura conferendi voluptas

ll. 1–12

['Before the statue of the Faculty of Medicine. Weep loudly, people! The world's wealth has gone! Alas, most generous Emperor! Death entered through so many windows, so many smallpox sores opened in the body of the ailing prince. So generous had Joseph been that, through his largesse, he removed any obstacle for suppliants, but never hope, even though he himself was always without hope; all the while nothing that he had been blessed with was excessive, except his delight in giving more'].

News of Joseph I's sudden death reached his brother Charles on 27 May (Torras i Ribé 1999: 291–2). Unsurprisingly given the presence of the emperor-to-be in the city, Barcelona similarly held official commemorative events for the deceased monarch. The ceremonies – on behalf of local political and religious representatives – took place on four different days across several locations. On 7 July a memorial was erected in the church of Santa Maria del Mar; four days later high-ranking clergy held funeral services in the cathedral, which were accompanied by illuminations; on 13 July 'the General Diputation' (*Diputació del General*), the permanent executive body of the Catalan parliament, marked the death of Joseph with a religious ceremony in Saint George's Hall, the principal ceremonial space in the Catalan government headquarters, the Palau de la Generalitat; the late emperor was finally honoured on 21 July with services and commemorative events held in the chapel of the Consulate of the Sea building (the *Llotja de Mar*), which the town hall put at Charles's disposal during his sojourn in Barcelona between 1705 and 1711.

Funerary orations in Spanish, Italian and Latin were composed for all these occasions.[26] The learned language was also the medium employed for the inscriptions carved on the memorials erected in Santa Maria del Mar and in the chapel of the Consulate of the Sea, at the behest of Archduke Charles and the local council respectively. Though the monuments have not survived, the texts engraved in the stone were reproduced in the so-called lapidary style in volumes published shortly after the funeral services.[27] As with the structures erected for the late emperor in Vienna, the funerary inscriptions prepared in Barcelona were clearly designed to contribute in a variety of ways to the shaping of the image of Joseph I. The inscriptions span a broad variety of genres (victory and funerary songs, chronograms, hieroglyphs and anagrams) and displayed, first and foremost, references to the War of the Spanish Succession, reminding mourners of the great deeds the late monarch accomplished in warfare. Though the field of battle features prominently among the inscriptions, the emperor's panegyrists responsible for the texts on the memorials also sought to emphasize Joseph I's other virtues, chiefly his sense of justice, clemency and piety, as illustrated by the following lines from one of the epitaphs:

> *Religioni ille natus et paci, iustitiae enutritus,*
> *fortitudine adultus;*
> *non his est ablatus sed nobis.*
> *En tamen quatuor istae virtutes lachrymantur.*
> . . .
> *Pro triplici ergo virtute gladium distrinxit,*
> *altera socia fortitudine.*
> *Haec in illo suas ita egit partes,*
> *ut in nullo Caesarum melius.*
> *Rhenus, Schelda, Padus, Ister et Iber testes.*
> *Qui numquam aquilas altius volantes compexere,*
> *numquam Gallos iisse demissius,*
> *quam cum IOSEPHI vel auspiciis vel ductu*
> *Germanae acies pugnarunt.*
> *Quid plura?*
> *Inviderunt Parcae tanto viro:*
> *et ne viveret amplius, imnortalitati donarunt.*
> *Invidiae est illum extollere, quem vult tollere.*
> *Pro encomiorum compendio:*
> *IOSEPHUS imperator fuit non primus, sed unus*

['Born to piety and reconciliation and nourished on justice, matured by fortitude; he was not parted from these but was taken from us. Behold! Those four virtues still shed tears ... For the sake of threefold virtue Joseph engaged his sword with further assistance from fortitude, which played its part for him better than for any other Caesar. The Rhine, the Scheldt, the Po, the Danube and the Ebro bear witness. They never saw eagles fly higher, nor Frenchmen flee more abjectly than when German armies fought under Joseph's auspices or leadership. What more could be said? The Fates envied such a great man: and lest he would not live longer they granted him immortality. It is envy's ability to extol those whom it wishes to remove. As a summary of our eulogies: Emperor Joseph was not the first, but the only one', in *Exequias del augustissimo señor . . .*, sign. C2r-v].

In addition, the allegorical representations of various provinces and territories both on the Spanish mainland and in central Europe were created to convey their respect for the deceased emperor. For example, in a poem in elegiacs 'devout Carinthia sings funeral songs to Joseph I' and in a composition in acrostics Tyrolean eagles erect an epitaph for the deceased emperor.[28]

Loyalty to the ruling dynasty also featured heavily in the funeral held at the Palau de la Generalitat, during which Fray Esteve Segarra, preacher to Charles III, delivered a sermon in Spanish in praise of Joseph, and poems in Catalan, Spanish and Latin by 'three grieving Muses of the Barcelona Parnassus' were recited.[29] The pieces written in the vernacular are in a broad range of poetic forms, popular and more cultivated alike, and a small number of bilingual compositions (Spanish and Latin) adds a slightly more playful twist to the otherwise mournful tone that pervades the collection. Variety is also favoured by the poets contributing Latin epitaphs, epigrams, elegiacs and acrostics. Most of the vernacular and Latin texts focus on a description of Joseph's death, lamenting his premature and unexpected departure from this world and expressing hope in the afterlife. That said, it is clear that at least some of the poets used the occasion to highlight other issues of more geopolitical significance. For example, the ceremony staged by the Generalitat was chiefly designed as a re-affirmation of Catalonia's allegiance to Charles at a time when parts of the principality (together with Majorca) were the only territory in Spain still loyal to the Habsburg claimant, and there was next to no prospect of Philip V being excluded from the throne. In this respect, a cluster of poems from the collection with this more political slant is especially noteworthy. The Catalan sonnet *Discurs politich sobre la inflamació interna de la C.M. de Joseph I* ('A political discussion of the internal inflammation suffered by his Imperial Majesty Joseph I', p. 60) casts doubt on the exact cause of Joseph's death, hinting that there may have been some involvement of espionage. In addition, a Latin epigram presents Catalonia's laments at the emperor's passing away as more heartfelt than those of any other territory under Habsburg rule:

Gens Gotholana gemis cum tristia fata Iosephi,
ostendis quantus sistat in orbe dolor:
adversis nam gente viges constantior omni;
multi sicque dolent anxia quando doles.
At mortem sentis, credo, vehementius istam,
vindictam gladio sumere quando nequis

p. 61

['As you, Catalan people, grieve for Joseph's bitter fate, you show how much pain may remain in the world. For you thrive in adversity, more resolutely than any other people. And thus many suffer seeing that you suffer in distress. Yet, I believe you feel this death more acutely when you cannot avenge it with the sword'].

Two further compositions in Catalan – *No sé per quin fonament* ('I do not know on which grounds', p. 68), and *Ab lo sentiment, Senyor* ('With our sorrow, Sir', p. 70) – seek to secure support for Charles as new Imperial ruler and to confirm the Principality's loyalty to the dynasty respectively.[30] Such depictions of Catalonia as a most faithful and sincere subject are also found in the Latin pieces, as we can see from the following epitaph:

En tibi adsum fidelissimi Principatus interque do
lentes principatum obtinentis vera imago, Ger
mani imperatoris funera, non praefica, lachrimosa
Iosephi primi Mnemosyne ad meos luctus (ut puto)
augendos nomen istud sortiti

p. 55

['Behold! A true image of the most faithful Principality and first among the mourners, I am here at the funeral rites for the (Holy) German Emperor, not as a woman hired to lead the mourning at a funeral, but as a tearful figure of Remembrance for Joseph I, who was given that name to increase (I think) my sorrow'].[31]

Following the new emperor's election, a series of Latin volumes were issued in the territories of the Holy Roman Empire to mark the death of Charles's immediate predecessors as well as to celebrate his own proclamation. A strong sense of continuity permeates these texts. As an example, in *Lessus funebris super praematura et inopinata morte Iosephi primi* of 1711 ('A funerary lament for the premature and unexpected death of Joseph I') the deceased emperor is depicted as 'living again' (*redividus*) in his successor.[32] Exaltation of the Habsburg dynasty and of its past and present members is also a key theme in a four-part volume entitled *Post nubila Phoebus* ('After clouds the sun') of the same year.[33] Unlike the Latin funerary programmes examined above, the book (as well as *Lessus funebris*) does not seem to be related to any structure erected in the territories of the Holy Roman Empire. The first section includes three epitaphs in memory of Cardinal Portocarrero (responsible for drafting Charles II's wills), of the heir to the French throne Louis of Bourbon (1661–1711) and of Charles II of Spain.[34] This is followed by *Luctus Austriacus* ('Austrian grief'), a collection of eight epitaphs dedicated to Leopold I. The first, in memory of Leopold, is an epitome of Imperial virtues, praising in particular the monarch's political wisdom in preserving the divinely preordained, hierarchical order, threatened by 'Machiavelli's principles' (sign. B1v).[35] A further epitaph in memory of Leopold, purporting to have been written by the knights of the Order of the Golden Fleece, glorifies his Imperial predecessors in a genealogy that claimed to have its ultimate origin in Antiquity.[36] Founded in 1430 by Philip the Good (1396–1467), an ancestor of the Austrian Habsburgs, the Order identified the Golden Fleece as Christ, the Lamb of God, and was co-opted to the Habsburgian cause by Philip II of Spain (Tanner 1993: 146–61). When the Spanish Habsburg dynasty died out, the Austrian line laid claim to the position of head of the order.[37] Directed against Leopold's critics, who reproached him for his excessive mildness, the epitaph depicts the late emperor as embodying the ideals of Christian clemency and humility, in clear contrast to the arrogance and hubris shown by Louis XIV. These two attributes are also the main focus of the last epitaph dedicated to Leopold (sign. C3r–v), who is the putative author of the piece, thus making him both the *laudandus* and the *laudator*. Three further epitaphs for Joseph I and four votive poems in honour of the new emperor make up parts three and four of the volume. The second of these epitaphs for Joseph I (sign. C4v–D1r), purported to have been written by the Holy Roman Empire itself, emphasizes the late emperor's military prowess at Landau in 1702, ultimately his most significant victory during the War of the Spanish Succession.[38]

The works we have looked at in the last two sections illustrate the central role played by Latin in the nuptial and funerary ceremonies organized by the Habsburg dynasty and how these in turn constitute an especially important element of its political propaganda during the War of the Spanish Succession. By contrast, parallel events and celebrations held on the Bourbon side (arguably, less frequent and fewer) seem not to have attracted a comparable degree of attention. To the best of my knowledge, the ratification of the royal wedding between Philip V and Maria Luisa Gabriella of Savoy in Figueres on 3 November 1701 was only celebrated – in engravings, operas and *epithalamia* – in the vernacular, both in Spain and in Spanish America (Alcoberro 2007: 59; Angulo and Pons 2017; Comas 1964: 560–1; and Olivas 2015: 202). A union through which Louis XIV sought to entice Victor Amadeus II to his cause, the wedding does not appear to have been politicized by the royal court, perhaps because the dynastic conflict was at the time only in its infancy and, in Spain, Philip's proclamation as king was to remain unchallenged until 1704 (Borreguero 2003: 98). Conversely, as military operations became rather adverse for Philip, the French court attempted to profit from any positive news with which to raise the morale of its subjects. Proof of this is afforded by the celebrations of the birth on 25 June 1704 of Louis, Duke of Brittany and Louis XIV's great-grandson.[39] Moreover, in the final stages of the war on the Spanish fronts, the death of Queen Maria Luisa Gabriella in February 1714 was exploited by the new administration through the delivery of sermons in Spanish, particularly in those territories like Aragon, which had returned to Philip's rule (Serrano Martín 2014).[40] Elsewhere in Europe the deaths of other members of the Bourbon household, such as those of the Grand and Petit Dauphins in April 1711 and February of the following year, elicited funerary orations in Latin, in which the potentially dangerous prospect of Philip V's accession to the French throne following both royal deaths is conveniently silenced in the interest of peacemaking.[41] More politically charged (and of more immediate consequence to the progress of war on the continent) was Louis XIV's recognition of James Francis Edward Stuart ('James III', 1688–1766) as the rightful heir to the English, Irish and Scottish thrones on his father's death in September 1701. The French court held funeral services for James II, in exile in Saint-Germain-en-Laye since the Glorious Revolution of 1688, and the virtues of the late monarch were celebrated in occasional writing in the vernacular and in Latin. In 1702 Henri-Emmanuel de Roquette (1655–1725) pronounced a funerary oration in French in honour of the Old Pretender and a year later Pierre Pestel (1651–c. 1725), professor of Eloquence at the Sorbonne, published in Paris a panegyric entitled *Iacobo secundo magnae Britanniae regi mausoleum* ('A mausoleum for James II, king of Great Britain').[42] Indeed, for several years Bourbon pamphleteers such as Patrick of Saint-John, active in Parisian academic circles between 1704 and 1710, continued to champion the Jacobite cause in Latin verse until it became a thorny issue in the Anglo-French negotiations for peace.[43] As peace talks gained momentum in 1712, French and Allied propagandists intensified their Latin campaign, as we shall see in the next section.

Peace at last

Marshal Villars's victories at Denain and Bouchain in July and October 1712 finally convinced the Allies that the War of the Spanish Succession could not be resolved through military means. France and England had been holding secret but substantive talks since 1711, but formal negotiations to bring the long conflict to an end had only begun on 29 January 1712, when the peace congress in Utrecht was ceremoniously opened 'at ten o'clock in the morning with the sound of trumpets' (Bruin et al. 2015 Introduction: 1).⁴⁴ The general congress included several different strands of negotiations, notably between the Allies, the United Provinces and Great Britain. Proceedings were however brought to a halt in August due to a spat between the French diplomat Nicolas Mesnager and Count Rechteren, the Dutch plenipotentiary, a circumstance which was cunningly exploited by Louis XIV to engage in bilateral talks with London and Madrid. The conference resumed, and on 30 January 1713 a first treaty was signed, granting the Dutch a military barrier in the Southern Netherlands, albeit in a less favourable position than the one promised in 1709. Despite continued Habsburg opposition to the peace congress, a treaty between England and France was signed on 31 March, and an agreement between France and the other Allies was reached on 11 April. Spain made peace with Savoy and Britain on 13 July, but progress in reaching a settlement with the Dutch was delayed until a further treaty was signed on 26 June 1714. Neither Austria nor the Holy Roman Empire accepted the terms of the April 1713 treaty and for almost a year fighting continued along the Rhine until Charles VI, after a series of military defeats, reopened negotiations and finally signed the Treaty of Rastatt with Louis XIV on 6 March 1714. Six months later the estates of the Holy Roman Empire joined the agreement by signing the Treaty of Baden, 'essentially a Latin translation of the Treaty of Rastatt, which Villars had insisted should be written in French' (Oury 2020: 383). The signing of the Treaty of Madrid between Spain and Portugal on 6 February 1715, and of the Treaty of The Hague of 17 February 1720 between Spain and Emperor Charles VI completed the process.

The Peace of Utrecht was welcomed and widely celebrated across Europe with festivities in many cities featuring fireworks, services of thanksgiving, masquerades, and theatre performances. As well as being the subject of political pamphlets in the vernacular, the Peace, and the several treaties within it, prompted a number of academic institutions to hold formal commemorations, in which Latin speeches and poems were recited. On 12 January 1713, as negotiations in Utrecht were gradually coming to a close, Charles Porée (1675–1741), professor of Rhetoric at the Collège Louis-le-Grand, delivered an oration 'congratulating the French on the return of victory' (*Gallis ob victoriam reducem gratulatio*).⁴⁵ After his introductory remarks, the speech is divided into two parts. The first one chronicles the making of peace. While acknowledging that military disputes between England and France in the past may have been justified, Porée insists that prolonging the present confrontation was, however, groundless, and even Queen Anne – 'the most foreseeing governess of the realm, most acquainted with the true glory, a second Pallas' (*moderatrix regni prudentissima, verae laudis scientissima . . . Pallas altera,* Porée 1747: 179) – realized that an end to the war was expedient. His speech includes some insightful remarks on British domestic and foreign politics, with Porée comparing France and England to Rome and Carthage. The second part, the core of the oration, deals with the conflict – both in antiquity and in the present hostilities – between the advocates of war and those seeking peace. Depicted as a 'new Hannibal', the hawkish British war general, the Duke of Marlborough, is rebuked for his wish to continue the fighting alongside his Whig allies (here dismissed as a modern 'Barca's faction', a reference to Hannibal's family). On the opposite dove side stands the Tory politician and Queen Anne's chief minister Robert Harley, earl of Oxford (1661–1724), 'a man of shrewd mind, a fervent patriot, in short a second Hanno the Carthaginian' (*vir ingenio sagax, patriae amantissimus, alter denique Carthaginensis Hanno*, p. 176), whose opposition to the conflict is reminiscent of Hanno II the Great's conciliatory policy towards Rome during the Second Punic War. Underlying Porée's depiction of France as a new Rome is his country's military superiority, which the author claims is the real reason why Britain eventually decided to engage in peace talks.

Unsurprisingly, the true hero of Porée's speech is Louis XIV. The orator condemns Dutch bellicosity, claiming that, unlike Britain who sought peace for her own benefit (*ex utilitate patriae*, p. 178), the United Provinces are to be blamed for unnecessarily prolonging hostilities. Porée identifies the failed negotiations at The Hague in 1709 as confirmation of a Dutch conspiracy against peace, and praises Louis XIV for his refusal to accede to the Allies' unreasonable and unjust peace proposals, above all their insistence that he supply military assistance to ensure the removal of his grandson, the Duke of Anjou, from the Spanish throne:

> *Sed omnes conditiones, omnia consilia, auctoritatem omnem [Batavi] aspernati sunt, sed nullam aequitatis, nullam humanitatis, nullam verecundiae rationem, in suis postulatis habendam esse censuerunt. Quam enim primam Ludovico magno posuerunt pacis legem? Ut Philippum V nepotem carissimum non modo relinqueret omnino indefensum, sed etiam ad ipsum e solio deturbandum arma impia cum eius hostibus infensissimis coiungeret (o scelus!)*
>
> Porée 1747: 180

['But (the Dutch) rejected all conditions, all suggestions, all authority and thought that no fairness, no humanity, no cause for respect was to be found in their demands. For which condition for peace did they impose on Louis XIV? Not only that he leave his dearest nephew Philip V totally unprotected but also that he take up unholy arms in league with his most bitter enemies to remove him from the throne (what a crime!)'].

Surprisingly rife with anti-Dutch sentiment given that a treaty with Holland would be signed only a few days later, the latter section (Porée 1747: 188–202) concentrates on Marshal Villars's campaign against the Dutch and the Imperial army through Flanders in the summer and autumn of 1712, which expedited peace negotiations. Vividness is key to the speech's delivery. The account begins with a pointed mockery of the enemy's arrogance and their taste for fine sparkling wine:

> Audivimus quo apparatu Batavi totam belli molem Galliae finibus admoverent ... qua spe aditus in provincias nostras facillimos designarent, qua cupiditate iam devorarent Campaniam, cuius (si iocari liceat in seriis) vina lectissima, submissis nuper Germanis, neque ignavi neque surdi palati hominibus praegustari iusserant ... qua iactatione verborum se Lutetiam pergere ibique de pace, quam alibi renuerant, acturos esse profiterentur
>
> Porée 1747: 190

> ['We heard about all the equipment the Dutch brought with them when they moved their whole army over the French border ... how hopefully they marked out the easiest points of entry to our provinces, how greedily they gulped down champagne, whose most excellent wines (if we may make a joke in such serious matters) they ordered to be tasted by the recently defeated Germans, men of neither lazy nor undiscerning palates; we heard how boastfully they declared that they would proceed to Paris and there press for the peace which they had formerly rejected'].⁴⁶

Military actions are about to commence (p. 192) but Porée assures his audience that they should not fear for 'France shall prevail'. There follows a detailed description of Villars's victorious offensive (pp. 193–7). The final episodes of the campaign (*nunc ad Duacum* ['now Douai'], *mox ad Quercetum* ['next Le Quesnoy'], *postremo ad Buccinium* ['finally Bouchain'], p. 198) are compared to a tragedy staged 'in that bloody theatre of Belgium' (*in illo cruento Belgii theatro*). French resilience 'puts on a show which is painful for the enemy but most pleasing for the French, whilst Britain remains silent, Spain applauds, Holland weeps, Germany growls, Portugal is struck with fear, Savoy bides its time and the whole of Europe stands by, amazed by the magnitude of the spectacle'.⁴⁷ Porée closes his speech by conceding that France has paid a high price for their efforts but then goes on to insist that they ought to be rewarded with peace. The enemy should come to terms and agree to end hostilities. The speech concludes with an exaltation of Louis XIV, the ultimate promoter of peace: 'Embrace the peace which Louis, mighty and peaceful in either situation, even now offers you' (*Pacem, quam Ludovicus in utraque fortuna magnus, in utraque pacificus, vobis etiamnum offert, admittite*, p. 201).

On 10 February, only a few weeks after Porée's speech had been pronounced, a fellow Jesuit at the Parisian Collège Louis-le-Grand, Noël-Étienne Sanadon, some of whose poetry we have already seen in Chapters 1 and 2, recited an eighty-line Sapphic ode addressed to the goddess of peace.[48] Though *Ad Pacem* features the occasional dig at the Allies, and the English and Dutch are ridiculed for their fondness for drinking and dams respectively, Sanadon eschews the patriotism that fuelled his earlier military pieces examined in the previous chapter, and the ode conveys a general sense of relief with respect to the impending end of the war.[49] The text begins with a description of Europe's yearning for peace after the long years of conflict ('Europe asks you for the spoils given to excessively harsh Mars. To you the Frenchman offers up his prayers, to you the suppliant Spaniard fervently offers up a thousand vows').[50] Almost all parties – including the Portuguese, 'whom the river Tajo enriches with enviable sand' – demand the cessation of hostilities, and the poet sardonically asks the divinity why he will not 'for the sake of pleasant peace banish the turbulent din of frenzied Mars and convey fear and trouble far away, to restless Ursa Major', in other words the north pole, in a reference to the ongoing Great Northern War between Sweden and Russia, which ended in 1721.[51] In stanzas six to eight, Sanadon reflects on Europe's deplorable state, which he likens to a wintry landscape: crops, trade and urban life have been completely devastated by Libitina, the goddess of corpses. Yet, 'after red Jupiter has caused the axes of the earth to tremble with his thundering right hand, the air often clears when the rain clouds have been dispelled'.[52]

The second section of the ode announces the arrival of spring, when delegates at the peace congress in Utrecht would ultimately ratify the treaty. Rebirth in the natural world is accompanied by the advent of Peace, whose chief remit is to persuade those powers still reluctant to embrace the negotiations – a tacit reference to Emperor Charles VI – to lay down their arms:

Nunc, ubi vernos Zephyrus tepores
cogitat pulsa revocare bruma,
prome formosum caput et iacentes
respice terras.
Vince discordes animos potentium;
arma deponant neque caecus ultra
obstinet regum furor immerentes
perdere gentes

ll. 37–44

['Now, when Zephyrus (a mild westerly wind) – once winter has been expelled – considers recalling the gentle warmth of spring, raise your handsome head and turn your attention to the dormant lands. Overcome the warring spirits of the powerful; may they lay down their arms and may the blind fury of kings not persist in further destroying their innocent subjects'].

After the calamities of the dreadful war have ceased, France will enjoy prosperity under the guidance of Louis XIV, and a new Golden Age will descend upon the realm.[53] In stanzas fifteen and sixteen, Sanadon depicts Peace with her traditional attributes: a laurel wreath, a horn of plenty and olive branches (*termes olivae*, possibly alluding to Horace, *Epod*. 16.45). Under the influence of Peace's rejuvenating light, the earth will deliver bounteous harvests, and 'faith, divine law and integrity fearful of deceit will return' (ll. 66–7).[54] Although the poet rejoices in the harmony and wealth that Peace will return to all of Europe, France is singled out as the best place to be. Like a second Corydon, Sanadon will celebrate this new peaceful age with his pipe and his verse.[55]

For Sanadon and other French pamphleteers, peace and prosperity in Europe were largely the result of Louis XIV's efforts to foster peace between his country and the Allies. As an example, in his *In solemnem abdicationem regnorum Franciae et Hispaniae factam in Parisiensi senatu die Mercurii 15 Martii 1713 ode* ('An ode to mark the solemn renunciation of the kingdoms of France and Spain held in the Parliament of Paris on Wednesday 15 March 1713') Claude-Louis Waltrin, whom we have already encountered in Chapter 2, praised the king's acceptance of Philip's renunciation of his claim to the French throne as a key factor in paving the way for the Peace of Utrecht.[56] As noted in the previous chapter, the Duke of Anjou formally waived his claim to the French throne on 5 November 1712. For their part, Philippe of Orléans, Louis XIV's nephew, and Charles of France, duke of Berry and Philip V's youngest brother (1686–1714), gave up their own rights to the Spanish crown on 19 and 24 November. The renunciations were accepted by Louis XIV in three letters issued on 10 March 1713 and read in the French Parliament five days later. All these events were chronicled in verse by Waltrin, whose ode describes the proceedings in detail, naming, for example, Guillaume-François Joly de Fleury (1675–1756), the king's attorney (l. 42), and Robert Harley and Charles Talbot (1660–1718), duke of Shrewsbury and Lord High Treasurer, the British politicians who were present at the assembly (l. 58). Couched in imagery drawn from classical myth and legend, Waltrin's piece extols the Bourbon administration as well as the monarch's generosity and high-mindedness. Though Greece may boast a Codrus, France rejoices in Orléans and Berry, a new Castor and Pollux (l.11), whose dignified renunciations may bring tranquillity and prosperity to the nation.[57] For his part, Philip – unlike Phaeton, who failed in his ill-conceived attempt to drive the sun's chariot – renounced his right to succeed the Sun King and, by so doing, prevented further war (ll. 13–16). Achieved with divine assistance (the end of the hostilities is regarded as a *bonum coeleste*, 'a gift from heaven', l. 64), the peace treaty is celebrated as a triumph of Louis XIV's peacemaking policies (ll. 37–40).

The Peace of Utrecht was also meant to usher in an era of prosperity for the Dutch Republic, where a large body of poetical and performative texts celebrating the treaty in the vernacular was commissioned by several local authorities. In most of these writings, peace is represented as a victory for the Netherlands and England over France, even if Dutch literary representations of the Peace of Utrecht bore little relation to reality: negotiators on behalf of the United Provinces were 'completely overshadowed by the other European powers, and the Dutch had little impact on the actual results' (Jensen 2015: 169). The same rhetoric of war and propaganda can be found in the numismatic collection issued by the Dutch to commemorate the Treaties of Utrecht, Rastatt and Baden, which was assembled and illustrated by Gerard Van Loon shortly after the end of the War of the Spanish Succession. Minted for the city councillors of Amsterdam, one of these medals (Van Loon 1717: 249) shows the Dutch lion, the heraldic representation of the United Provinces, together with Peace holding a shield in one hand and a spear in the other with which she points to a small olive tree growing in the foreground (Figure 6). The medal bears a Latin inscription, *Diva tegens Batavos, qua cuspide reppulit hostes, / nunc oleas pacis surgere signa iubet* ('With the spear with which she repelled the enemy the goddess protector of the Dutch commands the olive tree, symbol of peace, to rise'), a distich composed for the occasion by the Utrecht professor of History, Eloquence and Politics, Pieter Burman (Petrus Burmannus, 1668–1741).[58] On 22 May, in his official commemorative oration on the Peace of Utrecht 'settled between the mightiest king of France and the powerful orders of the United Provinces' first delivered in Latin and subsequently translated into Dutch, Burman showed rather more caution about the outcome of the negotiations. Here he commended those diplomats who had made every effort to seek peace but warned against signing the kind of treaties that would inevitably lead to further outbreaks of hostilities in the future.[59] Rather than defensive alliances, Burman advocated for the restoration of trade and saw Dutch republican values as the only reliable opposition to French monarchism and oppression (Burman 1713a: 35–6). He was particularly mistrustful of the Dutch Barrier in the Southern Netherlands granted by the

Figure 6 A medal minted for the city councillors of Amsterdam in 1714, bearing the inscription *Diva tegens Batavos, qua cuspide reppulit hostes, / nunc oleas pacis surgere signa iubet* ('With the spear with which she repelled the enemy the goddess protector of the Dutch commands the olive tree, symbol of peace, to rise'). Reproduced in Van Loon 1717: 249.

Peace of Utrecht which allowed the Dutch to garrison towns on its southern border with France, and which he believed would not prevent further conflict.

Though not unanimously welcomed in a climate of intense political factionalism, the Peace of Utrecht was also largely recognized as advantageous for Britain, which acquired trading rights in Spanish America and wrested the *asiento* (the word simply means 'contract' and refers to the monopoly on slave trade to the Spanish Empire) from the French. The signing of the treaty was marked by firework displays on the Thames, loyal toasts to Queen Anne, and religious ceremonies all over the country, most notably the public Thanksgiving held at St Paul's Cathedral in London on 7 July (Thompson 2014: 61–4). Three days later, the University of Oxford also decided to mark the occasion with a formal celebration in the Sheldonian Theatre. Members of the university recited speeches and verses in Latin which were later collected in a handsome commemorative volume.[60] Three texts address the freedom of the academic press, but the bulk of compositions included in the collection focus on the efforts made by Britain to secure peace, both on the battlefield and at the negotiating table. In *Exercitus exauctoratus* ('An army honourably discharged'), Charles Trelawney of Magdalen College celebrates the past military exploits of British troops and the advent of peace. Literary recreations of two articles from the London agreement leading to the suspension of arms with France in July 1712, *Regnum Galliae a Philippo renunciatum* ('Philip's renunciation of the Crown of

France') and *Dunquerca delenda* ('[The harbour and fortifications of] Dunkirk must be destroyed', playfully echoing Cato's famous *dictum* on Carthage) pay tribute to Britain's diplomatic skills and tactics at negotiating peace in the final months of the conflict. The peace-promoting machinations both in Parliament and abroad by two influential figures of the time – the Tory politician and Speaker of the House of Commons William Bromley (1663–1732), and John Robinson (1650–1723), bishop of Bristol, Lord Keeper of the Privy Seal and British ambassador at Utrecht – also attract comment in *Senatus Britannicus* and *Episcopus privati sigilli custos et legatus* respectively.[61] Several poems deal with the aftermath of war: Matthew Priaulx's *Aerarium repletum* ('Refilling of the treasury') describes the benefits that the British economy may reap at the expense of the Dutch, and two further pieces in the book, by the Barbados-born poets John Alleyn (1695–1730) and John Maynard (b. 1692), rejoice in the opportunities for South Sea trade awarded by the new peace.[62]

The central figures in the Oxford volume for the Peace of Utrecht are Queen Anne and her adherents, and several pieces in the collection seek to promote the monarch's political agenda in the face of the continuing animosity that surrounded the peace treaty in Britain. In Edmund Isham's opening speech *Pax Annae auspiciis instaurata* ('Peace restored under the auspices of Anne') Robert Harley is described as *Britannicus orbis pacator* ('British peace-maker of the earth'), and the monarch is commended for having procured a peace settlement for her war-weary nation (*Anna miserias populi sui perpendit* – 'Anne took careful note of the affliction of her people'). If only her Austrian ally had assisted Anne in her pursuits of peace, Charles VI's empire would still be free from danger.[63] By contrast, the Queen's valiant efforts to secure peace have been endorsed by her enemies: by Louis XIV, who, 'subdued by old age and all but broken by the exertions of a protracted conflict, may also request Anne's friendship and finally live out his old age securely', and by Spain, who, 'whilst admiring you as the bringer of the gifts of peace, willingly opens up her golden coffers for you and gladly pours the riches collected from both Indies into the British treasury every year'.[64] The piece concludes with a prophecy: after poring over volumes of ancient history and perusing Queen Boudicca's and Elizabeth I's illustrious deeds, future generations shall express their admiration at Anne's greater determination and bravery against her own male rivals. In *Ormondus imperator*, Richard Levet of Magdalen College praises the loyalty shown by Captain General James Butler, second duke of Ormonde, when he received his now notorious 'restraining orders' in May 1712. A poem in hexameters by Thomas Bromley of Christ Church, son of the Speaker, describes in great detail the grand procession from the Houses of Parliament to St

Paul's prior to the thanksgiving service in commemoration of peace, 'a ceremonial performance used by Queen Anne as a means of asserting her political authority' (Farguson 2015: 210).

David Money has made a strong case that such collections of Neo-Latin poetry published in Oxford offer 'a showcase of talent to the wider world and [provide] a useful means of asserting political loyalty' (2013: 389). Similar ideas and purposes resonate equally strongly in the verse collection produced by the University of Cambridge for the Peace of Utrecht, which includes pieces in Latin, Greek and Hebrew, most of them bearing no formal title.[65] The volume is noteworthy for the examples of individual flattery of Tory politicians, negotiators and commanders, 'contradicting the myth that Cambridge was predominantly Whig' (Money 1998: 236). A handful of poems are devoted to Harley and the Lord Chancellor Viscount Harcourt (1661–1727), to Bishop Robinson and the diplomat and poet Matthew Prior (1664–1721), and to Ormonde and William Drake, Lord of the Admiralty between 1710 and 1714.[66] As with its counterpart from Oxford, the Cambridge volume includes several compositions celebrating Utrecht that either list the material benefits to be obtained from the long-desired peace or praise Anne for having brought about the peace and having safeguarded Britain from her dangerous enemies. Echoing Horace's priamel in *Laudabunt alii* ('Others shall praise', *Od.* 1.7), in which the Roman poet refuses to sing of various great Greek cities in favour of the more modest Latin Tibur (Race 1982: 126), Adam Elliot – a fellow of King's College – expresses his intention to sing of the blessings of peace, rather than the military glories of the past:

> *Laudarunt alii felices Marte Britannos,*
> *venales et sanguine lauros;*
> *laudarunt merito; quis enim neget Anglus honores*
> *Malbrovio et victribus armis?*
> *Iam vero arma silent . . .*
>
> ll. 1–5

['Others praised Britons successful in war, and their triumphs won with blood. They praised them deservedly; for which Englishman will deny honours to Marlborough and to his victorious arms? Now their arms are indeed silent . . .'].

The reference to Marlborough is significant on two counts. Firstly, the former war general had been dismissed from office in 1711. But more importantly, alongside his Whig Cabinet allies, Marlborough was adamant that the fighting should continue even after Utrecht. By contrast, Queen Anne is celebrated by Elliot as a champion of peace, a new Minerva, who 'gave us our character, who gave us this peace' (l. 7).⁶⁷ Before his departure for Utrecht, Bishop Robinson is instructed by the monarch to seek a long-lasting peace agreement with war-weary France:

> 'I, legate Dei patriaeque, i, care, perenni
> Europen et foedere iungas.
> Gallia maesta diu gaudentes sanguine natos
> iam satiatos sanguine vidit'
>
> ll. 17–20

["'Go, ambassador of God and your country; go, my friend, and unite Europe in an everlasting alliance. Sorrowful France has seen that her children, who have long rejoiced in blood, have now had enough of it'"].

Anne then turns to her own subjects and urges 'mature Britain, nation most beloved of the gods, to prune her healthy laurel bushes and not shy away from being adorned with the decorous branch of the peaceful olive tree. She who conquers in all other things, should conquer herself'.⁶⁸ Underlying Anne's request is her longing for peace with her foreign enemies, but also her desire for civic harmony and national unity amidst the political acrimony caused partly by the Jacobite threat.

Elliot's distichs highlight the atmosphere of political distrust prevailing in Britain after the Utrecht settlement. The leaders of the Whig party were deeply suspicious of the Tory ministry's commitment to the Protestant succession.⁶⁹ As well as encapsulating a sense of the turmoil of the era, a few pieces included in the Cambridge book assert Anne's sovereign authority at this most critical time. For example, in his eight elegiacs under the title *Ad reginam*, John Exton of Trinity College promotes the first British monarch as a symbol of national unity, whose rule is admired even by her former rivals.⁷⁰ Two further poems in the collection take aim at those in Britain still averse to peace. In his Sapphic ode *In obnitentes paci* ('Against those who oppose peace'), John Bowtell of St John's College attacks his enemies 'for their lack of patriotism and, wrongly obstinate, for continuing to rage against the wish of their sovereign and the people' (... *neque consulentes / patriae pergant, male pertinaces! / principis votum populique contra / ire furentes*, ll. 1–4). He urges them not to boycott the peace ceremonies organized by the Crown, in which 'its subjects, the army and the church will all take part, happy in their service'.⁷¹ John Bolder's *Ad pacis oppugnatorem*, consisting of twenty-four elegiac couplets, is yet another example of an invective addressed 'to an attacker of peace'. The poem is built around a series of oppositions highlighting the benefits of peace enjoyed by Britain on the one hand, and the miseries in store for those still reluctant to embrace the treaty on the other. The contrast reaches its climax in the couplet 'Everything shines agreeably on my delightful face; only on yours do slaughter, blood and weapons look frightful' (*Omnia iucundo mihi suaviter ore renident; / uno horrent caedes, sanguis et arma tuo*, ll. 17–18). The tone thereafter is recriminatory: 'hence those tears' (*Hinc illae lacrymae*, l. 21, echoing Terence, *Andria*, 125). The foe is reminded that the Hanoverian succession, which was recognized in the treaty, guarantees stability for the nation:

> *Non domus Hannoviae illustris stabilitur in aevum?*
> *Non genus aeternum perpetuumque decus?*
>
> ll. 41–2

['Will the illustrious House of Hanover not be made stable for ever? Is its honour not eternal and everlasting?'].

Bolder goes on to invite the enemies of peace to flee the country if they do not feel content in England, and warns them against attempting to divide the nation, for 'it is wrong to provoke wars at home when there are none abroad' (*Si minus haec placeant, Anglis discede, nefandum est, / quum sunt nulla foras, bella ciere domi*, ll. 43–4). He strikes his final blow, adapting two lines from Martial, by bidding his enemy to fly away, yet reminding him he will never be better off anywhere else:

> *turbatum, furiate, cupis volitare per orbem;*
> *i, fuge; sed poteris tutior esse domi*
>
> ll. 47–8

['Enraged, you are eager to fly around a world in disorder. Go! Fly! Yet you will have been safer at home'].[72]

The peace process was completed by the congresses in Rastatt and Baden in March and September 1714 that were negotiated by Marshal Villars and Prince Eugene of Savoy. The medal issued by the French to commemorate the Treaty of Rastatt depicted two thunderbolts of battle giving Europe peace, with the inscription *Olim duo fulmina belli, nunc instrumenta quietis* ('Once two thunderbolts of war, now instruments of peace'), in a reference to the two head negotiators.[73] 'Most supreme prince in war and in peace', Eugene was also lavishly praised in a *Promotionsschrift* published by the University of Graz entitled *Laudis vectigal* ('Revenue of praise'), which consists of four short speeches penned by the class of Rhetoric expanding on the general's virtues – knowledge of warfare, valour, prestige and good fortune – as discussed by Cicero in his *Pro lege Manilia* (see Chapter 2).[74] At the end of the third oration, the foremost commander is urged 'to bring the peace negotiations to a satisfactory conclusion with the same prestige with which you have thus far endured the heaviest burden of war'.[75]

The preceding paragraphs have attempted to demonstrate how throughout Europe – except perhaps for Spain, where the initial treaty was met with much disquiet among political pamphleteers (Pérez Picazo 1966, I: 273–7) – the Peace of Utrecht provided an excellent opportunity for many European poets and prose writers to appropriate the achievement of peace and to portray it as a celebration of their own nation. With the same alacrity and pride they had rejoiced in the victories of their own commanders and armies on the battlefield during the conflict, authors of the Latin poetry and prose produced on the occasion of the Peace of Utrecht were eager to highlight and celebrate the contribution of their own nations to the peace negotiations in the face of opposition from other parties. As well as declaring their alliance to a particular individual, power or political faction, most writers utilized the peace process to further a broader political agenda in support of their own national interests. In most cases, the new and favourable conditions arising from Utrecht were presented as a result of royal (or republican) mercy, which had decided to put an end to the hostilities for the sake of the entire continent. In addition, in some of the texts examined above, war is coded as a divinely-assisted endeavour for peace, cooperation between nations is exalted, and enemies are depicted as potential friends. This conciliatory impulse also features in visual representations of the war, as shown in the *Repraesentatio belli ob successionem in regno Hispanico ... victoriosis armis usque ad pacem Badensem felicissime et fortissime gesti* ('Representation of the war caused by the succession in the kingdom of Spain ... auspiciously and heroically waged with victorious arms up to the Peace of Baden'), which was begun in 1712: granted the privilege of Imperial copyright three years later but not published until 1724, this series of plates included representations of both Allied and French victories, proof of a real change in the political climate as the dynastic conflict was gradually coming to an end.[76]

Conclusion

During the War of the Spanish Succession royal weddings and funerals, as well as the ceremonies to celebrate the Peace of Utrecht towards the end of the war, were orchestrated by the powers at play to enhance the status of their favoured candidate. Such grand public occasions prompted a rich body of Latin writing by teachers and pupils, clergymen, scholars and designers of coins and medals. The exigencies of the contemporary political situation and the rapid progress of war often forced them to produce their works (and have them printed or minted) in a very short period of time after the occasion they were describing or commenting on. Often arising from academic practice or related to a professional function or official duty, these texts became a central instrument of political propaganda during and in the aftermath of the conflict. In this chapter we have seen how nuptial, eulogistic and funerary pieces in verse and prose, though primarily anchored in the event they were meant to eternalize, were employed by both contenders within the dynastic feud to make a broader point and promote a more enduring vision of their cause beyond the particular occasion.

As with the literary celebrations of contemporary battles and military heroes examined elsewhere in this book, imitation of forms and sources from Greek and Roman literature is central to the texts under review in the present chapter. Yet, many of the Neo-Latin authors studied here are also to be credited for their ability both to adapt their ancient templates to more recent circumstances and to draw on non-classical models. Moreover, whilst some of the texts examined in the preceding pages were penned by individuals who had already made a name for themselves at court, in the church or in academia, other authors contributed occasional poems or orations either to establish or cement relationships with powerful rulers and patrons. Johann Werlhof and Anton von Öttl's *epithalamia* composed for the wedding of Archduke Charles and Elisabeth Christine of Brunswick-Wolfenbüttel in 1708 illustrate these two points well. Both men successfully embedded their Virgilian models – whether epic or pastoral – in a contemporary frame of reference but also supplemented them with historiographical or literary material extracted from medieval Latin chronicles of the House of Welf and the oral tradition respectively. For Werlhof, his *epithalamium* for Elisabeth Christine was the culmination of a long and distinguished career at the service of Prince Anton Ulrich of Brunswick-Wolfenbüttel, the dedicatee of his poem. Similarly, Öttl was clearly well aware of the possibilities of self-promotion within the Imperial court afforded by his encomiastic pieces for Elisabeth Christine (and Maria Anna of Austria): later in life he became *Hofkriegsrat* ('Court war councillor') and *Kaiserlicher Generalauditor* ('Imperial general auditor'). Unsurprisingly, he believed the staging of the valedictory ceremonies held in honour of both monarchs as the highlight of his tenure as rector of the University of Vienna (Klecker 2008: 53; Figure 7). With the taking of Majorca by the Bourbon army on 22 July 1715 and the end of all military operations, the sound of war-related ceremonies naturally ceased but the echo of the dynastic conflict continued to resonate across Europe. In this new political scenario Latin remained a key instrument of political discourse, as we shall see in the next chapter.

Figure 7 Rector Anton von Öttl's entry in the main register of the University of Vienna for the year 1708. Reproduced from the History of the University section of the Universität Wien website (accessed on 1 July 2022).

4

Latin Propaganda beyond the Dynastic Conflict (1715–1740)

On 19 March 1719 two members of the local Gymnasium at Neuseddin, near Berlin, held a formal academic debate or *disputatio*.[1] The subject up for discussion between the director Christoph Densovius and his respondent Tobias Heinrich Engelken was none other than the legal rights of Holy Roman Emperor Leopold I and King Louis XIV of France to place their favoured candidate on the throne of Spain in the long-gone year of 1703. In the text, the two colleagues at Neuseddin draw on some of the same legal and theological arguments employed years earlier by political propagandists on both sides of the dynastic dispute, which we have been examining in the three previous chapters. As with some of the pamphleteers at the service of either Charles of Austria or Philip of Anjou who have been quoted in the preceding pages, in their defences, both Densovius or Engelken resort to poetry in Latin and in several vernacular languages; chronograms, anagrams, riddles and sonnets on behalf of their chosen claimant provide further ideological ammunition in the debate.[2]

The Neuseddin *disputatio* is a good example of how the dynastic feud, four years after the end of the hostilities in the War of the Spanish Succession, continued to elicit attention in academic circles across Europe. More importantly, the text shows how the legitimate rights of Charles III and Philip V to the Spanish crown were still the subject of political debate, even though the treaties of Utrecht and Rastatt had to all intents and purposes settled the matter of the succession. In fact, even after Utrecht and Rastatt, Emperor Charles continued to nurture universalist dreams and did not give up hope of recovering more of his Spanish inheritance. As William O'Reilly rightly notes, Charles spent the rest of his life 'seeking to reconstitute the empire of his eponymous antecedent, Charles V' (2011: 66). The following paragraphs explore the ways in which Latin remained an instrument of political discourse in the aftermath of the dynastic dispute. The purpose of the first section of this chapter is to demonstrate how the learned language was the medium chosen by several Allied exiles, particularly by Catalan scholars established in Italy and Austria after 1713, where they worked towards restoring the state of affairs which had existed before the military conflict. The second part of the chapter examines the ways in which the Latin propaganda machine of Emperor Charles VI (and to a much lesser extent of King Philip V of Spain) continued to exploit the Spanish conflict after the proclamation of Charles VI as king of Sicily in 1720 and following the signing five years later of the Peace of Vienna, which officially marked the end of the dynastic feud of the War of the Spanish Succession.

Latin political propaganda and exile in the aftermath of the dynastic conflict

The Peace of Utrecht left only one issue unresolved, namely that of the 'case of the Catalans', who continued to support Charles of Austria (Albareda 2005). By the end of 1708 Philip V had taken control of practically the entire Spanish mainland territory, while Archduke Charles had been forced back to the Principality of Catalonia. In the ensuing years, Bourbon forces advanced further and further into Catalan territory until, following the Hospitalet Agreement of 22 June 1713, the Allied troops withdrew completely. On 6 July an assembly made up of the various segments within Catalan society pledged to resist, albeit with only the capital, Barcelona, and two fortified towns still opposing Philip V: Castellciutat, which surrendered on 27 September, and Cardona. Philip's army reached Barcelona on 25 July and a long siege ensued, culminating in the fall of the Catalan capital on 11 September 1714. After Cardona fell a week later, the leaders of the resistance were imprisoned and the Bourbon authorities suppressed all the institutions of the Catalan government, establishing an absolutist and centralist rule through the so-called Decree of the New Plant (passed on 16 January 1716). Catalonia was systematically stripped of the privileges it had preserved for so long and became a mere region of the new Bourbon state. In addition, between 25,000 and 30,000 people were forced into exile. They came from various groups in Catalonia and elsewhere in the Crown of Aragon (the neighbouring territories with long-standing ties to the Principality): those who were evacuated in the summer of 1713, those banished after September 1714, and those who fled secretly from then on right up until 1725. Most of them established themselves in the Italian possessions belonging to Emperor Charles VI, chiefly in Naples and Milan. The nobility and members of the upper echelons of the administration, however, joined the Imperial court in Vienna, where they formed the Councils of Spain (1713) and Flanders (1717) to monitor the former Spanish territories. These two institutions were used by the exiles as a platform for getting the 'case of the Catalans' back on the international agenda (Alcoberro 2002: 37–57).

One of those Viennese exiles was Marco Antonio San Marco, whom we encountered in Chapter 1. After accompanying Elisabeth Christine on her journey back to the Empire, on 21 May 1716 he completed a *Carmen historico-genethliacum* ('A historical birthday poem'), which came off the press of Simon Schmid in Vienna.[3] Dedicated to Count Rocco Stella (1662–1720), this piece in 445 hexameters was written to mark the recent birth of Charles VI's son Archduke Leopold Johann, whom San Marco addresses as 'Prince of Asturias' in his prefatory remarks (sign. A2v).[4] This reference to the title traditionally given to the heir to the Spanish throne might appear slightly out of place, almost in defiance of reality, given the outcome of the War of the Spanish Succession. Yet, it constitutes a manifest indication of how Imperial court propaganda continued to uphold Charles's claim to the Spanish crown in the aftermath of the dynastic conflict. Following Leopold Johann's sudden death on 4 November at the age of just seven months, the title of Prince of Asturias was again employed for the inscription on the sarcophagus built for the child in the Capuchin Crypt in Vienna (Hawlik-van de Water 1993: 129–30). San Marco's poem is a nostalgic and somewhat one-sided celebration of Habsburg military prowess during the dynastic conflict. It begins with a description of Charles's and Elisabeth Christine's wedding in Barcelona in 1708 (ll. 1–81), of the empress's pilgrimage to Mariazell upon her return to Vienna (ll. 81–94), and her ensuing pregnancy and the royal birth, which is celebrated by the Viennese populace (ll. 95–141). In this first section, the use of the second person is particularly dense, and Leopold Johann is repeatedly addressed by the author, who confers upon the new-born all the virtues pertaining to the Habsburg dynasty (ll. 141–81) and particularly his father's military courage and intellectual qualities (ll. 182–209).[5] The second part of the piece (ll. 210–438) presents a poetic chronicle of the circumstances leading to the outbreak of the War of the Spanish Succession and of the early episodes of the military conflict, both on the Iberian Peninsula and elsewhere in Europe, in which Charles and his troops distinguished themselves with their heroic performance. The text does not diverge from the conventional narrative employed in other pro-Habsburg writings examined in the preceding chapters: doubts are cast on the validity of Charles II's will (ll. 210–50) and Emperor Leopold and his elder son Joseph are praised for their decision to renounce their claims in favour of Charles, and for seeking legal justification for his actions (ll.

251–5). The following sections focus on Charles's voyage from England to Lisbon (ll. 256–302), on the two sieges of Barcelona during the Catalan campaigns (ll. 303–43), on the taking of Naples by Habsburg forces in 1707 (ll. 344–72) and on the siege of Toulon (ll. 373–409), which is celebrated as an Allied victory.[6] San Marco omits any reference to the defeats at Almansa or Villaviciosa and closes his account with an allusion to the Battle of Saragossa, in Aragon, won on 20 August 1710, praising Charles's military valour:

> ... non te Catalonia metis
> continet, angusto nec torpet limite virtus.
> Catellae, iucunda Valentia, Aragonas acri
> te stupet invictum bello cunctamque petisti
> victrici Hesperiam pompa partisque triumphis
>
> ll. 402–6

['And Catalonia does not restrain you within its boundaries, and your valour hardly diminishes. All Castile, pleasant Valencia and Aragon wonder at you, unvanquished in fierce war; you recovered all of Spain with victorious pomp and the triumphs you won'].

The following verses (ll. 410–38) introduce a critical note on Charles's political and military allies, who are accused of having abandoned the Habsburg pretender and sued for peace for the sake of economic gain. 'You alone, Charles,' – exclaims the poet – 'firm, faithful, you keep your alliances' (... *unus, / Carole, tu constans, tu fidus foedera servas*, ll. 419–20). Quoting Ovid's dictum 'There is a god within us', San Marco exhorts Archduke Leopold Johann to continue the dynasty's sacred mission, for 'Spain will finally recognise its ancient masters' (*antiquos tandem dominos Hispania noscet*, l. 438).[7] The poet then bids farewell to his young dedicatee (ll. 439–45).

Another exile who took refuge in Vienna after the evacuation of 1713 and the calamitous defeat of the following year was Francesc de Santacruz i Gener (d. 1730). A military engineer and sculptor who had witnessed the final siege of Barcelona, Santacruz produced a large engraving in 1716 under the title *Barcino magna parens* ('Barcelona, great mother').[8] Published two years later by Johann van Ghelen, 'printer to his Imperial Majesty and to his supreme Council of Spain', the work shows Barcelona from the north, closely besieged, with a detailed explanation in Latin and Spanish of the most important sites and episodes related to the long battle (Figure 8).[9] The echo of the valour and steadfastness shown by the citizens of Barcelona, who only surrendered in extremis, is remarkably resonant in the inscription on the shield which features in the bottom right corner of the drawing:

Augustissimo Romanorum Imperatori Carolo VI, semper invicto Hispaniarum Regi III Catholico, Barchinonensi Comiti et patri. Hanc Barchinonae ab ulterioris Hispaniae et Galliae coronis per decem et quatuor menses mari terraque obsessae et a propriis civibus strenue defensae, tandem deprecata ab obsessoribus capitulatione occupatae, delineationem in signum obsequiosissimae devotionis et reverentiae o(ffert) d(icat) c(onsecrat) Franciscus Santa Cruz, Catalanus 1716

['To Charles VI, most august Holy Roman Emperor, forever unvanquished Catholic King Charles III of Spain, count and father of Barcelona. As a sign of his most humble devotion and reverence Francesc de Santacruz, Catalan, offers, dedicates and devotes this sketch of Barcelona being besieged by the crowns of Castile and France during fourteen months by land and sea, bravely defended by its own citizens and finally occupied through capitulation implored by the besiegers. In 1716'].

The Council of Spain also sponsored the publication of works by Domènec Aguirre (fl. 1683–1734), upon whom Charles VI conferred the title of Count of Massot shortly after his arrival in the Imperial capital. In the 1690s, during his tenure as professor of Law at Barcelona University, Aguirre had penned his *Discursus super officiis venalibus Generalitatis Cathaloniae* ('A discourse on the purchasable offices of the Generalitat of Catalonia') as part of a larger tract on

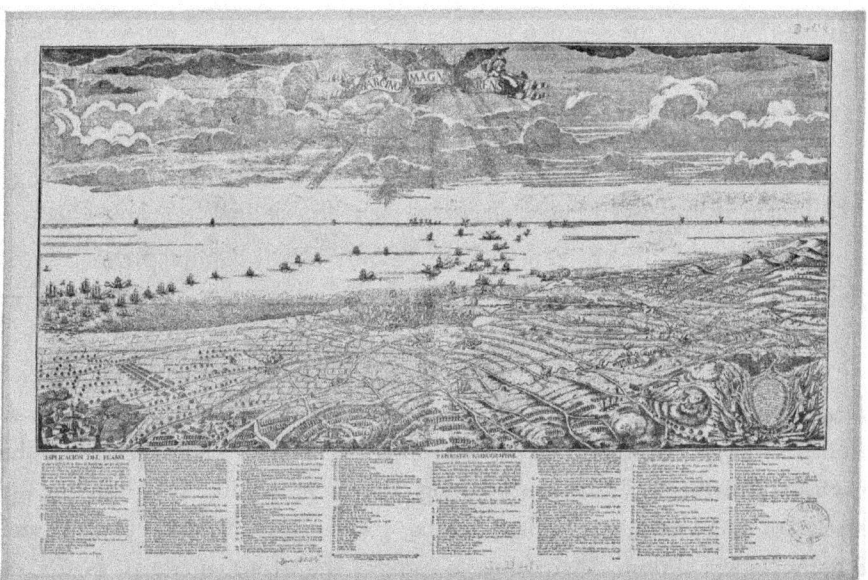

Figure 8 Francesc de Santacruz i Gener, *Barcino magna parens*, engraving, Arxiu Històric de la Ciutat de Barcelona, reg. 18265.

legal matters.¹⁰ Two decades later, 'compelled by necessity' (*necessitate compulsus*), he decided to bring it to the press at a moment when negotiations for the Treaty of Vienna between the Emperor and the Spanish king were well underway. The *Discursus* reflects the intense lobbying undertaken by Catalan exiles at the Imperial Court in Vienna to ensure that the new Bourbon government would respect Catalonia's liberties. Despite its rather specialized terminology and subject matter, Aguirre's work aims to preserve the memory of Catalonia's constitutions and privileges, which had been systematically abolished by the new Spanish administration. As boldly acknowledged on the title page, Aguirre's intention to publish his discourse in Vienna was 'also to preserve knowledge of things belonging to the fatherland' (*pro servanda quoque rei patriae notitia*) at a time when Catalonia's old political institutions had disappeared and political turmoil was rife. This point is highlighted in the preface to the work:

Sed cum hodie res Cathaloniae valde turbatae sint, maxime quae pertinent ad eius Generalitatem, cuius eximius magistratus suspensus reperitur, et notitiae horum officiorum ac eorum iurum facillime perire possint, propterea nunquam maiorem extitisse necessitatem huius edendi opusculi, quam nunc existimo, non quia ex se typis dignum esse diiudicem, sed ratione notitiarum tantum, ne tempore pereant, ut postea, Domino Deo miserente ac pervento optato casu, a viris doctis et sapientibus possit tanta res accuratius expediri

sign. b2r

['Yet, since today the situation in Catalonia is in great turmoil, above all with regard to the Generalitat [= the government of Catalonia], whose distinguished administration is currently suspended, and knowledge of these offices and of their jurisdiction may most easily be lost, for this reason I think that there has never been a greater need to publish this tract than right now, not because I consider my work worthy of being printed but rather for the sake of knowledge, so that it may not perish over time and later, with God's mercy and when the desired outcome is reached, such an important issue may be explained more accurately by wise and learned men'].

Aguirre's text includes a meticulous examination of the administrative machinery of the Catalan government, with which the author was well acquainted from his days as a magistrate of the Supreme Court in Catalonia before the beginning of the war. After an opening chapter presenting an outline of the history of the Generalitat, Aguirre's treatise goes on to describe its structure and different layers of power. According to Aguirre, the term 'Generalitat' is used to designate the entire Principality, and the institution itself consists of three branches, the ecclesiastical, the military and the royal, which is headed by the

Conseller en cap de la ciutat de Barcelona ('Councillor-in-chief of the city of Barcelona'). This meaning is not arbitrary but derives from the law, from juridical sources and from popular use.[11]

Nostalgia for Catalonia's lost constitutions and past glory is also the theme underlying the work of another Catalan exile, the jurist Josep Plantí (1681–1743). After holding administrative positions in Catalonia and Sardinia, Plantí was forced to flee to Vienna in 1717, when the island fell into Bourbon hands. In 1725 he was elected to the Senate of Milan, where he was active until his retirement in 1741 (Plantí 2019: 5–42). Sometime between 1719 and 1725 or shortly after he relocated to Milan, Plantí completed three Latin tracts, which, for all their Catalan and historicist slant, should be interpreted as essentially political manifestos in their own right, taking aim at the centralist policies of the Bourbon dynasty.[12] In his *Gothorum historia in Hispania* ('A History of the Goths in Spain') Plantí claimed that Catalan rights and liberties had been originally granted during the rule of the Goths between the fifth and the eighth centuries and, in an interesting reinterpretation of history on the author's part, were confirmed by their successors, the Habsburgs. The alleged Gothic ancestry of Catalonia also features in Plantí's second work, *De Cataloniae Principatu* ('On the Principality of Catalonia'). Plantí constructs specific sections of his tract according to the pattern of topics prescribed for the *laudes urbium*, geographical, ethnographical and historical accounts in praise of a city (or of any other territory) with a clear political intention, a genre made popular by Renaissance Latin humanism (Classen 2003: 332–55). He does so, however, in a rather peculiar way, by amassing evidence drawn exclusively from foreign sources, which Plantí claims are far more reliable than local documents.[13] The text first briefly deals with the origin of the name of Catalonia, then it provides a complete survey of the geographical features of the Principality, a political entity which, for Plantí, extends beyond the territory under the new Bourbon master, and includes 'the Counties of Roussillon and Cerdagne, which only by virtue of a peace agreement [the Treaty of the Pyrenees of 1659] passed to the French Crown' (*Principatus Cataloniae continens comitatum Ruscilionis ac Ceretaniae nam solum pacis tractatu ad coronam Gallicam transiere*, f. 120v). Attention is also given to buildings, history and famous events, and a general overview of Catalonia's government and political institutions, now regrettably defunct, is also provided. The tract ends with a discussion of the Catalan language and of Catalan contribution to scholarship.[14] Throughout his account Plantí conveys his deep-rooted belief in the relationship between the natural environment and human temperament. He stresses the advantages conferred on the territory by its geography and the beneficial impact of this on its inhabitants: Catalans are by nature loyal, noble, moderate and generous.[15]

Plantí's evocation of Catalonia's lost liberties and political institutions is at its most elaborate in his chronicle of the War of the Spanish Succession entitled *De morte Caroli secundi Hispaniarum regis et de excidio Cathaloniae necnon destructione Barcinonis quasi secuta* ('The death of King Charles II of Spain and the ruin of Catalonia as well as the virtual destruction of Barcelona which ensued'). The text covers the key military and political events between the death of Charles II in November 1700 and the fall of Sardinia to Bourbon troops in 1717, which forced Plantí into exile. He begins his account of the conflict by renewing the charge that Louis XIV had deceived the dying Charles II into accepting Philip of Anjou as his sole heir. The late monarch's testament was, therefore, invalid, and 'the always august Austrian royal family opposed, vehemently and courageously, the summons granted in the will and [Philip's] inheritance of the [Spanish] kingdom, electing Archduke Charles and ceding him their rights and claims' (*Praehabitae in testamento vocationi adeptaeque regni possessioni acriter viriliterque se opposuit Austriaca familia semper augusta, eligendo Carolum Archiducem huicque ei iura, praetensiones cedendo*, Plantí 2022: 58).[16] Plantí goes on to describe the formation of the Grand Alliance, a confederation dismissed by him – as it was by San Marco in his *Carmen historico-genethliacum* – as driven solely by a desire for financial profit. There follows an account of Charles's offensive on the Iberian Peninsula. Understandably, the focus of Plantí's description of the early stages of the war is the successful siege of Barcelona in 1705. This military operation resulted not only in the taking of the city but also in Charles's pledge to uphold Catalan privileges and rights at Catalonia's *Corts* or parliament, which was in effect an assembly of the Catalan estates. One of the most far-reaching decisions announced at the parliamentary session was 'the exclusion in perpetuity of the Bourbon family from the succession of the kingdoms of Spain' ([*excludendo*] *Borbonicam familiam in perpetuo a successione regnorum Hispaniae*, Plantí 2022: 76). This resolution was made 'according to the constitution in which the king makes the proposal and the *Corts* agree to it' (*in constitutione, in qua rex loquitur et curiae consentiunt*, Plantí 2022: 76), in a reference to the equal relationship between the monarch and his subjects, based on negotiation, which Plantí claims had constituted an essential component of Catalan political life since the Middle Ages until the defeat of 1714. The adverse course of war, for which Plantí holds the Allies, the pope and the Catalans themselves responsible, was exacerbated by Joseph I's sudden death in April 1711. From then on, the Allies turned their backs on

Catalonia, which was excluded from the peace negotiations between France, Spain and the Allies at Utrecht and Rastatt, and was therefore compelled to continue the fight alone and eventually surrender. Plantí justifies Catalan resistance after Utrecht on the grounds that Catalonia was at that time a free state, with no ties to Charles VI and unbound by any pact to Philip V:

> *Catalonia, autem, a suo patrono manumissa, a confoederatis fallita, a potentioribus in pacis tractatu neglecta, praesentiens et praevidens quae praeparabantur ab Hispanis ad eius destructionem, quae iam per longum ante tempus attendebatur attendensque Catalonia suam impotentiam quodque dispositum referebatur in conventu seu pacis tractatu, iam non in statu representandi et, quod sicut nec audita nec adiuvata poterat existimari, iudicans considerans que se esse liberam, tamquam nulli principi subjecta nec obstricta nulloque iuris vinculo alicui principi obnoxia, non Philippo per Caroli dominationem, non Carolo per eius abdicationem*
>
> Plantí 2022: 112

['Catalonia, however, freed by her former master, deceived by the Allies, neglected by the more powerful in the peace treaty, presaged and foresaw everything which was prepared for her destruction by the Spaniards. Close attention was paid to these matters for a long time, and Catalonia – considering her impotence and the arrangements proposed in the agreement or in the peace treaty, being unrepresented and regarding herself as unheard and unaided – judged and considered herself free, as if she was not subject or bound by oath to any prince, nor beholden to any prince by any legal obligation, neither to Philip, on account of Charles's sovereignty, nor to Charles, on account of his abdication'].

Plantí was fully aware of his historical position. As with Aguirre, he was writing about his country, in order to ensure that recent events in Catalonia would not be lost over time. Rather solemnly, he declares he 'shall not die silent . . ., having been impelled to write by my love of truth and the glory of our nation' (*ne mutus obeam . . ., ad scribendum me adigunt et veritatis amor et gentis nostrae gloria*, Plantí 2022: 138). In this respect, Plantí's choice of Latin was doubtless prompted by his intention to reach an international readership following the defeat of 1714, as observed by Alcoberro (2002: 204–5). Even though they ultimately remained unpublished (an issue which is hardly taken into account by scholars of Catalan exile in the aftermath of the dynastic feud), Plantí's histories were undoubtedly intended to give voice to Catalan discontent in the wake of Utrecht as a reaction to the arguments proffered by the Spanish diplomacy of the time.[17] In his chronicle of the war Plantí dismisses, for example, those political thinkers and pamphleteers who attack Catalonia.[18] In this respect, he refers specifically to a treatise in Spanish entitled *Monarchia hebrea* (1719) by the politician and Spanish ambassador at Utrecht, Vincenzo Bacallar (1669–1726), to whom I shall return later in this chapter (Plantí 2022: 150). But Plantí was also writing autobiographically. At times, he places his reader in the settings he conjures up. 'As an eyewitness' – he claims – 'I am bound to describe whatever I saw' (*Tamquam ocularis testis describere quaeque vidi sum constrictus*, Plantí 2022: 70), as with his account of the meteorite which fell near Barcelona on Christmas Day 1704, an astronomical phenomenon interpreted by Plantí as an ominous sign in the context of war. Occasionally his voice and individual experience can be heard, and he explicitly refers to his predicament.[19] The experience of exile must have doubtless also determined Plantí's linguistic choice: he wrote about his homeland because he was in exile, and perhaps it was his exiled perspective and status that influenced his choice of language – and led him to write in Latin. Plantí constitutes yet another example of how Latin at the time became the acquired speech of an élite community that identified itself by this linguistic marker (Burke 2004).

The combination of recriminatory remarks against the Allies (Britain in particular), focus on recent history and thorough knowledge of Catalonia's legal system and political institutions that we find in Plantí's historiographical writings all feature as well in the anonymous *Record de la aliança fet al serm. Jordi-Augusto, rey de la Gran-Bretaña . . . ab una carta del Principat de Cataluña y ciutat de Barcelona* ('A reminder to most serene George August, King of Great Britain, of the alliance, together with a letter from the Principality of Catalonia and the city of Barcelona').[20] In this fictive bilingual letter in Catalan and Latin King George II (1683–1760) is reminded of the commitments made by his forebears to Catalonia under the Pact of Genoa in 1705. The original Catalan text of the epistle addressed to the British monarch is alleged to have been rendered into Latin and annotated by a certain 'Alan Albion, Oxonian lawyer' (*Alanus Albion, advocatus Oxoniensis*), clearly a nom de plume for either an individual or a group of anonymous pamphleteers. The text has a threefold structure: an overview of the history of Catalonia is followed by a chronicle of the early military episodes in the War of the Spanish Succession and then by an account of the negotiations leading to the Pact of Genoa as well as the promises made by England to Catalan politicians. The volume includes copies in French of the instructions given by Queen Anne to her ministers granting them permission to negotiate with the Catalan delegates at Genoa. A copy of the final 1705 agreement in Spanish and Latin is also appended. Alabrús (2001: 408–11) convincingly relates the text to attempts by Catalan exiles to restore relations with Britain after the end of the War of the Polish Succession in 1735. By contrast, the Latin culture exhibited by the putative editor in his annotations does not seem to have attracted much interest from historians of the Catalan exile in the aftermath of the War of the Spanish Succession. In the *Record de la aliança* Latin sources are always employed to bolster the historical and political authority of the arguments deployed by the author(s). Here Latin is the learned language. The Latin text of the *Record de la aliança* is thus the appropriately scholarly document to back up the argument put forward, namely to persuade Britain to resume her commitment to the Catalan case. The philological and historical apparatus prepared by the annotator includes a large number of supporting quotations from biblical passages as well as legal tracts. Pride of place is given to the Dutchman Hugo Grotius (1583–1645), whose *De iure belli et pacis* ('On the law of war and peace', 1625) is often quoted to reinforce arguments regarding the legal status of the war waged against Philip.[21] But Albion also draws on other more literary sources. In note 13, the episode in Sallust's *Jugurthine War* involving Sulla and King Bocchus, in which the former states that 'the Roman people from the beginning of their rule have preferred to seek friends rather than slaves and have thought it safer to govern by consent than by compulsion' (102.6), provides a historical parallel to contemporary Habsburg rule, praised as more lenient than Bourbon government.[22] The metaphor of the ship of state is echoed on the title page through a quotation from one of Alciato's emblems: *Innumeris agitur respublica nostra procellis! / Spesque venturae sola salutis adest* ('Our state is shaken by innumerable storms, and there is only one hope for its future safety', 43). Hope in the future of Catalonia is further conveyed in the putative editor's preliminary letter 'to the reader, be this an Englishman or who you will' (*lectori sive Anglo sive cuilibet*), through quotations from Erasmus's adage *Spes pertinax* ('Tenacious hope'), Petrarch's dialogue *De expectatione meliorum temporum* ('Expectation of better times') in his *De remediis utriusque fortunae* ('Remedies for Fortune fair and foul', 1.115), and Virgil's fourth *Eclogue* announcing the coming of a Golden Age.[23]

Alongside works of similar subject matter in the vernacular circulating both in Catalonia and abroad which reveal continuing support for the House of Austria well into the 1730s, the Latin writings produced by Catalan exiles in the aftermath of the dynastic feud played an important role in early modern Catalonia. Indeed, this body of texts helped preserve a sense of political and historical consciousness which later generations were to exploit more effectively. When Catalan nationalism, or Catalanism, became a fully-fledged political movement in the last decade of the nineteenth century, it re-imagined traditions that hark back to the Habsburg-

Bourbon conflict discussed in this book and drew heavily upon the imagery and discourse of Catalan historians and political thinkers from the first four decades of the eighteenth century. Thus 11 September, of all days, was declared Catalonia's national day in remembrance of the defeat of 1714. Furthermore, by way of reprints of some of the texts examined above, contemporary Catalanism also revaluated many of the issues tackled by these authors who some two hundred years earlier had proudly invoked Catalonia's unrivalled liberty in order to oppose Spain's centralist policies.[24] In the end, the political awareness of writers such as the anonymous author(s) of the *Record de la aliança* set a precedent for those intellectuals and politicians who at the turn of the twentieth century brought their discontent with Spain to the forefront of their political vision for the future.

A new king of Sicily, the Peace of Vienna and the emperor's final years

As a result of the first phase of the Peace of Utrecht in 1713, Sicily was ceded by Philip V to Victor Amadeus II of Savoy, an ally of the Empire, and Sardinia to Austria. In November 1717 Spanish forces re-established control of Sardinia and following the capture of the island landed in Sicily in July of the following year. This prompted Britain, France, Austria and the Dutch Republic to form a Quadruple Alliance on 2 August, which then declared war on Spain. The subsequent conflict ended less than two years later with the Treaty of The Hague, signed on 20 January 1720. Under the terms of this new agreement, Victor Amadeus was forced to exchange Sicily for Sardinia. The former was granted to Charles VI, who held it until 1734, when the Habsburgs were expelled by Philip V's son Charles of Bourbon, the future Charles III of Spain (1716–88). In the aftermath of the War of the Spanish Succession (and the ensuing conflict over Sardinia and Sicily), the proclamation in 1720 of Charles VI as the new king of Sicily was also exploited by the Habsburg propaganda machine.[25] The royal title was not a mere formality: it had significant far-reaching implications, for the island – which remained loyal to the Bourbon cause during the military conflict – had been in Spanish hands for several centuries. In Palermo, the festivities to celebrate the official proclamation of the new king began on 29 September and included a decorative and iconographic programme which was intended 'to give expression to Charles VI's political ambitions for this region of his empire' (Grönert 2011: 132). The new monarch's accession was also marked with the publication of several festival books recording the ceremonies held in the city for the occasion. One such volume, in Italian and Latin, was issued under the patronage of the Jesuits and was authored by Domenico Turano under the title *Apparato fatto in Palermo … in occasione della solenne acclamazione dell'imnperator Carlo VI e III re delle Spagne e di Sicilia* ('A display built in Palermo on the occasion of the solemn acclamation of Emperor Charles VI, King Charles III of Spain and Sicily').[26] The book provides detailed descriptions of the temporary constructions and decorations installed at the local Jesuit college for 1 October, the emperor's birthday. In his examination of coronation festivals and rituals in early eighteenth-century Palermo, Pablo González Tornel regards the work as a chronicle 'aimed at recording the festival, rather than a genuine propaganda article', on the grounds that the *Apparato* was published 'with no involvement of external authorities' (2021: 42). Yet, as explored elsewhere in this book, the (very often unprompted) political role played by the Jesuit congregation in several European territories in promoting royal power during the dynastic conflict should not be underestimated. As with the ceremonies organized to celebrate Philip V's proclamation in 1701 and his military victories in Castile nine years later, in 1720 the fathers of the Society of Jesus in Palermo chose to extol the deeds of the reigning monarch, in this instance with a series of fourteen boards (*tabelloni*) displaying Latin epigrams and inscriptions. The texts chronicle the history of the new ruling dynasty on the island, from Rudolf I to his last heir Charles VI, with the clear purpose of emphasizing the continuity of the Habsburg line on the throne of Sicily. Echoing Martial's epigram in praise of Domitian, Turano describes the late Emperor Joseph as 'one who expanded his kingdoms' (*regnorum amplificator*) through successful military campaigns in Italy, Flanders and the Mediterranean during the War of the Spanish Succession. The acquisition of Sicily by Charles following the War of the Quadruple Alliance is also recognized as having enhanced Habsburg power in Europe:

> *Sceptra vide sceptris et regnis addita regna*
>   *et nova post palmas ut cito palma venit.*
> *Subditur Eridanus, socians Ticinus et undas,*
>   *subditur amplexis Mantua fortis aquis.*
> *Et Sardi et Belgae, Balearis et utraque funda*
>   *inclita et Hesperiis regna subacta plagis.*
> *Tu quoque, Parthenope, ante Italas pulcherrima nimphas*
>   *inseris optato mitia colla iugo.*
> *Hi tibi communes, Caesar, cum fratre triumphi,*
>   *quae datur ex Siculis laurea, tota tua est*
>
>   Turano 1720: 23

['Behold sceptres added to sceptres and kingdoms added to kingdoms, as a new victory quickly follows others. The Po is subdued, and also the Ticino, which joins its waters; Mantua, firm thanks to its surrounding waters (the town's defence system), is subdued. And so are the by the illustrious double slingshot the Sardinians, the Belgians and the Balearic islands as well as the kingdoms brought under the Spanish regions. You too, Parthenope [Naples], the most beautiful of Italian nymphs, introduce your gentle neck into the chosen yoke. These triumphs, Caesar, you share with your brother; the laurel which is given from the conquest of the Sicilians is all your own'].[27]

After 1720 it became increasingly expedient for Austria and Spain to work towards establishing a bilateral peace. Negotiations culminated in the Peace of Vienna, a series of four treaties signed between 30 April and 5 November 1725, which officially marked the end of the dynastic feud of the War of the Spanish Succession. In this new treaty, the Habsburg dynasty relinquished all formal claims to the Spanish throne, while Bourbon Spain removed its contention in the Southern Netherlands. At the start of the previous year, on 14 January 1724, Philip V had abdicated the throne and the Spanish crown had passed to his sixteen-year-old son Prince Louis (the future Louis I). However, the newly enthroned king fell victim to smallpox on 31 August, and Philip found himself king once more. He remained on the throne until his death in 1746. At the time of the abdication there was considerable controversy regarding the reasons that led Philip V to renounce the throne in favour of his son, and this controversy was reflected in the Latin and vernacular literature of the age.[28] While authors from the rival political camp suggested that the monarch's true ambition was to be able to exercise his dynastic rights to become king of France, Bourbon propagandists claimed that Philip V had decided to abdicate in order to withdraw from public life and devote the rest of his time to prayer and meditation.[29] In the wake of the royal abdication and in the midst of the negotiations that were to culminate in the Peace of Vienna, the Sardinian aristocrat (and Spanish ambassador at Utrecht, as mentioned earlier) Vincenzo Bacallar was commissioned by Philip V to write a history of the War of the Spanish Succession, which he entitled *Comentarios de la guerra de España e historia de su rey Phelipe V el animoso* ('Commentaries on the war of Spain and history of her king Philip V, the brave'). Published in Genoa by Matteo Garvizza in 1725, Bacallar's chronicle draws on extensive documentation as well as the author's direct knowledge of the events described. That same year the Jesuit Giulio Cesare Brusati (d. 1743) translated a portion of the text into Latin, the first five books of the twenty-four that make up the commentaries covering the period from 1699 to 1705 (Alabrús 2001: 75).[30] The reasons why Brusati translated only a section of the volume remain unclear but the project may have been hampered by the king himself, concerned that a complete Latin translation of the work may have helped disseminate in Europe a version of the dynastic conflict with which he was not entirely satisfied. After all, Philip V forbade publication of the original *Comentarios* in Spain 'due to the excessive sincerity of a historical narrative that laid bare the dynastic ambitions of Philip's second wife Elisabeth Farnese, 1692–1766' (Pasolini 2008: 260). Entitled *De foederatorum contra Philippum quintum, Hispaniarum regem, bello commentaria* ('Commentaries on the war of the Allies against Philip V, king of Spain'), Brusati's partial version at times amplifies and embellishes the original Spanish text. Here is Bacallar's description of various episodes from the siege of Barcelona of 1705, highlighting the deceitfulness shown by the Catalans to Viceroy Fernández de Velasco:

> *y al Virrey de Cataluña D. Francisco Fernández de Velasco le faltaba un todo para la defensa y lo que es más la fidelidad del país. Avivaba la llama de la sedición el Veguer de la ciudad con gran cautela y se tenían las juntas en casa de un carnicero... permaneció traidoramente fiel la provincia; por lo menos, lo parecía porque todos ofrecieron al Virrey no excusar peligro ni gasto a la defensa de la ciudad*
>
> Bacallar 1725a: 258–9

['and the viceroy of Catalonia, Francisco Fernández de Velasco, lacked everything for the defence of the city and, what is more, the trust of the country. The city's *Veguer* fanned the flame of sedition with great caution and gatherings were held in a butcher's house ... the province remained treacherously faithful; at least, it seemed so because everybody vowed to spare no danger or expense in the defence of the city'].

And this is how Brusati renders the passage in a more vivid manner:

> *Veruntamen Francisco Velasqueo (nam in povinciis vicarius regis est) nihil non ad defensionem durat atque in primis provincialium fides. Conciliabula passim nobilium caeterorumque virorum, in quibus erat ipse urbis praefectus (vicarium vocant), in tenuiorum tabernis, ne res efferretur, atque in macello, quod pudeat, agitabantur ... At Catalauni quidem perfidiam simulatione praeclare tegentes apud regis vicarium frequentes profitentur nullum se periculum communis salutis causa recusare*
>
> Bacallar 1725b: 410–12

['However, Francisco Fernández de Velasco (for in the provinces there is a viceroy) had nothing at his disposal for the enduring defence of the city and, above all, he lacked the trust of the inhabitants of the province. Secret gatherings of noblemen and other men, at which the governor of the city himself (whom they call *Veguer*) was present, were held in different places, in the shops of the poor, so that the matter should not be known about, and in a butcher's house, something which was shameful … But the Catalans, concealing very clearly their perfidy with deceit, continuously assured the viceroy that they would not refuse any danger for the sake of common safety'].

The signing of the Peace of Vienna was also exploited by the Habsburg side. The treaty was celebrated through medals, a much-favoured medium of political propaganda within the Imperial court. The volume *Nummi augustorum Caroli VI et Elisabethae Christinae Viennae Austriae cusi* ('Medals of august Charles VI and Elisabeth Christine, struck in Vienna in Austria') assembles a series of twenty-eight medals designed by Imperial numismatist Carl Gustav Heraeus to chronicle the life and reign of Charles VI from his elevation to the Spanish throne to the year 1725.[31] A response to the *Histoire du regne de Louis le Grand par les medailles* ('History of the reign of Louis XIV through his medals', Paris, 1689) by Claude-François Ménestrier (1631–1705), this *historia metallica* focuses principally on Charles's piety, his generosity as patron of the arts and on the achievements of his armies during the 1716–18 Austro-Turkish War. However, the collection also includes several items related to the dynastic conflict and its outcome. The first medal shows an effigy of Charles and bears the inscription *CAROLVS VI CAESAR AVGVSTVS*. The description which follows focuses on Charles's Catalan and Valencian campaign during the War of the Spanish Succession and highlights the loyalty shown by the newly-elected emperor to his subjects when he left his spouse in Barcelona as Lieutenant and Captain General of Catalonia in September 1711: *Perstitit hic etiam post discessum Caroli ad Imperium Romanum; pignus nobile, quo neque maius neque carius apud fideles Catalaunos relinquere rex potuit* ('Elisabeth Christine continued steadfastly here even after Charles's departure for the Empire; the king could hardly have left a greater and more precious noble pledge among their loyal Catalans', p. 8). On the piece commemorating the signing of the Treaty of Rastatt the inscription *PAX AVGVSTI* is placed under a representation of the Temple of Janus, famously closed three times under Augustus in periods of complete peace in ancient Rome. The accompanying text praises not only Charles but also the late Louis XIV for their peace-making endeavours in 1714. By contrast, this rather more conciliatory tone is absent from the descriptions of medals twenty and twenty-three, which feature, respectively, the inscriptions *PRO QVIETE PVBLICA* ('For the sake of public tranquillity') and *VTRAQUE SICILIA ADSERTA* ('The kingdom of the two Sicilies claimed'), relating to the forming of the Quadruple Alliance and the transfer of Sicily to the Habsburgs, who had already ruled Naples since 1707. Here the target is not the Bourbon dynasty but the old enemy, Philip of Spain, for his refusal to accept the terms of the Peace of Utrecht and for his ill-conceived plans to occupy Sicily. Bearing the inscription *CONCORDI PACE LIGAVIT* ('He joined them in harmonious peace') and depicting the previously irreconcilable opponents shaking hands in the presence of Mercury, the penultimate medal in the series celebrates the signing of the treaties of Vienna as well as Charles VI's contribution to peace in Europe. In the accompanying text the emperor, who is still referred to by his Spanish title, is credited with convening a secret peace conference and having fostered the final agreement. Though presented as deeply concerned about how little progress was made at the Congress of Cambrai between 1722 and 1725, Charles was, in truth, fully aware of Philip V's weak negotiating position at Cambrai and knew how to seize the opportunity:

Discessit, ut meminimus, ab armis Hispanus: hac tamen discessione pax non illico coaluit. Agebatur illa Cameraci; verum impedimenta plura eam remorabantur, in annos se plures iam trahebat. Interea Augustissimus, ut est pacis amans, idem negotium Viennae sub rosa auspicatur, rem quam fieri poterat arcanissime tractari iubet. Et, vero pace celerrime cum plenipotentiario, quem Hispania occulte submiserat, transacta, mirum! subito fama insonat: 'pax! pax!' 'Fama prius falso similis' [Claudian, *Against Eutropius*, 1.345] *visa est. Ubi constitit de veritate, incredibile dictu est quanta ea res laetitia ac plausu excepta sit, quam laetis vocibus acclamatum sit Carolo pacatori III*

p. 95

['As we recalled, the Spaniard laid down his arms. Yet peace did not immediately become established from this. Peace was negotiated at Cambrai but many obstacles delayed it and [the conference] dragged on for many years. In the meantime, the most august one, since he is a lover of peace, formally initiated the same business in Vienna confidentially and ordered the matter to be dealt with as privately as possible. And, once peace was agreed upon with the utmost speed with a plenipotentiary [John William, Duke of Ripperdá, 1684–1737] whom Spain had sent in secret, oh wonder, rumour suddenly resounds: "Peace! Peace!" 'At first the rumour seemed false'. When truth was revealed, it is incredible to say with what extraordinary joy and applause this matter was received and with what joyful voices Charles III was acclaimed as peacemaker'].

In the last years of Emperor Charles VI's reign episodes from the War of the Spanish Succession continued to provide propaganda material for the Habsburg dynasty even though hostilities had, by then, long since ceased and the original dynastic dispute had been resolved. As an example, on Saturday 12 May 1736 the following entry was recorded in Charles's private diary: *Barcelona, heut 30 Jahr*

('Barcelona thirty years today').[32] The words refer to the lifting of the Bourbon siege of the Catalan capital in the spring of 1706, a potent indication that the key episodes from the War of the Spanish Succession continued to be preserved in Charles's memory three decades after they had taken place. In that same year of 1736 Maria Theresa Voigtin, widow of the printer to the University of Vienna, issued an edition of *Fasti Austriae* ('On the Austrian calendar'), a *Promotionsschrift* consisting of twelve compositions in elegiacs clearly modelled on Ovid's poetical calendar of the Roman year. This volume purports to sing of the glories and virtues of the House of Habsburg month by month.[33] As with Ovid's own *Fasti*, the month of March (*Martius*) is dedicated to the Roman god of war, and it celebrates the dynasty's heroic performance on the battlefields of Europe. The capture of Barcelona in the autumn of 1705 – a military operation in which Archduke Charles was not directly involved – merits praise from the poet, who compares the current emperor to his illustrious predecessor Charles V:

> *Vidimus et Carolos (testor mea gaudia) binos,*
> *quintum, illum et sextum, qui modo sceptra rotat.*
> *Magnus uterque animo, gestis quoque magnus, Iberis*
> *praesenti invictum prodidit ore iubar.*
> *Ille Abylam Calpenque suis superando triumphis*
> *plus ultra Herculeum scribere iussit opus.*
> *Hic Cataloniacos gnarus defendere campos,*
> *Barcellona, tua victor ab arce redit*
>
> 3.73–80

['We saw two Charles at the time (I bear witness to my joy), the fifth and the sixth who recently brandishes the sceptre. Both magnanimous towards the Spaniards, both notable for their deeds, they project an invincible splendour on their propitious faces. The former, going further beyond Abylla and Calpe with his triumphs, commissioned a Herculean work. The latter, skilful in defending the Catalan heartland, returns triumphant, Barcelona, from your fortress (Montjuïc)'].[34]

Entitled *Constantia et fortitudo Austriaca* ('Austrian firmness and bravery') in a clear reference to Charles's Imperial motto *Constantia et fortitudine*, the tenth poem in the collection constitutes a sort of *genethliacon* ('a birthday poem'). The piece is devoted to October, the month when Charles was born, which the poet – following the examples of July and August – proposes should be renamed *Carolinus* in honour of the monarch. In the text allusions to Charles's heroic deeds during the War of the Spanish Succession are intertwined with central events from his biography, all of them occurring in the month of October. The surrender of Barcelona in 1705 and Charles's election to the Imperial throne six years later are heralded as high points in the sovereign's early life:

Haec notat Hesperio decus ortum nobile regno,
Barcino te regem dum venerata suum.
Inde alia abstractum, cari post funera fratris,
imperii summum monstrat adiisse gradum.
Absentemque habuit Genuaeque in littora pulsum
lux, quae concordi sydere vota tulit

10.43–8

['This day marks the noble honour obtained in the kingdom of Spain when Barcelona revered you as its king. The other day indicates that Charles, drawn away from that place following the funeral of his dear brother, assumed the highest rank of the empire. And the daylight which brought news of the votes cast with the heavens in agreement reached him when he was absent, having been driven to the shores of Genoa'].[35]

The deaths of Charles VI on 20 October 1740 and of Elisabeth Christine a decade later provided Habsburg propagandists with the last opportunity to attempt to legitimize once again the dynastic conflict and to emphasize the Imperial couple's commitment to the Spanish cause. Between 22 and 24 March 1741 the University of Vienna held funeral services for the deceased emperor in St Stephen's Cathedral, where a temporary structure was erected (Brix 1973: 265, no. 46). As described in a volume which also includes the university's official funerary oration by Rector Johann Adam Gerster von Gerstorff (1681–1747), the monument consisted of four statues on behalf of the faculties within the university, each one celebrating an Imperial virtue.[36] The structure was also decorated with a relief depicting the successful siege of Belgrade by Austrian troops against the Turks in August 1717 and with four shields, each bearing inscriptions. They represent the Holy Roman Empire, Bohemia, Hungary as well as, significantly, Charles's Spanish kingdoms, which, according to Habsburg propaganda, the late emperor had continued to be entitled to by hereditary right. In an interesting twist, the text of the inscription carved 'on the shield of Spain' (*in scuto Hispaniae*) praises Charles for his determination to leave Spain despite the (favourable?) course of war and to return to Vienna after his brother's premature and unexpected death in 1711:

CAROLO
HISPANIARUM REGI
    PURO VETERUM SACRORUM CULTU
APOSTOLICAE SEDIS REVERENTIA

>   ILLUSTRIBUS PROBITATIS EXEMPLIS
> CATHOLICO
>   QUI
> AMPLISSIMA REGNA
>   IURE HAEREDITARIO QUAESIVIT
> VIRTUTE OBTINUIT
> MEDIUM VICTORIARUM CURSUM
> AMORE PATRIAE RUPIT
>   INTER ADVERSA ET PROSPERA
> MAIESTATEM ANIMI OSTENDIT
>   REGNIS MAIOREM

['To Charles, Catholic king of Spain through chaste worship of the old sacred rites, through reverence of the Apostolic See, through illustrious examples of probity, who sought most magnificent kingdoms by hereditary right and obtained them by courage, who interrupted the undecided progress of victories because of his love of the fatherland, who amidst adverse and prosperous times showed his kingdoms greater dignity of mind', p. 2].

Following Elisabeth Christine's death in 1750, a sarcophagus was built for the late empress and placed in the Capuchin Crypt. Motifs relating to the War of the Spanish Succession were yet again employed in the decoration of the sovereign's resting place, and the relief and the inscriptions on the sarcophagus included written and visual references to Elisabeth Christine's voyage to Catalonia in 1708 as well as her military and political engagement during the Spanish conflict (Hawlik-van de Water 1993: 158–62).[37] Finally, in 1752 Empress Maria Theresa (1717–80) commissioned a new sarcophagus for her late father, which, apart from depicting the coats of arms of the Holy Roman Empire, Castile, Bohemia and Hungary, was decorated with a scene from the Battle of Saragossa in August 1710, Charles's last victory on the Peninsular front during the War of the Spanish Succession (Hawlik-van de Water 1993: 152–8).[38]

Conclusion

The outcome of the Spanish dynastic conflict as sanctioned by the Peace of Utrecht and subsequent conciliatory treaties did not put an end to the hostilities between the Habsburg and Bourbon families nor did it resolve all the issues at the heart of the dynastic feud. Philip V wished to overturn a peace settlement which he believed had been imposed upon him. Losses in Italy were deeply felt by the Spanish king, who was determined to regain Sardinia and Sicily at the earliest opportunity. Following the departure of Allied troops by sea from Catalonia in 1713 and the fall of Barcelona to the Bourbon army the following year, large groups of Catalan clergymen, nobility and high officials were forced into exile in Europe. Despite what was agreed at Utrecht and Rastatt, the restoration of the global empire of Charles V remained alive in his eponymous descendant, who never gave up hope of bringing together all the lands once under Habsburg rule. Such claims were upheld in the propaganda and art of the Viennese court, even after military operations in the War of the Spanish Succession had long since ceased in the summer of 1715. In the new political and diplomatic scenario arising from the peace negotiations of 1713 and 1714, Latin continued to function as an instrument of political discourse. In this chapter I have demonstrated how Latin was the medium chosen by a group of Catalan savants in exile in Italy and Vienna, where they sought to preserve the memory of Catalonia's constitutions and privileges. The learned language also assisted Habsburg propagandists when Emperor Charles VI was proclaimed new king of Sicily in 1720 in the wake of the War of the Quadruple Alliance. Moreover, the texts presented here show how the echo of the war of Spain is remarkably resonant in several Neo-Latin antiquarian tracts published at the time of the signing of the Peace of Vienna of 1725 and in the last years of Charles's reign in which the emperor's rights to the Spanish throne are still invoked. These texts constitute a potent reminder of the continuing fascination the dynastic feud exerted on Charles VI's household even when the Spanish conflict had long since faded from memory.

Conclusions

'This is the battle of Poultousk which we are told was a great victory, but in my opinion was nothing of the kind. We civilians, as you know, have a bad habit of making up our minds as to whether a battle is lost or won. The side that retires after the fight, has been beaten we say; and that being so, we lost the battle of Poultousk. After fighting we retire; but we send off a courier to St. Petersburg with a report of victory.'

Leo Tolstoy, *War and Peace*, Book 5, Chapter 9

On 4 October 1734 a conference was held in Vienna to discuss the creation of a colony for Spanish exiles from the War of the Spanish Succession in the sparsely populated Banat of Temesvar, near the site of the modern-day Serbian town of Zrenjanin, in an area which had been ceded by the Ottoman Empire sixteen years earlier. Known as New Barcelona, the settlement was intended to house groups of exiles who had lived in Vienna since the end of the dynastic conflict or had recently relocated to the Imperial capital following the seizure of Naples and Sicily by the Bourbon authorities in 1734. The first group of settlers arrived in the autumn of 1735, and by 1737 there were about 800 exiles in Banat. Among them, the most numerous were those who came from Catalonia, followed by others from the former territories of the Crown of Aragon, together with a small contingent of Italian pensioners originating from Sicily and Naples. Despite Imperial financial assistance the experiment was short-lived, partly because of the proximity of the Ottoman threat to the region and partly because of the outbreak of the Great Plague of 1738, which worsened the living conditions of the colonists, most of whom were elderly. By 1740 many exiles had already relocated to Buda and Vienna and the colony was officially closed (Alcoberro 2002: 99–114).

Though the foundation of New Barcelona was ultimately prompted by Charles VI's decision to dispense with the Council of Spain and by the Bourbon occupation of Italy's southern kingdoms, proposals for the establishment of a colony for Spanish exiles had been laid before the Habsburg administration long before, indeed as early as 1714. Around 1725 the Catalan jurist Josep Plantí drafted a document in Spanish – his only work not written in Latin – entitled *Nueva colonia española ideada* ('A programme for a new Spanish colony'). In his text, Plantí described a composite state in a region bounded by the Danube River, the natural border of the empire, to be inhabited by Spanish exiles and ruled according to the constitutional principles of the territories that were formerly part of the Crown of Aragon (Alcoberro 2002: 210–18). The text is prefaced by one hundred and fifteen *Hemistichia ex Virgilio, lib[er] 1 Aeneidos* ('Half-lines from Virgil's first book of the *Aeneid*'), a *cento* – 'a patchwork' – comparing Aeneas's heroic deeds and the mythical foundation of Rome to the creation of a new colony for Spanish exiles under the auspices of Charles VI, 'fairer than whom there has been no other, nor any greater in piety, war and arms' (*quo iustior alter / nec pietate fuit nec bello maior et armis*, ll. 1–2, quoting *Aen.* 1.544–5, reproduced in Plantí 2022: 156 and also examined by O'Reilly 2023: 116).

As with Josep Plantí, most Latin authors and anonymous works examined in this book frequently used analogies from classical history and literature to frame their own narratives of the War of the Spanish Succession. One of the guiding premises of this study has been that the ancient world offered different means of expression, narrative structures and literary formats with which Latin political propagandists on both sides of the dynastic feud could champion their own cause. This is hardly surprising, given that close acquaintance with classical texts and the composition of Latin (and, at times, Greek) poetry and prose were integral to the (bilingual or trilingual) literary culture of early eighteenth-century Europe, as befitting a society whose literary tastes were still moulded by Roman and Greek literature. Latin writers of the age instinctively employed classical *exempla* and *topoi* in the poems, speeches, historical and juridical tracts, medals and letters they produced in the context of the War of the Spanish Succession. The classical templates, in short, served all these authors fairly well, and the ancient world remained a fruitful source. It should be noted, however, that all these models were always used for a specific purpose, rather than slavishly adhered to. Neo-Latin reflected, after all, modern life. Most eighteenth-century poets and prose writers featured in this study relied on their knowledge of Greco-Roman history and literature to eulogize and legitimize their favoured suitor, to persuade their audience of the dangers posed by their dynastic foe, and – as with the Russian diplomat Bilibin in Tolstoy's *War and Peace* – to spin military setbacks as victories, or to present military episodes which otherwise bore no lasting consequences on the outcome of the conflict as decisive battles.

This examination of the key role played by Latin and the classical tradition in the construction of political identity and the dissemination of propaganda during the war offers a truly pan-European map of early modern Latinity across a broad range of literary genres. It also reveals a vast intellectual landscape which could be further explored in the wake of the present enquiry. By illustrating the dynamism demonstrated by eighteenth-century Latin, this book endeavours to rehabilitate a surprisingly varied corpus of political-ideological writing which has to date been largely overlooked by scholars of Neo-Latin studies. It also constitutes a potent reminder of the perils of distorting European literary identity by ignoring the rich Latin tradition which ran in tandem with its often more widely appreciated vernacular counterpart. If the War of the Spanish Succession has been the subject of important reassessments in recent years and it certainly no longer deserves to be regarded as a 'forgotten war', it is to be hoped that this investigation of Latin propaganda material further contributes to a fuller and more satisfactory picture of the conflict.

Appendix 1

The Spanish Succession: A Dynastic Table

The Spanish Succession

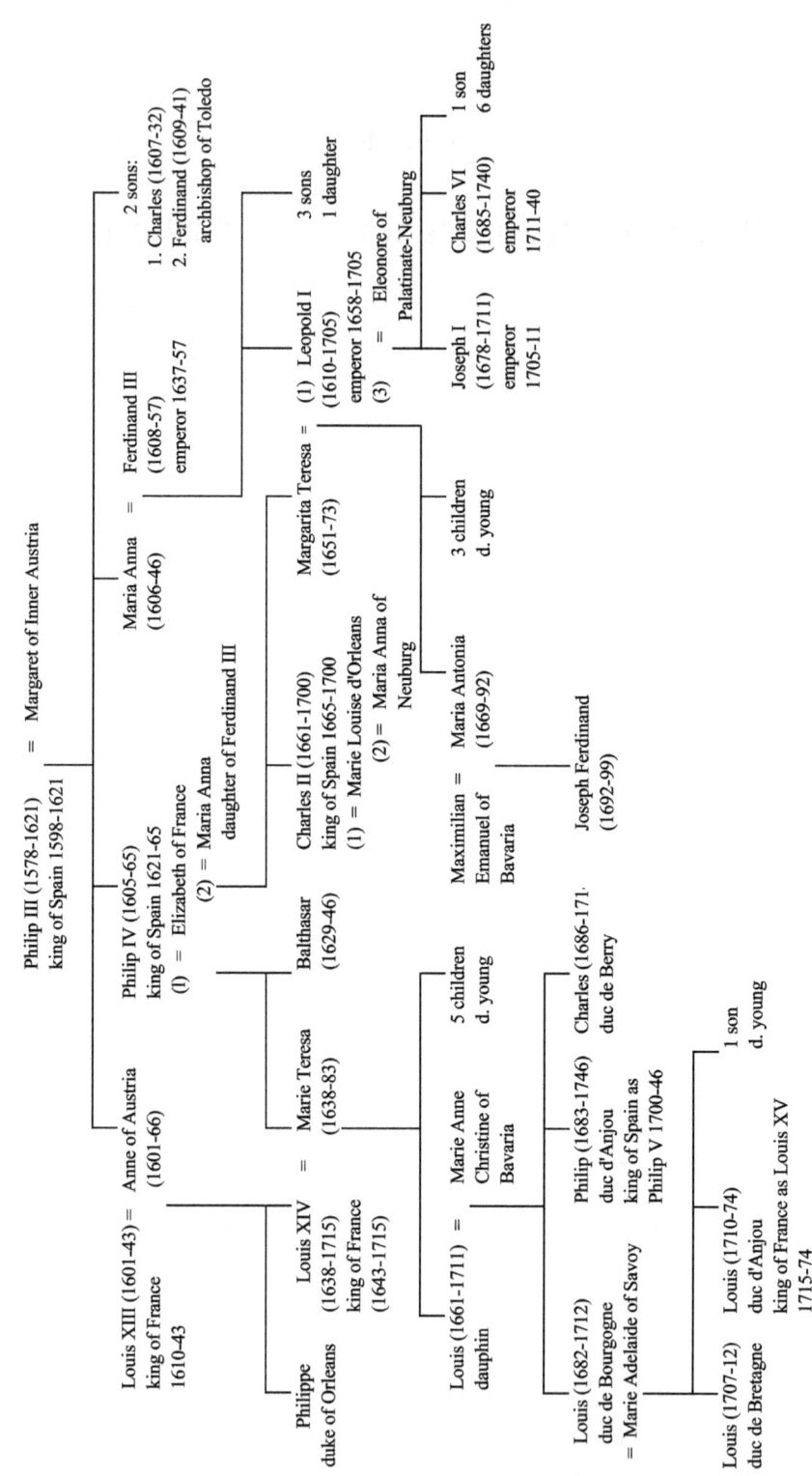

Appendix 2

Texts from Chapters 1 and 2

Since the body of the book deals extensively with the texts included in Appendices 2 and 3 and translates large parts of them, I have not deemed it necessary to provide translations here.

Appendix 2.1: Jean Le Comte, *Ad iustitiam ode* (Paris, 1701, BnF, Yc. 3414).

Diva, quam sancti comitem pudoris
aureum vidit genus, innocentis
hospitam mundi populosque amica
    pace beantem,

non diu terris propria haec dedisti   5
munera, humanis vitiis iniquam
te cito in caelum revolare adegit
    decolor aetas.

Inde, quos votis miserorum et aegro
annuit paucos Deus aequus orbi,   10
longa post tandem revocasse visi
    tempora Cyrusque

et Numa et Spartae columen Lycurgus
et Solon, nunc te pietate cunctis
regibus maior Lodoïcus alto,   15
    diva, volentem

elicit caelo, tibi sceptra, lauros,
vota submittit, sociam gerendis
rebus et belli mediamque pacis
    gaudet adesse.   20

Lenibus pollens monitis, verendi,
assides regis solio; unde centum
temperas urbes populisque iura
    dividis aequa.

Te cliens, fraudis metuens avarae,   25
te patre amisso puer audientem
sensit et rapto male tuta inopsque
    nupta marito.

Fama te semper bona veritasque
et cohors legum veneranda cingit,   30
ense terrentem nimium superbas
    vindice vires.

Nuper Hispanam miserata gentem,
anxiis quae te precibus vocabat
supplices fundens lacrymas, nec uno   35
    pressa timore,

Caroli ad sacrum caput adstitisti,
protinus menti nova lux oborta,
fata tum regnis stupuit canentem
    flebilis aula: 40

'Qui puer mixtas adolescit inter
liliis lauros', ait, 'et sub umbra
crescit ingenti, mea iustus illi
    sceptra resigno'.

Dixerat, regi placido ore, diva,   45
annuis durisque animam exsolutam
ilicet vinclis, rapido volatu in
    astra reportas.

Principis iusti pia vox dolorem
publicum lenit, Tagus ex arenis   50
aureum tollit caput, in superbos
    versa triumphos

funera, immenso fremuere plausu
celsa Pyrenes iuga, quem Padusque
et Mosa et totis mare personantem   55
    audiit undis.

Semper o! magnum sobolemque magni
aemulam patris foveas Philippum.
O! novum per te melioris aevi
      affluat aurum.   60

Appendix 2.2: Johann Jakob Haake, *Carolo III Austriaco, Hispaniarum atque Indiarum regi, regnorum avitorum vindici ac assertori, terra marique triumphanti, sacrum* (s.l, 1706, BC, Fons Bonsoms, 8088).

Nomina magna ducum memores extollite, fasti,
Hectora, Pompeium, statuis et in aere perennent;
fortis et accedat soboles Argiva Philippi,
triste gemens, arcto nimium quod limite mundi
bella gerat, victore novos pede maior in orbes   5
prosultura manuque patris pugnace triumphis
addita; tuque, cui duodenos fama labores
totque trophaea canit praesignia, claviger heros!,
huc ades et victis Erymanthi robore monstris
et Nemeae Lernaeque feris, caput infere caelo.   10
    Ite, nec invideo, propriae quos laudis anhelus
urit amor posuitque quibus monumenta vetustas;
ite, duces, pigri cineres, quibus unica belli
causa erat ambitio latrociniumque superbum,
nulla seu juris seu facti nobilis umbra   15
testi, perversis tantum saecli artibus acti.
Cedite, dum Martis patulum subit ille theatrum,
Austria cui primas populis plaudentibus auras,
cui dedit excelsas heroica dextera lauros,
Carolus armorumque potens animique severus   20
miles, imago ducis iure et vincentis et armis;
quem virtus antiqua patrum, quem sanguinis altum
quaesitumque suum ius, mores gentis Iberae
atque salus populi regem ultoremque sacrarunt!
Mars stetit attonitus, digitis cecidere remissis   25
mox flagra Bellonae, cristis trepidantibus haesit
Gallus, ut, accipiter rapidis dum fulminat alis,
corde pavet metuensque truces se proripit ungues,
raptibus ipse suis diffisus, Alastoris ausis!

Unus Iber, patria praestans gravitate, suavi 30
obvius Austriaco, 'Felix', ait, 'advena, salve!
Hoc iter ingresso gratulantur regna, coronae;
asperum id, at victis inimicis suave futurum:
hospes eris numquam rediturus, iura daturus
regia te populo veneranti regis Iberi 35
nomine; te geminus regem polus, orbis uterque
accipit, arridens Nemesis novitque probatque
imperium, numquam tanto rectore labascens!
Rex! age Catholicus, pietas quoque regnat in armis.
Rex cape magne animum, virtus quo suadet eundum! 40
Per vada, per scopulos, per iniquas ire Charybdes
ne fuge, divinis efflant tua carbasa ventis;
naufraga saxa nihil metuas, bona causa triumphat,
queis periit Pharao, Moyses it liber in undis'.
  Dixerat omnis Iber. Nemesis tibi, Carole, dixit: 45
'Scande ratem positoque metu te fluctibus infer,
nil nocitura tibi dicrimina spondet aquarum.
Respice ad Hesperides, valeant regnentque Latini!
Fallor? Amara maris meditato pectore versas,
Carole, te cari retinent spes altera stirpis 50
Austriacae magnusque parens materque verenda
rexque simul frater tuus (nunc maximus Atlas
imperii); poteras et amore metuque teneri
et poteras precibus, poteras et fletibus aures,
rex, dare vincendas. At, inexorabilis heros, 55
inquis, avete, Lares patrii, res spesque valete!
Certat amor certatque timor; quo gloria ducit,
nolle sequi, o! quantum reputanda piacula credis?
Carolus aggrederis vitreo dare carbasa ponto
Aeolidumque minis et aquarum turbine maior 60
vela facis, Lusitana tenens hinc littora, lusis
artibus et remoris, vacua quas fraude pararat
livor iners positis et inertia livida technis!
Nec stetit hic ausus generosi pectoris, ultra
Herculeas audes victor penetrare columnas 65
et maris indomitas armis tibi iungere fauces!
  Tenditur ulterius, bona sors fit sola viarum
arbitra duxque simul, socia dum Barcino classis
vi petitur ruptisque seris tibi, Carole, iurat

atque tui ingressu mox felix cingula laxat. 70
Iamque tibi Catalonus ager quasi fidus Achates
clamat ovans: "Vindex vivat! Mea vincla revinxit
Carolus, ut liceat manumisso plaudere; servus
ante fui Gallo, canitur modo faustior ode.
Galle, vale; servire tibi fuit aenea moles, 75
aurea successit, placidus moderatur habenas,
iniussi sequimur, faciles regale tributum
pendimus et vitam regi sacramus avitam!"
Verba nec esse putes! Conclamat ad arma gregatim
nobilitas, cives et agris assueta iuventus. 80
Fit via vi, Gallus trepidis procul avolat alis,
cuius adhuc pavido Catalonia stercore foetet.
Io triumphe! tuis devota Valentia iussis
paret et Arragones magno cum pectore pergunt
arma sequi, iurare fidem tibi, Carole, princeps 85
optime! Neapolis motus ciet usque faventes,
vespera Siciliac Gallo renovanda minatur;
utraque Castiliae regio tibi servat apertas
portas teque suum omnis adorat Iberia regem,
qui regat imperio populos, qui iura reducat 90
pulsa, novis iamiam sublatus ad astra trophaeis!
Nobilis eventus! sequitur quem gloria lauris
inclyta, quam merito tellusque polusque tuentur!
    Perge bonis avibus, dum Barcino salva triumphat
Gallica dumque cadunt horrendas arma sub umbras, 95
nempe die, solem qua solis ferre pudebat
ac spectare fugae foedos tristesque labores.
Dedecus hicque tulit sceleris, diadema sed alter!
Carole, perge tuam iam fusis hostibus urbem
denique Madriturn regali sede fovere! 100
    Eia, age, rumpe moras, virtus Carolina resurgit
auspiciis, Auguste, tuis fasque omne fugatum
gestit in Hesperios portus et regna redire;
scande triumphales currus iurisque paterni
ter, vindex coelestis, ova terraque marique 105
victor ab utrovis solium iam sole capesse!
    Sed tu tolle, Philippe, citum fugiture caballum
et cede haeredi iusto, cui militat Anna,
cui Batavi ac Angli veniunt in classica venti!'

[*In Emanuelem, victum ac proscriptum electorem Bavariae.*] 110
Dicitur Emmanuel comedens cum melle butyrum,
    ut reprobare malum norit, amare bonum.
Miscuit incantans Ludovicus melle venenum,
    ludis amatores sic, Ludovice, tuos!

Appendix 2.3: Noël-Étienne Sanadon, *Philippo quinto Hispaniae regi vaticinium de filio ipsi nascituro* (in *Natalis Stephani Sanadonis e Societate Iesu carminum libri quatuor*, Paris, 1715, pp. 37–9, BnF, Yc. 8607).

At non probroso, Musa, silentio
vocem obligasti. Da tripodas, pater,
    da, Phoebe, lauros: nil profanum,
        nil humili meditor Camena.

Philippe, regno, quod geris, altior, 5
dis cura regum est. Quidlibet insolens
    Fortuna volvat, non refiget
        impositam capiti coronam.

Non (si Batavo iunxerit ultimos
orbis Britannos, Teutonas Insubri) 10
    timebis obluctantem iniquis
        bella movere odiosa divis.

Urit nitenti scilicet aemulos
fulgore gentis Borboniae decus,
    avique patrisque in nepotes 15
        usque novos abitura virtus.

Sic est, inani nec mea Delius
adstavit augur pectora numine;
    quem vota poscunt Ludovicum
        est tibi mox paritura coniux. 20

Hunc sospitalis coelitum favor
iam nunc amico lumine respicit
    lateque regnandam perenni
        Hesperiam tibi firmat aevo.

Hoc spondet hostili ebria sanguine 25
Almansa, quando iam prope transfugam

victoriam ad nostras coegit
    Barvikius revolare partes.

Atque pudendae fervidus Allobrox
purgare cladis dedecus adparat,   30
    Telonis obsessas ahenis
        fulminibus iaculatus arces,

frustra. Repressus numine non suo
iam damnat ausum, iam laceras fugax
    turmes removit foederatis   35
        pollicitus meliora prínceps.

Getula qualis praedae avidus leo
Obit voraci gutture pascua,
    iam iamque securas cruento
        destinat exitio capellas   40

si fors odora nare sagax canis
latravit hostem, protinus exciti
    ad arma pastores, ad arma
        praecipiti properant tumultu.

At ille (quamquam saeva premit fames   45
pectusque torquet magnanimum pudor)
    festinat aeternum sub altis
        opprobium occultuisse sylvis.

Appendix 2.4: *Ode Sapphica serenissimo Eugenio sacra* (Vienna, 1709, ÖNB, 307098-B).

Laureas Canto tIbI, fortIs heros,
et saCros aVsVs tItVLosqVe Veros:
gaLLIa fraCta, Cape IUre ViVas
            MartIs oLIVas.

qVa nItens tItan properat qVa DrIgIs   5
atqVe se VertIt Vaga LVna bIgIs,
eVgenI fortIs, tVa se LeVabat,
            faMa VoLabat.

Cor saCra pLenVM fLVat hIppoCrene,
aestVat gratIs neqVeoqVe pLene   10

eXeqVI pLaVsVs CeLebres sonorae,
    teVtonIs orae.

ConCInVnt AngLVs, bataVVs DeCores,
DebItos LaetI resonant honores:
qVIsqVe VICtrICI tVa gesta LaVro   15
    InserIt aVro.

aVget appLaVsVs ItalVs per aLpes
et per eXCeLsae IVga Magna CaLpes
ferVet hIspanVs tVa ferre faCta
    fortIVs aCta.   20

QVas per astVtas tenVere fraVDes,
EVgenI! saCras tIbI IVre LaVDes
aCCInVnt GaLLi, fVgIVnt Cohortes
    PrInCIpe fortes.

approbat sCaLDIs roseVs rVbore,   25
gaLLVs hVnC tInXIt noCVo CrVore:
herCVLes noster tIbI, franCe, VeLLit,
    LILLIa peLLit.

qVID VoLo VICtas CeCInIsse gentes?
saepe qVas CoeCa rabIe fVrentes   30
EVgenI prInCeps! tVa DeXtra fregIt,
    forte sVbegIt.

qVantVs es! saeVo pyroente veCtVs,
ense praeCInCtus gaLeaqVe teCtVs:
si regIs DeXtra phaLerIs DeCora   35
    aVrea Lora.

herCVLes DICVnt, VehItVr CabaLLo,
sI tVIs DVX es, reboante VaLLo,
barbara LInqVIt tIbI strage pLenas,
    hostIs arenas.   40

eVgenI! LaVrIs tItuVLIsqVe CLare,
gentIbVs CVnCtIs sVperIqVe Chare,
fLoreas Laete, sIne fIne Vernes,
    arMa gVbernes.

Ita DeMIsse aCCInVIt
W.E.G. Presbyter

Appendix 3

Two Eighteenth-Century Latin Poets at Work

The aim of this appendix is to illustrate the mechanics of imitation through two texts examined in Chapters 2 and 3 respectively: the anonymous *Carolus III invictissimus Hispaniarum rex* (s.l., s.d. but surely 1706; Biblioteca de l'Abadia de Montserrat, Res. 4° 1/32), and Johann Werlhof's *Epithalamium potentissimi Hispaniarum regis Catholici Caroli III et serenissimae principis Brunsuico-Luneburgicae Elisabethae Christinae augusto connubio* (Helmstedt, 1708; HAB, Q 165 Helmst. 2°, 20).

Carolus III invictissimus Hispaniarum rex

The author of *Carolus III invictissimus Hispaniarum rex* reuses substantial portions of text from, chiefly, Livio Vitale Orosio's *silva* in praise of Francesco Maria II della Rovere (henceforth *LVO*), and Gunther of Pairis's *Ligurinus*. These passages are, in turn, partly based on Virgil's *Aeneid*. Italics denotes reused text, with the exact source indicated in the endnote. Roman font indicates (apparently) original text.

> Caesaris Augustam lustrat praesentia regis
> et gentes cunctae felici murmure plaudunt:
> 'Hic vir, hic est, [Aen. 6.791] *nobis concessus munere divum,*
> Carolus *est princeps, quo non praestantior alter,*
> *qui regat imperio populos et legibus aequis.*[1]   5
> Rex noster decesit, dira tyrannide fati,
> Carolus excelsus, nulli pietate secundus,
> tertius insequitur, miro solamine missus;
> *hic velut eximium post tristia nubila tandem*
> *sydus adest, hic bella fugat pacemque reducit.*[2]   10
> *Si dotes animi spectes, coelestia dona;*
> *ingenium cernes, formatum Paladis arte;*

ideo adeo celeri mundi primordia mente
concipit et quascumque oculis natura negavit
occultas rerum causas; cur denique rerum 15
accipiat genitura novam per sydera formam;
scit tabulas etiam legum, scit condita iura,
scit licitum, novit vetitum quae poena sequatur.
Nec tamen ignorat laudatas corporis artes,
nam tubicen quandoque canit decedere circo [Aen. 5.551], 20
infusam turbam et campos iubet esse patentes [Aen. 5.552];
tum lecti iuvenes, armis ostroque superbi,
fraenatis lucent in equis [Aen. 5.554] *ac ordine longo*
robora dura ferunt, praefixa hastilia ferro [Aen. 5.557].
Heros marmoreo tandem se limine promit,[3] 25
quem pulchris tinctus maculis sub Baetica natus [Aen. 9.49]
portat equus [Aen. 5.566], *fulvum mandens in dentibus aurum* [Aen. 7.279],[4]
collectosque praemens tumidis ex naribus ignes [Valerius Flaccus, *Argonautica*,
I.221: . . . *tumidis taurorum e naribus ignis!*];
atque ubi Misenus clangoribus aetera pulsat
et vocat ad pugnam; ferrata calce fatigat [Aen.11.714] 30
cornipedem; dat lora manu, se flectit in armos
fraxineamque trabem certus praetendit et omnes
quos habet adversos cursuque ictuque lacessit.'[5]
Qualis erit? Quantusve putas? Quae gloria regni?
Quis decor imperii tanto sub principe surget?[6] 35
Iam nunc testantur post tot discrimina belli
Tarraco et ostrifero superaddita Barcino ponto,[7]
sicque Valentinus sospes, sic liber Iberus,
cum pius Augustam restaurat nomine Caesar,
quae agnoscit dominum supplex regemque fatetur;[8] 40
qui tunc ad cunctos sedato pectore fatur [Aen.9.740 and 10.556]:
'*Quod nos in vestras bellum convertimus oras;*
nil mirum: clamant causae sub iudice iusto;
non fuit hoc animo neque enim mihi quaero triumphos,
antiquas repeto sedes et avita tueri 45
regia iura volo:[9] *procedam Marte benigno*'.
Obtulit et princeps hostes auferre tyrannos,
ulcisci scelerum noxas, punire nocentes,
oppressos relevare manu, fraenare superbos[10]
et totum clemens festinans opere complet; 50
sancta et plena suo sunt regia pondere verba,

dicta semel nullum patiuntur iure recursum.¹¹
O vere magni proles generosa parentis,
o vere felix dulci de stipite fructus,
o vere famosa domus, cui totus ab ortu 55
solis ad occiduas mundus subtenditur undas;¹²
iam solum nobis *grates persolvere* [*Aen*.1.600] restat
et genibus pronis votum proferre rogantes.
Omnia virtutis sunt haec spectacula summae
*et celebris numquam peritura insignia laudis;*¹³ 60
nec de tam multis generosi principis actis,
credidimus nobis tenui tentanda Camaena;¹⁴
non est exigui de tanto principe vatis
scribere; magnificum desiderat ille poetam,
nos animo tenues et nullo robore fulti 65
sudamus facilem magno sub fasce laborem.¹⁵
Hispani tandem laetantur sorte beata:
'Vivat, nam vivet regnorum gloria semper,
cum sit cunctorum quos cernunt sydera regum,
maximus et toto nulli cessurus in orbe'.¹⁶

Johann Werlhof, *Epithalamium potentissimi Hispaniarum regis Catholici Caroli III et serenissimae principis Brunsuico-Luneburgicae Elisabethae Christinae augusto connubio*

Here I edit two long passages from Werlhof's nuptial poem. The texts provide an insight into the quality of Werlhof's Latin as well as his debt to Virgil and Ovid.

Description of the seize of Gibraltar by Allied troops in August 1704 and the subsequent siege of Barcelona by Archduke Charles in 1705 (ll. 378–97). In this first text, it is not overly difficult to detect the influence of Virgil in the description of Aurora.

Et sic, prima novo ceu spargit lumine terras 378
Tithoni croceum linquens Aurora cubile¹⁷
humentemque polo pedetentim dimovet umbram,¹⁸ 380
magni etiam Carolo surgunt cunabula regni,
paulatim Hesperiae Iove discutiente tenebras.
Tu quondam Herculea Calpe decorata columna,
Mauram Abylam contra, magnorum meta laborum
Alcidae, occiduus Titan ubi mergitur undis,

tu Leopoldigenae prima urbes inter Iberas
principium es creperae lucis. Patuere Britannis
claustra freti ac toties sulcandum classibus aequor,
infusum mediis quod terris littora lambit
Hispana et circum Balearica regna profundo   390
fluctisono bullat. roseis ast lutea bigis
puniceisque invecta rotis Aurora rubere[19]
occiduae conspecta plagae, cum Barcino capta,
prima novi Carolo sedes et gloria regni
Hesperii, excussitque iugum Catalaunia, priscae
libertatis amans dudumque invita capistrum
durius Andini mordens [...]   397

Description of Elisabeth Christine's arrival in Vienna in May 1707 (ll. 641–77). The image of the future queen's chariot drawn by two turtle doves occurs in Ovid (*Met.* 14.597: *perque leves auras iunctis invecta columbis*).

Exsultans Cytherea agitat bis mille choreas   641
Salzdali et, nisi connubium, nil pectore versat
felicis Caroli. Carolo ut vicinior adsit
et coram Austriacos vultus moresque verendam
maiestatem orbi divinaque Caesaris ora
Iosephi adspiciat fratremque agnoscat Elisa
ex fratre Augusto, secum petat illa Viennam
suggerit et genitor placido annuit ore benignus.
      Sic adeo nostris longum pulcherrima terris
Guelphis Elisa vale, sic aulae dicis avitae,   650
quam roseas madefacta genas! Coelestia roris
lumina ferviduli quam stillant humida guttis?
Haeccine iam postrema dabis calida oscula caro
dulcis avo? Nunquamne iterum, quos moesta relinquis,
te cernent genitor genitrixque et sanguine eodem
Guelphiaco geniti? Certe, si corpore visum
destituis nostrum, praesens animo inclyta virtus
permanet atque oculis divina recurret imago.
      Excipit aurato nympham dea Cypria curru,
quem volucrem geminae iunctim duxere columbae,   660
saepe sibi infixis torquentes oscula linguis,
bissenae niveaeque omnes, at colla coloris
purpurei incinctae perpulchris orbibus auri

permixti varie multo fulgore coruscis,
perque leves Zephyro molli comitante per auras,
Austriacam, celeres alis, vexere Viennam.
    Hic ego quid referam, magno quam Caesari Elisa
accepta exstiterit, toti quam Caesaris aulae?
Quid procerum plausus? Populi quid gaudia? Et undis
fluctisonis ipsum spumantem laetius Istrum?   670
Iosepho placuisse sat est. Miratur Elisam
Caesar et haec orbis primo omnia principe digna
Caesare in Augusto. Cunctas it Fama per urbes
Austriacas, late quae omnes sermone replevit
multiplici populos, genitam de semine Guelpho
advenisse deam, Veneris quae tota lepores
spiret et aurati mereatur proemia pomi.   677

Notes

Introduction

1 For discussions of new methodological approaches to the study of the War of the Spanish Succession and for surveys of recent bibliographical material on the conflict see Oury 2020: 9–14, Scott 2018 and Seitschek and Hertel 2020: 1–7.
2 The dramatic potential afforded by some of the events which took place in Barcelona in the summer and autumn of 1705 must have been recognised by Voltaire, who set the beginning of his *Histoire de Jenni* (1775) during the military episode.
3 This is an argument repeatedly employed by Catalan historiography of the dynastic conflict. See, for example, Alabrús 2001 and, particularly, Alcoberro (2002, 2003, 2021 and 2022), who has examined the contents of some of the Neo-Latin tracts discussed in Chapter Four within an otherwise impressive historical enquiry into the politics of exile following the end of the war.
4 The volume edited by Enenkel, Laureys and Pieper (2012) constitutes an extremely valuable tool for the study of the connections between Neo-Latin literature and political-ideological discourse in the early modern period. The chronological framework covered by the essays included in the book does not extend, however, beyond 1700. The same holds true of general surveys of Neo-Latin epic poetry and of the function of Neo-Latin literature as an instrument of political power, as with Braun 2007.
5 Though it unearths previously unexplored material, the study by Coroleu and Paredes is restricted to Catalonia; combining attention to military history and to the imitation of classical and contemporary vernacular texts, Money's volumes analyse (chiefly British) Neo-Latin prose and verse responses to the battles of Ramillies and Oudenarde; Klecker's discussion of a cluster of texts from the 1700s in praise of Archduke Charles of Austria is part of an extremely valuable and wide-ranging survey of Neo-Latin writing produced at the University of Vienna across several centuries.
6 Exceptions to this universal rule are Haskell 2013, Laird 2020, and Verhaart and Brockliss 2023.

1 Praise and Blame: Legitimizing the New Kings' Old Dynasties

1 *Serenissimo principi . . . Carolo archiduci Austriae . . . hoc genethliacum munusculum . . . dicatur et consecratur* ('This brief birthday poem is dedicated and devoted to the most serene prince, Archduke Charles of Austria'), Vienna, 1700, from the copy at ÖNB, 35465-B. I have not been able to find any further information on Scharff, who does not feature among those instructors responsible for the young archduke's education at the Imperial court (Kalmár 2020).

2 *Plures anno eo, quo natus, Carole, / contra Thracicam lunam partae sunt victoriae* ('Many victories against the Thracian moon were accomplished in the year in which you, Charles, were born', ll. 38–9) and *[Carolum] ominosum, / ominosum inquam, quia eo tempore / in lucem editus es, / quo secundantibus armis nostris / expugnatum est Novarinum* ('portentous Charles, portentous I say because you first saw the light of day when Pylos was captured by our favoured troops', ll. 151–5). Historically also known as Navarino, the town of Pylos on the Peloponnese was recaptured from the Turks in July 1685 during the early stages of the Morean War in the context of the Great Turkish War (1683–99).

3 The months leading to Charles II's death provided several occasions on which Archduke Charles's dynastic claims to the Spanish throne could be unequivocally endorsed through the use of Latin and references to classical antiquity. As an example, a medal displaying the inscription *CVIVS ET ANNIS ET GENERI FATVM INDVLGET QVEM NVMINA POSCVNT [INGREDERE]* ('[You, Aeneas], whose years and race fate indulges, whom the gods call, [advance]'), *Aen.* 8.511–12, reproduced in Sabatier 2007: 75, was struck in Nuremberg at the time of the Second Partition Treaty between France, Great Britain and the United Provinces (London, 17–25 March 1700), which however failed to prevent the outbreak of war.

4 Though restricted to vernacular sources and focusing on Spain, in an important study González Cruz 2009b offers an excellent typology of the legitimization strategies employed by both sides during the dynastic conflict. For Britain see Griffin 2005.

5 *La bonaventura que diguè la gitana imaginaria al duch de Anjou al partirse de Paris per lo regnat de Espanya* ('The fortune told by the illusory Gypsy girl to the Duke of Anjou as he departed from Paris for his reign in Spain'), Barcelona: Josep Llopis, 1707, copy at BC, Fons Bonsoms, 5659; and *Lletres curioses de la bonaventura que diguè una gitana a Carlos tercer quant partí de Viena a Espanya* ('Mysterious letters on the fortune told by a Gypsy girl to Charles III as he departed from Vienna for Spain'), Barcelona: Francesc Guasch, 1707, copy at BC, Fons Bonsoms, 5663. Antoni Comas (1964: 51–2) relates these pieces to further examples of popular prophetic literature in Catalan in support of Archduke Charles or directed against Philip of Anjou.

6 In the early modern period, these texts – which in antiquity were restricted to the occasion of a departure of a friend and had a standard set of topics codified by Menander Rhetor and other late rhetoricians – tended to fuse the worlds of academia and politics. The Neo-Latin *propempticon* seems to have been especially popular in the German-speaking areas (Viiding 2006).

7 For contemporary accounts of the French leg of the royal journey, see Levantal 1996. A later account of the journey in Spanish is provided by Royal secretary Antonio Ubilla y Medina (*Succession del rey D. Phelipe V, nuestro Señor en la corona de España: diario de sus viages desde Versalles a Madrid, el que executó para su feliz casamiento, jornada a Nápoles, a Milan, y a su exercito, successos de la campaña, y su buelta a Madrid*, Madrid, 1704).

8 *Philippo Franciae Hispaniarum regi dum iter in Hispanias Aurelia faceret comitantibus regiis principibus fratribus suis duce Burgundiae et duce Bituricensi offerebat Collegium regium Aurelianense Societatis Iesu* ('The Royal College of the Society of Jesus at Orleans offered [these poems] to Philip of France, king of Spain, as he passed through Orleans on his way to Spain accompanied by the royal princes, his brothers the Duke of Burgundy and the Duke of Berry'), *s.l.*, 1700, copy inspected: BnF, Yc. 911 (88); and *Philippo quinto Hispaniarum regi et serenissimis eius fratribus Blesis transeuntibus regium Blesense Societatis Iesu Collegium gratulatur* ('The Royal College of the Society of Jesus at Blois manifests its joy to Philip V, king of Spain, and his most serene brothers as they travel through Blois'), *s.l.*, 1700, copy inspected: BnF, Yc. 11927.

9 Gibert's tenure at the Collège Mazarin, where D'Alembert was one of his pupils between 1731 and 1733, is very well documented (Ben Messaoud 2005) but I have not been able to find any record of the speech referred to in the title of Le Comte's ode: *Ad iustitiam cum ob delatam Philippo, duci Andegavensi, Ludovici magni nepoti, Hispanicorum regnorum hereditatem M. Baltazar Gibert, rhetorum alter, utrique regi oratione publica gratularetur in Collegio Mazarinaeo die ultima Decembris anni 1700 ode* ('An ode to Justice, as M. Balthasar Gibert, one of two rhetoricians, congratulated Philip, duke of Anjou, grandson of Louis XIV, on the transfer of the inheritance of the kingdoms of Spain in a public speech [delivered] at the Collège Mazarin on the last day of December of 1700'), Paris, 1701, copy inspected: BnF, Yc. 3414, reproduced in Appendix 2.1. In the text the goddess of Justice – 'after having recently taken pity on the Spanish people, who summoned you with anxious prayers' (*Nuper Hispanam miserata gentem, / anxiis quae te precibus vocabat*, ll. 33–4) – is praised for 'having descended upon Charles II's sacred head' (*Caroli ad sacrum caput adstitisti*, l. 37).

10 *Hispanis et Gallis gratulatio, habita Parisiis, cum Philippus, dux Andegavensis, Hispaniarum rex renuntiatus est* ('A congratulation held in Paris for the Spaniards and the French as Philip, duke of Anjou, is proclaimed king of Spain'), Paris, 1701, copy inspected: BnF, 8-Z Le Senne-8437.

11 *Philippo quinto regi Catholico in Hispaniam abeunti Musarum gratulatio in regio Ludovici magni Collegio Societatis Iesu*, Paris, 1700, copy inspected: BnF, Yc. 3895. On Commire, see Vissac 1862: 19.
12 In the text the poet identifies Charles V through his coat of arms depicting the two-headed eagle of the Holy Roman Empire, from Ausonia, a reference to the Italian territories inherited from his grandfather Ferdinand, and the Pillars of Hercules, with the motto *plus ultra* ('further beyond') to indicate the crown's New World territories.
13 The full title of the volume is *Musae iuveniles rhetorum in regio Ludovici magni Collegio Societatis Iesu Philippo Andegavensium duci ad Hispaniarum regna evocato felicitatem gratulantur* ('The youthful muses of the Rhetoric class at the Royal Collège Louis-le-Grand of the Society of Jesus manifest their joy to Philip, duke of Anjou, summoned to the kingdoms of Spain'), second edition, Paris, 1701, copy inspected: BnF, 8-Z Le Senne-11360 (1). Prepared by Gabriel François Le Jay (1657–1734), the first edition was published earlier that year by Antoine Lambin's widow and is considerably shorter. The BnF catalogue attributes the second edition (by Louis Sevestre) also to Le Jay but the volume itself provides no conclusive proof of this.
14 BC, MS 3566, ff. 46r–55v (Chapter 4, on Philip and King David). I owe this reference to Maria Toldrà. The text must have been written in the very early months of Philip's reign for it includes no references whatsoever to the dynastic conflict. In the final lines of the preliminary epigram (f. 4r) 'the Crown [of Spain] believes it will not be restored to these Austrians but will originate from highest prophetic heaven' (*Nec se restitui putat his corona Austriacis / sed nasci e summo praesagiente caelo*, ll. 7–8).
15 *Festiva, gratulatoria proclamatio pro regali et Oscensi Divi Vincentii Martyris Collegio, ex Philippis quinto Hispaniarum regi Philippo, Ibereos praecurrenti, dicata* ('A festive, congratulatory proclamation on behalf of the Royal College of Saint Vincent Martyr in Huesca, dedicated to King Philip of Spain, the fifth Philip, foremost of the Iberians'), s.l. (but surely Huesca and most likely published by Joseph Lorenzo de Larumbe, printer to the university), 1701?, copy inspected: Saragossa University Library, G-74–17 [32]. The adjective *Sertorianus* refers to the Roman general and statesman Quintus Sertorius (c. 126–73 BCE), who – according to Plutarch's *Life of Sertorius*, 14 – established a school in Huesca, where he died. Founded in 1354, from the late sixteenth century onwards the University of Huesca was known as *Universitas Sertoriana* (Garcés Manau 2002). On Estarrués, who also wrote a Latin funerary poem for Charles II in 1700, see Gómez Uriel 1884: 1.448– 9 (I owe this reference and further information on eighteenth-century Huesca to José Enrique Laplana).
16 [*Philippus*] *cum Aragonensium suffragiis promunitur et votis . . . sacris adstat Fori legibus*, sign. A2v.
17 Estarrués must have included this quotation from Ovid to provide a suitably erudite image from classical literature of a person unable to move. Although the original

describes Niobe, brought to a standstill by grief at seeing her family slaughtered, there is nothing in the Latin to indicate the subject is female. However, in translating it into English, a gendered possessive adjective must be provided, which poses a problem. I have opted for the masculine because contemporary readers must surely have read the quotation as referring to Philip. I am grateful to David Barnett for drawing my attention to this point.

18 It is tempting to speculate on the reasons for choosing this day, which falls on the same date on which Ferdinand II of Aragon gave an address to the parliament at Naples in 1507, and 'stressed his right to the kingdom by inheritance, rather than conquest' (Shaw 2022: 179). The proclamation of the new king preceded the royal funeral rites for Charles II at Palermo Cathedral on 18 April 1701 (Mínguez Cornelles et al. 2014: 127).

19 The inscription is reproduced in Antonio Mongitore, *Il Trionfo Palermitano, nella solenne acclamazione del cattolico re delle Spagne e di Sicilia Filippo V, festeggiata in Palermo a 30 di Gennaro 1701* ('Palermitan triumph, on the occasion of the solemn acclamation of Philip V, Catholic king of Spain and Sicily, celebrated in Palermo on 30 January 1701'), Palermo, 1701, pp. 47–8. This brief text is transcribed, but with several Latin errors, and discussed in Mínguez Cornelles et al. (2014: 139).

20 The insurrection on behalf of the Austrian interest came to be known as the 'Conspiracy of Macchia', named after Gaetano Gambacorta (1657–1703), prince of Macchia, who was one of its leaders. The events took place on 22 and 23 September 1701 and were chronicled most notably by Giambattista Vico (1668–1744) in his *De coniuratione principum Neapolitanorum* ('The conspiracy of the Neapolitan noblemen'), a text 'written soon after the conspiracy and certainly before Naples came under Austrian rule in 1707' (Marshall 2006: 86). It is worth noting that Vico himself had composed a Latin panegyric to mark Philip's entry into Naples in May 1702 (Naddeo 2011: 21–2).

21 The royal entry was celebrated in several Latin speeches, such as Oronzio Palladio's *Oratio panegirica de Philippo V, invictissimo Neapolitani regni atque Hispaniarum rege* ('A panegyric speech on Philip V, most invincible king of the kingdom of Naples and Spain'), Naples, 1702.

22 Hengerer describes the declaration of Archduke Charles as king of Spain as 'articulated in a restrained and peaceable way' (2018: 220). Yet, some of the pamphlets published to mark the new king's departure for war examined in the following paragraphs seem to paint a rather different picture, perhaps because military operations across Europe were no longer in their early stages. For this purpose, the Habsburg side did not hesitate to engage luminaries such as Gottfried Wilhelm Leibniz, whose *Manifeste contenant les droits de Charles III, Roi d'Espagne, et les justes motifs de son expédition* ('A manifest presenting the rights of Charles III, king of Spain, and the just reasons for his expedition') was published in The Hague in 1704.

23 The volume is entitled *Austriacum vale et Hispanicum ave dictum augusto Carolo tertio Hispaniarum regi declarato, Caroli secundi vero et legitimo in monarchiam Hispanicam successori ac haeredi, dum e domo paterna ad capessendum monarchiae suae thronum regnorum invitatu in Hispaniam proficisceretur* ('An Austrian farewell and a Spanish greeting uttered for august Charles III, declared king of Spain, true and legitimate heir and successor of Charles II to the Spanish monarchy, as he travelled from his paternal home to Spain to take up the throne at the invitation of his kingdoms'), Vienna, 1703, copy at ÖNB, 305764-C. On Charles's pilgrimage to Mariazell between 15 and 17 September 1703, see Matsche 1981: 172.
24 See *Wiener Zeitung*, no. 13, 20 September 1703, p. 7 (accessible through *AustriaN Newspapers Online* at ÖNB).
25 *Ad serenissimum ac potentissimum Carolum tertium Hispaniarum et utriusque Indiae monarcham, regem Catholicum, Archiducem Austriae, dum ad capessendum haereditarium Hispaniarum regnum Vienna discederet, suprema ac festiva acclamatio ab antiquissima ac celeberrima Universitate Viennensi* ('A supreme and festive acclamation by the most ancient and famous University of Vienna for the most serene and mightiest Charles III, king of Spain and both Indies, archduke of Austria, as he departed from Vienna to take up the inherited throne of Spain'), Vienna, 1703, ÖNB, 303388-C.Adl.4; and *Serenissimo ac potentissimo Hispaniarum ac Indiarum neo-regi Carolo III, Archiduci Austriae, principi ac domino domino suo clementissimo dum Viennae in Austria declaratus regnum adiret* ('To the most serene and mightiest Charles III, new king of Spain and the Indies, archduke of Austria, prince and lord, to the most clement lord, as, having been declared king in Vienna in Austria, he took possession of his kingdom'), Vienna, 1703, copy at Passau, Staatliche Bibliothek – S nv/a K (b) 2, available through the online catalogue of MBSB, accessed on 5 August 2021. The first text is cited by Klecker 2008: 52. I have not been able to find any further information on Hunoldt.
26 As with Haake's poem examined in Chapter 2 where the French also soil themselves in terror as they retreat, Hunoldt exploits the idea that the French are 'unclean' as a further propaganda motif.
27 I owe this reference to Klecker 2008: 69. The volume was published in Vienna in 1704 by Leopold Voigt, printer to the university (I use the copy at ÖNB, 296339-A. Adl.6.). The title of the collection echoes Aeneas's words in *Aen.* 1.94: *O terque quaterque beati!* ('O thrice, four times happy they [the Trojans]').
28 See Klecker 2008: 56–8 for a discussion of the typographical features of these volumes, and of problems with their authorial attribution.
29 Archduke Charles is also presented as *LIBERATOR ET VLTOR* ('liberator and avenger') on another Viennese medal struck to commemorate his landing in Lisbon (Sabatier 2007: 79).
30 Elected on 23 November 1700, Pope Clement XI first recognized Philip, thereby angering Emperor Leopold I. After Leopold I's death in 1705, his son Joseph I

invaded the Papal States, taking Parma and Piacenza and besieging Ferrara. The Pope initially countered the attacks but then backed down and on 15 January 1709 he recognized Charles (Martín Marcos 2011).

31 Philip's official entry into Madrid on 14 April 1701 was marked with a medal bearing the inscription *PHILIPPO V CODICE CAROLI II HISPANIARVM INDIARVM REGI CATHOLICO A LVDOVICO XIV APPROBATO* ('For Philip V, Catholic King of Spain and the Indies through the testament of Charles II, approved by Louis XIV'), included in Sabatier 2007: 74.

32 Pamphleteers on the pro-Austrian side claimed that, at the time of rewriting his will, an enfeebled Charles II had been a victim of political intrigue. For the depiction among Allied propagandists of Philip V as usurper see González Cruz 2009b: 173–4.

33 The *Synopsis* was published sometime after 1700 (s.l., copy at MBSB, 4 J.publ.e.256); Seilern's text was published by Johannes Jakob Kürner in Vienna in 1701 (copy at ÖNB, 36.B.21) and reprinted two years later, most likely to coincide with Charles's proclamation as king of Spain. Similar arguments to those adduced by Seilern and the anonymous author of the *Synopsis* were employed by Johann Christoph Beckmann (1641–1717) in his *Ius Austriacum in successione regnorum Hispaniae vindicatum* ('The vindication in Austrian law of the succession to the kingdoms of Spain'), Vienna?, 1704.

34 *dum hi [Galli] ad excludendum omnes plane feminas non tantum a Franciae regno, sed etiam ab iis ditionibus, quae per feminas ad Galliae reges pervenerunt, variis titulis connisi masculam regiae familiae successionem secundum lineas iam dudum acerrime propugnarunt* (p. 7).

35 Mínguez Cornelles et al. (2014: 126) provide several examples of political pamphlets in support of Philip published at the time in Naples but written in Spanish or Italian.

36 A reaction to the publication of the aforementioned *Ius Austriacum in monarchiam Hispanicam assertum*, which is explicitly mentioned in the preface (p. 7), Biscardi's letter is framed as having been written by *Philalethes* ('Lover-of-truth') and addressed to *Dicaeophilus* ('Lover-of-justice'). The volume was first published in Naples by Giuseppe Roselli in 1703 and was reprinted in 1734, when Naples returned to Bourbon hands. I have inspected the copy held at BC, Toda 11-III-36.

37 Biscardi returns to this issue in one of the final sections of his tract, entitled *Nullam extare legem, quae repellat feminas et earum descendentes a successione regnorum Hispaniarum* ('There should be no law debarring women and their descendants from the succession to the kingdoms of Spain'), pp. 121–7.

38 I use the copy held at BC, Toda 13-II-4. I have not been able to find any further information on Verderosa, who is described on the title page as a 'defence advocate working in the Naples court of justice' (*Partenopes in foro causarum patronus*). Significantly, his tract was also reprinted in 1734 (see note 36 above).

39 Consisting of 106 hexameters, the text is included in the collection *De Philippo V potentissimo Hispaniarum rege ... carmina*, sign. A1r–A4v (Naples, 1704, copy at the

Biblioteca de l'Abadia de Montserrat, C XXXIX 8° 12). On Caracciolo see Crispi 1720: 2, 43–6. I owe this reference to Fulvio Delle Donne.

40 Contemporary political propaganda written in Latin in support of Philip seems to have been particularly concerned with retelling this most delicate episode of the last years of Spanish rule in Naples. See, for example, the Franciscan and Scotist philosopher Girolamo de Montefortino (c. 1662–1738), who devoted a long section of his *Pro Philippo quinto Catholico, Hispaniarum ac Indiarum monarcha piissimo, oratio panegirica* ('A panegyric oration on behalf of Catholic Philip V, most pious monarch of Spain and the Indies'), Naples, 1704, pp. 52–89, to chronicle the insurrection in terms and style reminiscent of Sallust's *Conspiracy of Catiline*.

41 Philip's participation in the Italian campaign in the summer of 1702 is the central subject of the third epyllion included in the volume, entitled *Philippo V Hispaniarum regi invictissimo epinicium* ('Victory song for most invincible Philip V, king of Spain', sign. E1r–L3r), whose contents will be examined in the following chapter.

42 To designate the Duchy of Savoy and other territories in northern Italy, Caracciolo here uses the term *Insubria*, a region around Milan which rebelled against Rome in 225 BCE and was subsequently defeated. See the following section and Chapter 2 for further recurrences of the term and of the related *Insuber, -bris* ('Insubrian', 'belonging to Insubria') in anti-Habsburg propaganda during the War of the Spanish Succession.

43 Naples, 1705, copy at BUB, 07 C-250/5/7.

44 Amsterdam, 1705, copy at BUB, 07 XVIII-8101. An abridged German version of the text under the title *Gründliche Anzeige und Vorstellung des Frantzösischen Unfugs und der Oesterreichischen Befugniß zur Spanischen Succession* ('Careful declaration and presentation of French nonsense and Austrian right regarding the Spanish Succession') was published in 1707, probably in Vienna. On Álvares da Costa, who was a member of the final court of appeal and of the Royal Academy of History in Lisbon, see Barbosa Machado 1786: 2, 255–6.

45 Petersen's poem came off the press of Ulrich Liebpert in Coloniae Brandenburgicae (Köln an der Spree, now part of Berlin), and May's commentary was printed in Kiel by Johann Sebastian Riechel. I use the copies held at HAB, Gl 4 Kapsel 2 (3) and MBSB, 4 Austr. 87, respectively.

46 In May 1703 a revolt led by the aristocrat Ferenc Rákóczi II (1676–1735) began in Hungary, with French support and finance, against the process of Germanization and Catholicization that had been championed by the Habsburgs since the late seventeenth century.

47 *Anagrammatismus augustissimo et sacratissimo imperatori Carolo VI, Hispaniarum et Indiarum regi, sacer* ('A sacred poem in anagrams for the holiest and most august emperor Charles VI, king of Spain and the Indies'), Brunswick, 1712. A copy of the text is held at HAB, Gl 4 Kapsel 1 (9). The poem is partly reproduced and discussed by Helander (2004: 459–63), from whom the following remarks are drawn.

48 Friedrich August Hackemann, *Programma solenni orationi in coronationem augustissimi et sacratissimi imperatoris Caroli sexti* ('Programme for the solemn oration to commemorate the coronation of the most august and sacred emperor Charles VI'), Helmstedt, 1711, sign. A4v, from the copy at HAB, H: 11 Helmst. Dr. (50).

49 *Serenissimo, potentissimo invictissimoque principi ac domino domino Carolo VI electo Romanorum imperatori . . . gratulatur Iustus Christophorus Böhmer* ('Justus Christoph Böhmer manifests his joy to the most serene, mighty and invincible prince and lord, lord Charles VI, elected Holy Roman Emperor'), Helmstedt, 1711, from the copy at HAB, 164.2 Helmst.

50 *Universae vastissimaeque Hispanicae monarchiae rex est legitimus, gentilitio iure, transferente patre, concedente fratre* (sign. B2v). As noted in the Introduction, during the proclamation ceremony held in Vienna in September 1703 Emperor Leopold and his firstborn son ceded their rights to the crown of Spain to Charles.

51 *In celebratione coronationis Caroli sexti . . . in laudem Elisabeth Christinae . . . oratio panegyrica* ('A panegyric in prose to mark the coronation of Charles VI and in praise of Elisabeth Christine'), Barcelona, 1712, from the copy at BUB, C-240/6//20-3. Information on San Marco is scarce: in the preface to a birthday poem composed in 1716 for Charles's son Leopold Johann, Archduke of Austria, to which I will return in Chapter 4, he describes himself as a native of Francavilla, in the region of the Abruzzi. San Marco may have followed the Imperial entourage, first in Barcelona and subsequently in Vienna, where the piece was published.

52 For the medal minted at Nuremberg, see Lauffer 1742: 83 and 249, and for the symbolism of Charles's stay in the city, see Matsche 1981: 26. For Regensburg, see *Vota orientis anni Caesareae Maiestati dicata Ratisbonae* ('Vows of the year that begins dedicated to his Imperial Majesty in Regensburg'), s.l., 1705, from the copy at HAB, Gl 4 Kapsel 1 (17).

53 See *Wiener Zeitung*, no. 886, 27–29 January 1712, p. 1. The title of Schlittern's speech reads *Oratio gratulatoria ob auspicatum in Austriam reditum ad Carolum sextum* ('A congratulatory oration for Charles VI on account of his auspicious return to Austria'), Vienna, 1712, copy at ÖNB, 240142-C.

54 *Oratio solennis, qua . . . Carolo VI Romano imperatori . . . gratulatur Georgius Fridericus a Tann*, Meiningen, 1712, from the copy at MBSB, 2 P.o.lat. 81, 14. The volume includes in an appendix a letter from the theologian and professor of Greek at the Gymnasium Casimirianum, Philipp Theodor Verpoorten (1677–1712), addressed to his colleagues, in which he praises Pope Clement XI for his decision to recognize Charles as Spanish king in 1709. On Charles VI as a new Charlemagne, see Matsche 1981: 294–5.

55 Schlittern's text is briefly discussed in Klecker 2008: 51. Another Latin text published by Voigt on the occasion of Charles's coronation is *Germania vetus selectis*

quaestionibus illustrata ('Ancient Germany illustrated through selected themes'), Vienna, 1712. As persuasively argued by Klecker (2008: 71–2), this description of ancient Germany is, in reality, an anti-French pamphlet and constitutes an excellent example of the political exploitation of antiquarianism during the War of the Spanish Succession. Other contemporary booklets of similar subject matter – as with *To Plus ultra columnae Herculis in Carolo VI augustissimo Romanorum imperatore figuratae* ('The further beyond of the column of Hercules represented in Charles VI, most august Holy Roman emperor', Prague, 1712) – are further proof of the political functions served by antiquarianism at the time of the Imperial coronation. Texts such as *To Plus ultra columnae*... were clearly written to coincide with Charles VI's adoption of the device of his predecessor Charles V, the two columns of Hercules and the motto *plus ultra*.

2 'Bellonae et Martis genitus': Mapping the Spanish Conflict in Latin Verse and Prose (1701–1712)

1 *Annus primus belli Italici* was dedicated to the graduating doctors in Philosophy and the graduation ceremony was organized by a *promotor*, here the Jesuit Andreas Magerl, professor of Philosophy until 1703. I use the copy of the text held at ÖNB, BE 7 T 84. On Staindl, who was rector of the University of Graz between 1725 and 1728, see Peinlich 1864: 89. I am grateful to Lav Šubarić for information on the University of Graz in the early eighteenth century.
2 *Falx, falcis* denotes a military implement shaped like a sickle, used in sieges to pull down walls or enemy soldiers stationed on battlements.
3 As late as the 1740s Eugene's raid on Cremona still elicited responses from Neo-Latin panegyrists (Korenjak 2008). I am grateful to Martin Korenjak for drawing my attention to his article.
4 Latin played an important role in the festivities following the victory of the Anglo-Dutch fleet on the bay of Vigo: the battle was the subject of several poems included in *Epinicion Oxoniense* ('An Oxonian victory song', Oxford, 1702, copy at BL, 837.m.26), and it was celebrated with a firework display in The Hague featuring 'metaphorical scenes and animals, and well-known Latin devices' (Frijhoff 2015: 241).
5 These French successes were celebrated at the Collège de Louis-le-Grand by André Le Camus, whom we have already encountered in the previous chapter, in a Latin oration entitled *Imago nascentis herois* ('Image of a born hero', Paris, 1703, copy at BNF, RES-LB37–4225). The speech was dedicated to Philip V's elder brother and Louis XIV's grandson, Louis Duke of Burgundy, who in 1702 still 'had to prove that he would be a warlike king' (Oury 2020: 93).

6   The Tyrolean campaign of 1703 was still celebrated in Latin prose by pro-Habsburg writers and publishers in Vienna and Amsterdam as late as, respectively, 1709 and 1710 (Schaffenrath and Tilg 2004).
7   *Solve Europa comas, luctusque exponere dolorem, / da lachrymas, nullo tempore maesta magis* are the opening lines of the anonymous *Conspectus Europae Anno 1704*, available in Dahlberg 2014: 57–8.
8   See for example *Plausus Musarum Oxoniensis sive gratulatio Academiae ob res prospere terra marique gestas* ('Applause from Oxonian Muses or a rejoicing offered by the university for the deeds successfully undertaken on land and at sea', Oxford, 1704; copy at BL, 837.m.27).
9   Caracciolo provides, for example, specific information on Eugene's order of battle into two lines, the left under Visconti and Charles, prince of Commercy, the right under Prince Vaudémont (1670–1704), while Eugene himself commanded the centre (ll. 648–52).
10 It is worth noting that the expression *rerum inviolata potestas* used to describe God is a borrowing from Caracciolo's fellow Neapolitan Neo-Latin poet Jacopo Sannazaro (1458–1530), one of the sources explicitly acknowledged in Caracciolo's preface (p. 6). The expression can be found in Sannazaro's *De partu Virginis* ('The Virgin's birth'), 3, 2.
11 *tu, qui posthabitis aliis me sceptra tueri / nobilis Hesperiae et tantis succedere regnis / iussisiti moriens.*
12 Lines 814–15 (*praepetibus pennis extra Garamantas et Indos, / extra anni solisque vies . . .*) draw on *Aen.* 6.794 and 796, respectively.
13 This text does not, of course, constitute an isolated case in this respect. As shown by González Cruz in his examination of vernacular sources (2002: 25–36), it was common for Habsburg propagandists to present Charles as 'Catholic king' in response to Philip's claim that the Archduke was aided by heretical England and Holland.
14 Another example of propagandistic fictive letters written during the dynastic conflict is afforded by Anton Kiffer's *Epistolae heroum et heroidum ex augustissima domo Austriaca* ('Letters by heroes and heroines from the most august House of Austria', Graz, 1705). Modelled on Ovid's *Heroides*, this collection includes epistles purported to have been written by the pope as well as male and female members of the Imperial family in praise of the Allied cause (Mörschbacher 2015).
15 In Book 5 of his *Politicorum sive civilis doctrinae libri sex* ('Six Books on Politics or Civil Doctrine', Leiden, 1589), Justus Lipsius deals with military prudence.
16 Francisco Fernández de Velasco, Duke of Frías, first became viceroy of Catalonia in July 1696, and was recalled from the post fourteen months later. He was reappointed in 1703.
17 I use the copy held at the Arxiu Històric de la Ciutat de Barcelona (4 op. 1566). A further copy of the text has been preserved in the Biblioteca de l'Abadia de

Montserrat (Res. 4° 1/33). For a discussion of Latin medals celebrating the taking of Barcelona in 1705 see Sabatier 2007: 79.

18 *Hostibus armatis currit fortissimus heros / Armstati Princeps, moenia pandit ovans; / qui, ut primum coepit montem expugnare, triumphat, / extemplo moritur; distat utrumque nihil* ('The bravest hero, Prince George of Hesse-Darmstadt runs against the armed enemies and, rejoicing, lays the walls open. As soon he storms the mountain, he celebrates his triumph but immediately dies; there is no difference in either thing', ll. 21–4). For examples of funerary verse on Prince George of Hesse-Darmstadt in Latin, Catalan and Spanish, see Alabrús 2001: 173–6.

19 Since the late fifteenth century the mythical foundation of Barcelona had been attributed to Hercules, son of Jupiter. The poet was clearly aware of the symbolism underlying the false etymology of the name 'Montjuïc' as Jupiter's Mountain. For Charles as Hercules see Matsche 1981: 343–57.

20 See, for example, the broadsheets *Clamors de Barcelona al tirà govern de Velasco* ('Cries of Barcelona against Velasco's tyrannical government', Barcelona, 1705?) and *Invectiva al político govierno de don Francisco Velasco* ('Invective against Francisco Velasco's political government', Barcelona, 1705). On these pamphlets see Alabrús 2001: 177–8.

21 It is tempting to interpret the words *Destruxit dominans urbem feritate* as a rebuke of Fernández de Velasco's coat of arms featuring the motto *Sapiens liberavit urbem* ('He saved the city by his wisdom', Eccl. 9.15), as can be seen in an engraving of 1704 commemorating the successful defence of Barcelona by the viceroy (Museu Nacional d'Art de Catalunya, GDG 3343-G9, reproduced in Alcoberro 2007: 62).

22 The motto is a direct quotation from Paulus Orosius (*Hist.* 7.35) misquoting in turn Claudian's lines discussed below. The medal is reproduced and described in Fontcuberta i Famadas 2014: 103.

23 Understandably, Vienna also witnessed celebrations of the victory by means of illuminations in St Augustine's church decorated with Latin emblems by Abraham a Sancta Clara (1644–1709), as noted in *Fasti Austriae* 1736 [2015]: 159.

24 The complex circumstances surrounding the erection of the statue are expertly reconstructed and documented in Mollfulleda 2007, who, however, mistranscribes the text of the inscription. The statue was destroyed by the new Bourbon authorities in May 1716.

25 See, for example, *Goigs de la Purissima Concepcio de Maria Santissima collocada en la Real Columna, que en lo Born de la Excellentissima Ciutat de Barcelona erigí la Catolica Magestat de Carlos Tercer (que Deu guarde) Rey de las Espanyas, Die 20 de Iuny de 1076* ('Joyful songs in praise of the Purest Conception of the most blessed Virgin Mary, honoured on the Royal column erected in the Born in the most excellent city of Barcelona by his Catholic Majesty Charles III (May God protect him), King of Spain, on 20 June 1706', Barcelona, 1706). For further examples of *Goigs* at the service of Charles, see Campabadal i Bertran 2003: 2, 199–201.

26 *Exemplares acciones de devoción y culto* ('Exemplary acts of devotion and cult'), Barcelona, 1706, p. 4. In the version of the document quoted by Voltes Bou (1963: 115) the first three lines read as follows: *Caroli III Regis Catholici Anathema / proprio Marte, arte et manu / in Monte Serrato affixum* ('An offering from the Catholic King Charles III placed by his own efforts, his skill and his hand at Montserrat').
27 For Ferdinand and Leopold's *pietas Mariana*, see Matsche 1981: 159-72.
28 *Iuverit Aeneam mater, Saturnia Turnum, / a socia tulerit Pallade Graius opem. / Quid nisi mentitae sunt argumenta Camaenae? / Pugnat in auxiliis fabula nulla tuis* ('Aeneas would have been assisted by his mother, Turnus by Saturn's daughter and the Greek would have carried support from allied Pallas. What but lies are poetry's plots? No fable is fighting to your aid', ll. 167-70).
29 For further examples of (chiefly British) Latin verse in praise of Queen Anne's role during the War of the Spanish Succession, see Gilmore 2008.
30 I have not been able to find any further information on Affatighi. In the last poem to Queen Anne, he mentions that he is suffering from gout (perhaps due to old age?). The *subscriptio* which follows Poem 7 describes him as a member of the convent of Santa Maria Novella in Florence.
31 For the full text of Affatighi's seven Latin poems, see Coroleu 2006.
32 I use the only copy known to me (BC, Fons Bonsoms, 8088), which does not include any details of place of publication or printer. The poem is edited in Appendix 2.2. On Haake see Flood (2006: 748).
33 Claudian, *Cons. Hon.*, 7.96-8: *O nimium dilecte deo, cui fundit ab antris / Aeolus armatas hiemes, cui militat aether / et coniurati veniunt ad classica venti* ('O you exceedingly loved by a god, for whom Aeolus frees the armed tempests from his caves, for whom heaven is fighting and the winds come, sworn to obey, at the call of your trumpets').
34 *Amore et timore* ('Through love and fear') was Joseph's motto. *Virtute patrum* ('Through the valour of his ancestors') was Charles's motto during his time as Spanish king. After being crowned emperor in 1711, he adopted the mottos *Constanter continet orbem* – 'Firmly he holds the world together', and *Constantia et fortitudine* – 'Through firmness and bravery' (Hartmann and Schnith 1996: 587).
35 Livio Vitale Orosio's poem is included in Simon de Pretis's *De ultimarum voluntatum interpretatione tractatus amplissimus* ('A most distinguished treatise on the interpretation of last wills', Frankfurt am Main, 1583), sign. A3r-A4r.
36 The wording is reminiscent of the terms in which Charles – in a letter of 19 June 1706 addressed to the citizens of Saragossa (BC, Fons Bonsoms, 5738) – declared his willingness to respect 'the charters, entitlements and privileges which, because of your loyalty, you deserved from my illustrious ancestors' (*los fueros, gracias y privilegios, que por leales merecisteis de mis gloriosos antecessores*).
37 Johann Baptist Schönwetter, *Eugenio, duci Sabaudiae, . . . post expeditionem in Italia feliciter peractam, in urbem Viennam . . . reduci applausus emblematicus*, Vienna?,

1707 ('Applause in emblems for Eugene, duke of Savoy, on his return to Vienna after having auspiciously undertaken his campaign in Italy', ÖNB, 100938-B). The volume reproduces the emblems from *Elogia heroum Caesareorum in Italia* discussed above (p. 46) and includes new verses by the author in praise of Eugene.

38 I have consulted the copy from MBSB, 4 Mil.g. 157 m.

39 The title of Reusch's speech reads *Oratio solennis qua felicissimam summorum foederatorum expeditionem bellicam in Catalonia, Brabantia et Italia, anno seculi huius sexto confectam, in illustri Academia Altdorfina. . .prosecutus est Erhardus Reusch* ('A solemn oration held in the illustrious University of Altdorf in which Erhard Reusch has chronicled the most auspicious campaign of the Allied troops in Catalonia, Brabant and Italy in 1706', Nuremberg, 1707). I use the copy at HAB, Q 165 Helmst. 2° (29). On Reusch see Flood 2006: 1653–4.

40 This is a crucial point made by Dahlberg 2018 in her examination of how Neo-Latin poets around the Great Northern War transformed official reports from the conflict into literary celebrations of Sweden's most recent military successes.

41 I use the copy from BC, Fons Bonsoms 11957 (s.l: s.t., 1706).

42 For the different political interpretations given to the solar eclipse in contemporary propagandistic literature, see González Cruz 2002: 122–4.

43 The role played by women during the siege of Barcelona of 1706 and its relation to religious imagery and Marian devotion during the dynastic conflict has been examined by Alabrús 2010, who limits her enquiry to vernacular sources.

44 Alabrús 2007 examines vernacular responses to Almansa on the Allied and Bourbon sides. After the seizure of Valencia by Berwick's troops three weeks after Almansa, José María Miñana (1671–1730), professor of Rhetoric at the local university, began to write a pro-Bourbon chronicle of the war in the Kingdom of Valencia (*De bello rustico Valentino*) which was first published in 1752 (Pérez Durà and Estellés 1985).

45 A biographical sketch of Sanadon is provided by Mertz, Murphy and IJsewijn 1989: 168–9. The ode *Philippo quinto Hispaniae regi vaticinium de filio ipsi nascituro* ('A prophecy for Philip V, king of Spain, on the imminent birth of his son') was included in Sanadon's edition of his own poetry (Paris, 1715, pp. 37–9, BnF, YC-8607). León Sanz (2020: 153) persuasively argues that the announcement on 18 August 1707 of Charles's betrothal to Elisabeth Christine (see note 58 below) was deliberately made ahead of the impending birth of Philip's son.

46 *Non (si Batavo iunxerit ultimos / orbis Britannos, Teutonas Insubri) / timebis obluctantem iniquis / bella movere odiosa divis* ('Even if fortune will have bound the remotest Britons of the world to the Dutch and the Teutons to the Insubrian, you shall not fear that, fighting with help from hostile divinities, it moves hateful wars').

47 Sanadon must have taken inspiration from Horace, *Epodes*, XVI, 6, where he describes the Allobrogian tribe as *infidelis* ('treacherous'). In 1728 Sanadon published a French translation of Horace's *Odes* (Krasser and Schmidt 1996: 15).

48 These are available in Sanadon's edition of his own poetry (see n. 45 above), pp. 48–52, pp. 57–61 and pp. 113–16.
49 See ll. 45–8: *Vitales qua luce subit Lodoicus in auras, / tunc rebus visa est spes rediisse tuis. / Vestra Deus laeto cumulat connubia partu / illa, qua Lodoix scandit in astra, die* ('Hope seemed to return to your fortune the day when Louis ascended to the vital breezes; God crowns your marriage with a joyous birth the day when Louis rose to the stars').
50 In Newton's letters, speeches and poems 'the war is an intermittent theme' (Binns 2008: 103). As an example, a prophecy in 159 hexameters – included in a separate section towards the end of his works and dated 1 June 1706 – alludes to the Catalan campaign and to military operations around Turin (Newton 1710, sign. D2r–E1v, from the copy at MBSB, 4 Epist. 126 m).
51 *Dum Hispania, quae Caroli est, aegre ac vix spiritum trahat et de Catalonia poene desperandum fuerit, ni laboranti provinciae praesto aderint nostra Palatini militis ex Italia auxilia* (Newton 1710: 92–3).
52 The speech was pronounced on 31 December 1707 and printed a few weeks later in Paris (copy at BL, 1090.g.9.(3.)). I quote the text from Le Jay's *Bibliotheca rhetorum praecepta et exempla complectens* (Venice, 1747, pp. 492–504), from the copy at Barcelona, Biblioteca Pública Episcopal, 106141.
53 *Hic forte mirari vobis contingat, auditores, aut etiam expostulare nullam factam esse a me Bervichii mentionem, qui tantam in tanto opere partem sibi vindicat* ('Here it may perhaps happen that you, my audience, are surprised or even complain that I have not made any reference to Berwick, who in such an important affair demands such an important part for himself', p. 501). Praise of Berwick is preceded by a description of the Duke of Orleans's military virtues.
54 *Liceat et illud, auditores, inter adversa nostra computare quod intactas adhuc Galliae provincias oppugnare hostes praesumpserint* (p. 502).
55 The text is available in three eighteenth-century copies (BUB, B-54/1/1; BNE, VE/1463/12; and HAB, Gi 4° 3) and in a modern edition with Catalan translation in *Barcelona atacada pels francesos* 2014. The dedication (ff. 3–4) is signed by a certain I. C. Collus, who exhorts Charles to live and rule according to the principles of the Christian faith.
56 The proem is followed by a description of Barcelona which echoes the opening of the *Aeneid*: the Catalan capital (*Urbs antiqua manet princeps*, l. 9) and the fortress of Montjuïc ([*rupes*] *quam veteres olim dixere coloni*, l. 17), are compared to the Carthaginian city of Tyre, featured at the beginning of Virgil's epic: *Urbs antiqua fuit (Tyrii tenuere coloni)* – 'There was an ancient city the Tyrean colonists held', *Aen.* 1.12).
57 The programmatic words *dicere fert animus* (1.3) and *Musa mihi carmen praesta* (1.5) draw on, respectively, Ovid, *Met.* 1.1, *fert animus . . . dicere*, and Virgil, *Aen.*1.8, *Musa, mihi causas memora*. For the former, see also Lucan, *Pharsalia* 1.67: *fert*

animus causas tantarum expromere rerum. Other intertextual echoes are: *Qui flammis omnia lustras* (1.3) – *Sol, qui terrarum flammis opera omnia lustras* (*Aen.* 4.607); *fama super aethera tollit* (1.73) – *fama super aethera notus* (*Aen.* 1.378); *milite complent* (1.73) – *armato milite complent* (*Aen.* 2.20); *pueri innuptaeque puellae* (1.228) – *pueri circum innuptaeque puellae* (*Aen.* 2.238); *disiecti fractique hostes ultroque repulsi* (2.238) – *incipiam. Fracti belli fatisque repulsi* (*Aen.* 2.13); *Ut patrios fines et dulcia visent arva* (2.6) – *nos patriae finis et dulcia linquimus arva* (Virg., *Eclogues* 2.3); *Iam flumina sanguinis ibant* (1.175) – *iam flumina nectaris ibant* (Ov., *Met.* 1.111); *Lactea nomen habet* (1.238) draws on Ov., *Met.* 1.169. See also the previous note.

58 *haec pacem vobis et candida tempora reddet, / et pulchra Carolum faciet te prole parentem* (II. 293–4). In the previous two lines II. [291–2: ... *orBi / EST IRIS CAELI (vertatur lettera) NATA* ('the goddess of the rainbow of the sky (rearrange the letters) has been born for the world')], the letters in capitals make up the Latin name *Elisabet(h)a C(h)ristina*. The text of the letter sent to the people of Barcelona is preserved in BC, Fons Bonsoms, 5758, and was edited by Fernández–Xesta y Vázquez 2018. For the counter-propagandistic function served by the document after defeat at Almansa, see León Sanz 2020: 153.

59 As noted by León Sanz (2020: 161), the arrival of Elisabeth Christine and the celebration of the royal wedding ushered in a sense of euphoria among the Catalan ruling classes and institutions, which led Figueró to describe 1708 as a 'triumphant year'.

60 It is worth remembering that examples of this practice can also be found in the Bourbon camp, as explored elsewhere in this book.

61 I have inspected the copy held at ÖNB, 305019-A. The nine texts in *Laureae novi saeculi* also feature in *Leopoldi magni et Iosephi primi Caesarum invictissimorum victoriae praecipuae* ('Distinguished victories of the unvanquished emperors Leopold I and Joseph I', Vienna, 1708, pp. 106–43), a collection describing Austrian victories against the Turks and the French, which went through several reprints by 1720.

62 See, for example, the depiction of Prince Eugene of Savoy leading his troops on the French redoubts in *The Battle of Malplaquet*, oil on plaster, by Louis Laguerre (1663–1721) and assistants, *c*. 1713–14, a painting decorating one of the two flanking staircases of Marlborough House, the London residence of the Duke and Duchess of Marlborough (Royal Collection Trust, RCIN 408438; Figure 5 but b/w). It should be noted that contemporary French accounts of the battle also present it as a Bourbon victory (Fogel 1989: 448–50).

63 The ode may have been recited on a public occasion, as attested by the subscription *Ita demisse accinuit W. E. G. Presbyter* ('Thus W. E. G., Priest, humbly sang').

64 Oury describes Villaviciosa as the 'chef-d'oeuvre du duc de Vendôme', featuring in the 'galerie de Batailles' at Versailles (2020: 339). Significantly, the battle was celebrated by the Habsburg as a victory (Hengerer 2018: 218, n. 43).

65 Interestingly, Brihuega was celebrated by the Austrians as a victory in a brief report addressed to Charles by Starhemberg in early 1711 (HAB, M: Gi 207).
66 On the role of the local senate in organizing civic festivals in eighteenth-century Palermo see Di Fede 2005–6.
67 See, for example, the following marble inscription on the façade of the Senate Palace recorded by Vitale: *PHILIPPO V Regi, victori per Castellanam fortitudinem et Gallicam virtutem infensis hostibus ad Brihuegam exterritis, captis; ad Villam vitiosam contritis, caesis; ad Gerundam pulsis, deletis, brevi dierum intervallo; eadem festinatione maximum S. P. Q. Panormitanus triumphum decrevit* ['To King Philip V, victorious after the threatening enemies were terrified and captured at Brihuega through Castilian fortitude and Gallic valour; after they were crushed and beaten at Villaviciosa; after they were expelled and destroyed at Girona after a short interval of days. With the same promptness the Senate and People of Palermo ordained lavish triumphal festivities', p. 112, from the copy held at the Biblioteca Nazionale Centrale di Firenze, (3) 1711 (R)].
68 *Philippo V Hispaniarum regi Catholico ob caesos acie pulsosque occupatis urbibus ac regnis hostes epinicia in regio Ludovici magni Collegio* (Paris, 1711, copy at Paris, Bibliothèque de la Sorbonne, U 60).
69 Noailles's campaign in northern Catalonia is also the subject of an Alcaic ode in Latin by Claude-Louis Waltrin, O.S.A. (fl. 1713), entitled *Mars Russinonaeus* ('The Mars from the Roussillon', s.l., s.d.), which is available in a copy at Lyon, Bibliothèque Municipale, 358017.
70 *Non antevertunt ora victoris minae / comesque vindictae furor, / sed gratia et pax atque post iniuriam / oblita poenae lenitas. Gerunda testis quique Germano datam / Sycoris recantavit fidem* ('The threats of the vanquisher do not place themselves before your faces, nor does fear, companion of revenge, but, after you affront, grace, peace and gentleness forgetful of your punishment. Witness are Girona and the Segre [flowing through Lleida], which revoked the fidelity given to the German', ll. 41–6).
71 *At si imperantis mite detrectas iugum / dominumque male sana abnuis, / post ferrum et ignes, post face ambustas domos / turresque adaequatas solo, / sera dolebis, Barcino, admissum nefas / purgasse poenitentia*. In Loungeval's ode examined above, Barcelona – 'ill passion of war' – is addressed by the poet in similar terms: 'Why do you not lay down your arms, whilst there is time to repent? (*quin arma ponis, dum veniae locus?*, l. 58 [p. 9]).
72 Pro-Bourbon propagandists also employed the vernacular in their efforts to persuade the authorities in Barcelona to surrender to Philip V [see, for example, the pamphlets *Exortació catholica dirigida a la nació catalana* ('Catholic exhortation addressed to the Catalan nation'), s.l., c. 1711, BC, Fons Bonsoms, 627, in Catalan, and *Copia de carta escrita por un vezino de Barcelona, amonestandola...a que se*

entregue a su legítimo rey Phelipe V ('A copy of the letter written by a citizen of Barcelona urging the city to surrender to its legitimate king, Philip V'), Madrid, c. 1713, BC, Fons Bonsoms, 7538, in Spanish].

73 *Agnosce regem, perfida Barcino. / Nam quid paventes nunc aquilas foves? / Dabis ruinam concidesque / sub laceris male tuta pennis.*

74 Colonel von Fresen's heroic defence was celebrated in *Laureae novi saeculi*, as mentioned in the previous section.

75 The text is also included in Sanadon's complete poems (see n. 45 above, pp. 69–74), accompanied by two French translations of the same piece (see n. 45 above, pp. 255–62 and pp. 263–7). One of these versions, by the poet and playwright Gilles de Caux de Montlebert (c. 1682–1733), had been printed separately by Collombat a month after his own edition of the original Latin text, which provides a good indication of the wide circulation of Sanadon's encomiastic poetry in contemporary Paris. I have consulted the 1712 Latin edition in the copy at BnF, YC-12262.

76 *Olim talis erat, quum Momorancios, / Turrenas, Catinatios / ducebat rapido fida comes gradu / inter funera nobilem / mercari impavidos sanguine lauream* (ll. 16–20). Here Sanadon refers to Henri de Turenne, Nicolas Catinat and François-Henri de Montmorency, duke of Luxembourg, three illustrious French commanders of the Louis XIV era.

77 The *pré carré* was a double line of fortresses guarding the French border.

78 *Qua Villartius ingruit, / hostiles Libitina immiserabili / proturbat cuneos manu.* See also ll. 103–5: *Instat Martigenae alitis / fidens auxilio victor, inutiles / murorum exuperat minas* ('Courageous with assistance from Mars' bird the vanquisher threatens and surmounts the useless menaces of the walls'). Both passages may be interpreted as an implicit rebuke of Villars's tactics, which cost him 2,100 casualties, most in the initial assault on the Allied entrenchments (Lynn 1999: 354).

79 *Nequiquam temerariis / obstat consiliis Anna, Britannicum / quae nutu mare temperat, / pacales oleas* [probably alluding to Ovid, *Met.* 6.101] *lauricomis amans / interponere frondibus* (ll. 47–51).

80 This phenomenon applies not just to the corpus of texts written in Latin but to the total output in all languages.

3 Latin Writing between Court, Church and Academia during the War of the Spanish Succession

1 For the circumstances surrounding Elisabeth Christine's controversial conversion to Catholicism, see Peper 2010: 113–84. For the symbolism attached to Whit Sunday, the date chosen by the Imperial court for the celebration, see Matsche 1981: 179. For contemporary accounts of the new queen's journey to Barcelona, see Koch 2004.

2   As recorded by the catalogues of several European libraries (BC, Biblioteca Nacional de Portugal and HAB, *ss.vv.* Charles VI, Elisabeth Christine of Brunswick-Wolfenbüttel and Maria Anna of Austria), as early as April 1707 congratulatory orations as well as musical and literary *epithalamia* in the vernacular were published in Barcelona, Halle, Helmstedt and Lisbon to commemorate both the engagements and the official wedding ceremonies. For the texts produced in Barcelona, see Casademunt i Fiol 2011 and Chapter 2 above, pp. 75–6. The festivities in the Catalan capital included a firework display and the staging of two operas in Italian (Carreras i Bulbena 1902: 113–30). It is worth noting that Elisabeth Christine landed in Mataró, north of Barcelona, on 25 July 1708. The date was no coincidence, for 25 July is the Feast of St. James, patron saint of Spain (see Serrano Méndez 2008 for a description of the welcome reception in Mataró).

3   These are Öttl 1708a and Öttl 1708b. The volumes bear the titles *Festiva acclamatio serenissimae ac potentissimae Elisabethae Christinae ... dum ad ineundum cum Carolo III rege Catholico connubium Vienna discederet* ('A festive acclamation for the most serene and mightiest Elisabeth Christine ... as she departed from Vienna to join Charles, Catholic king, in matrimony', Vienna, 1708, copy at ÖNB, 303388-C.Adl.5), and *Syncharisticon amoris imperio reginae Mariae Annae archiduci Austriae, dum felici nuptiali faedere serenissimo ac potentissimo Lusitaniae et Algarbiae regi Ioanni V illigata sub idem amoris imperium iret ter fausto connubio orbi gaudium paritura* ('A greeting poem under the rule of love for Queen Maria Anna, archduchess of Austria whilst, bound in joyful nuptial alliance to John V, most serene and mightiest king of Portugal and Algarve, she departed to the same rule of love to bring joy to the world in thrice propitious matrimony'), Vienna, 1708, copy at ÖNB, 303388-C.Adl.6. Both texts are briefly mentioned in Klecker 2008: 52–3. Two further examples of Latin valedictory writing in honour of Maria Anna of Austria are Anton Steyerer's chronogrammatic collection of votive poems *Mariae Annae archiduci ad augustas Portugalliae coronas ex Austria proficiscenti felix iter!* ('Joyful journey for Archduchess Maria Anna as she departed from Austria for the august kingdom of Portugal!'), Vienna, 1708 (ÖNB, 303388-C.Adl.7), and Johann Müller's *Vota academica* ('Academic vows'), s.l., 1708, a speech pronounced in Prague on the occasion of Maria Anna's passing through the city, available online at ELTE Digital Institutional Repository (EDIT) and accessed on 28 February 2021.

4   See, for example, *Wiener Zeitung*, no. 493, 21–4 April 1708, p. 2, and no. 515, 7–10 July 1708, p. 2.

5   *Bella gerant alii, tu felix Austria nube* is based on Ovid, *Heroides*, XII, 84: *bella gerant alii, Protesilaus amet* ('Let others wage wars; let Protesilaus love!'), and XVII, 254: *bella gerant fortes, tu, Pari, semper ama!* ('Let the valiant wage wars; you, Paris, ever love').

6 *Syncharisticon* 1708, sign. C1v: *novus orbis reperiendus trans Atlanticum, cum Philippum Austriacum Ferdinandi Castellae regis haeredem instituerent coeli, ut, dum crescere Austriaca gens orbi non posset magnitudine, genti illi orbes crescerent. Talium tu, regina serenissima, sanguis es et serus, ut fructus existas tot gloriosorum saeculorum et parentum ac velut mare tantorum fluviorum unum compendium* ('A new world was to be found beyond the Atlantic as heaven proclaimed Austrian Philip heir to Ferdinand, king of Castile, so that, whilst the Austrian people could not expand in the world, those worlds would expand for them. You, most serene queen, are also a late descendant of these so you may prove to be the fruit of so many glorious centuries and ancestors, as the sea is a single amalgam of so many rivers').

7 For Austrian interests (of a religious and intellectual kind, rather than economic and political ones) in the colonial sphere, see Auer 2018.

8 For the political implications of the union of the House of Habsburg and the House of Bragança, see León Sanz 2008.

9 The full line reads: *iam nova progenies coelo demittitur alto* ('a new lineage is sent down from high heaven'). The so-called Sibylline books, in which a new Golden Age was prophesied, were said to contain the utterances of a Sibyl or prophetess who operated in Cumae, near Naples, in the sixth century BCE.

10 *Tagrus* is the Latin name of a mountain in Portugal, just north of the Cape of Roca (Varro, *De re rustica*, 2, 1, 19).

11 *Ioannis, exple pectus amoribus / caroque nexu connubii liga* (ll. 125–6).

12 A common literary motif both in the vernacular tradition and in Neo-Latin verse and prose, the legend survives in various versions, one of which features the lovers as a young man from Antequera and a woman from nearby Archidona (Maestre Maestre 1994).

13 Words in this opening line are reminiscent of Lucretius' invocation in *De rerum natura* to 'nourishing Venus' (*alma Venus*, 1.2), and of Ovid's *Metamorphoses* in which the chariot of the goddess is described as 'drawn through the light air by two turtle doves' (*perque leves auras iunctis invecta columbis*, 14.597).

14 Virgil's second eclogue begins with the line *Formosum pastor Corydon ardebat Alexin* ('The shepherd Corydon burned with love for the handsome Alexis').

15 I use the copy at HAB, Q 165 Helmst. 2°, 20. A reprint of the text was included in the first volume of Johann Tobias Rönick's compilation of German Neo-Latin verse (*Recentiorum poetarum Germanorum carmina latina selectiora*, Helmstedt, 1749, pp. 39–70). As confirmed both by the poem's title (*in panegyri publica humilime dicatum* – 'humbly pronounced in a public festival oration') and Werlhof's obituary (Friedrich August Hackemann, *Programma orationi solenni in obitum . . . Werlhofii*, Helmstedt, 1711, sign. A3v), the *epithalamium* was recited, partly or in its entirety, at the University of Helmstedt on 31 August 1708 during an official ceremony at which

a congratulatory oration in German was also pronounced by Justus Christoph Böhmer, whom we have encountered in Chapter 1. On the eve of the ceremony Werlhof, at the time rector of the university, wrote a formal invitation in Latin to Böhmer's speech (*Pro-Rector Academiae Iuliae Iohannes Werlhofius civibvs academicis S. P. D.*, Helmstedt, 1708).

16 In a remarkable meeting between contemporary journalism and this mythologically inspired literary fiction, the *Wiener Zeitung* (no. 439, 15–18 October 1707, p. 2) reports that on 18 October 1707 the Spanish ambassador to the Imperial court in Vienna presented Princess Elisabeth Christine with a letter from Charles and a painting of the bridegroom. Though the royal pair had been engaged since 1704, this was the day when their marriage was officially announced in the Austrian capital.

17 For a more detailed analysis of Werlhof's verse technique as well as his Virgilian and Ovidian models see Appendix 3 and Coroleu 2019.

18 This rather intricate passage focuses on Kunigunde of Altdorf (*c.* 1020–54), the first wife of Azzo II of Este with whom she had one son, Welf IV (*c.* 1037–1101). She was the only daughter of Welf II, count of Altdorf, and her brother was Welf III, duke of Carinthia. Kunigunde was also the ancestress of the younger House of Welf (Schneidmüller 2000: 123).

19 Ovid (*Met.* 15.753) speaks of 'sea-girt Britons' (*aequoreos Britannos*) when describing Caesar's exploits. For the Sicambri, see Chapter 2 above, p. 83.

20 Boge and Bogner (1999: 524–33) record at least twelve orations, mostly in the vernacular or in bilingual versions, pronounced in several German towns shortly after Joseph's death. Pompous obsequies were also organized by the Roman Collegium Germanicum Hungaricum, where Heinrich Truchseß, Count of Zeil and a fellow of the college between 1707 and 1711, was responsible for the funerary oration *Causae doloris in obitu Iosephi I Romanorum imperatoris oratio* ('Grounds for sorrow upon the death of Holy Roman Emperor Joseph I, an oration'), Rome, 1711 (copy at MBSB, 2 P.o.lat. 81, 15). On Truchseß see Steinhuber 1895: 2, 245.

21 For Latin funerary orations on Leopold I, see Goloubeva 2000: 209–10; for similar works in German, see Dauga-Casarotto 2018. For an example of the temporary structures erected for Leopold I in Vienna, see Brix 1973: 260, no. 30.

22 The full title of the volume reads *Memoria posthuma Iosephi primi in magnifico Caesarearum virtutum monumento adumbrata* ('Posthumous memorial to Joseph I, represented on a magnificent monument to Caesarean virtues'), Vienna, 1711, copy at ÖNB, 167698-C Alt Mag.

23 *Theatrum gloriae Iosephi primi*, Vienna, 1711, copy at ÖNB, 219618-C Alt. The oration is included on pp. 1–29 and the inscriptions, on pp. 30–7.

24 It is worth noting that Pliny the Younger and other Roman panegyrists were the model for Francesc Solanes's *El emperador politico y política de emperadores* ('The politic emperor and the policy of emperors'), a life of Trajan printed at Barcelona in

1700 and 1706 and dedicated to the ruling monarch (first to Charles II and to Charles III six years later).

25 *O Europa! / Quam tranquillum sperasses statum imperii, / dum bilancem tenuisset, / diutius si vixisset / tam iustus Caesar* (p. 36).

26 See the following funerary orations (all of them were published in Barcelona in 1711): Antoni Abad, *Oracion funebre en las exequias del emperador Joseph primero*; Gian Battista Ancioni, *Nell'essequie di Gioseppe il generoso re di Germania e romano imperatore orazione funebre panegirica*; Domingo Pérez, *Oratio in augustissimi imperatoris Iosephi primi regio fraterno funere*; and Juan Bautista Sicardo, *Oratio in obitu augustissimi Caesaris Iosephi huius nominis primi*. On Abad's text, which was delivered in the cathedral, see Popelka 1999: 12–13.

27 For the funeral services and related events at Santa Maria del Mar see *Apparatus et symmetria exequialium inscriptionum, quibus tum soluto, tum ligato stylo omnifariam distinctum et illustratum fuit Iosephi primi imperatoris cenotaphium, iussu Caroli tertii regis Hispaniarum extructum in Basilica Sanctae Mariae ad Mare Barcinone pridie nonas Quintiles et nonis Quintilibus currentis anni Christi Domini* ('Display and structure of the funerary inscriptions with which the memorial of Emperor Joseph I, constructed in the church of Santa Maria del Mar in Barcelona at the behest of Charles III, king of Spain, was distinguished and embellished in all cases, both in loose [i.e., not having its flow impeded by metrical laws] and bound style, on 6 and 7 July of the current year of Our Lord Jesus Christ', Barcelona, 1711, copy at BUB, C-239/6/7). The religious ceremony held at the Consulate of the Sea was recorded in *Exequias del augustissimo señor emperador Josepho primero, celebradas por el magnifico magistrado de la Lonja del Mar de la ciudad de Barcelona en su capilla de dicha Lonja el dia 21 de iulio de 1711 e ilustradas con varias inscripciones latinas* ('Obsequies of the most august Emperor Joseph I, conducted by the honourable magistrate of the Consulate of the Sea of the city of Barcelona in the chapel of the aforesaid Consulate on 21 July 1711 and illustrated with several Latin inscriptions', Barcelona, 1711, copy at BUB, B-45/2/19), which also includes an oration in Spanish by Tomás Marín (1673–1730), read at the funeral service. It is most likely that only a selection of the texts included in the books would have featured on the memorials.

28 *Apparatus et symmetria exequialium . . .*, sign. B7v (*Iosepho primo devota Carinthia naenias canit*) and sign. B8r.

29 *Panegyrico funeral que de orden del excelentissimo y fidelissimo consistorio de la Deputación del Principado de Cathaluña predicó Fray Esteve Segarra, predicador de su Magestad en las ostentosas exequias por la muerte del augustissimo Emperador Joseph primero de Austria* ('A funerary panegyric pronounced by Friar Esteve Segarra, preacher to his Majesty, at the behest of the most excellent and faithful consistory of the Diputation of the Principality of Catalonia during the elaborate funeral held to

mark the death of most august Emperor Joseph I of Austria', Barcelona, 1711, copy at BUB, 07 B-39/4/14-1). The *Dolorosos acentos de tres afligidas Musas del barcelonés Parnasso* ('Sorrowful songs by three grieving Muses of the Barcelona Parnassus') constitutes an appendix to the panegyric (pp. 53-76). The text is briefly mentioned by Popelka (1999: 22).

30 See Comas 1964: 554-5 for a brief analysis of these pieces.

31 This last line is obscure. I don't understand the link between Joseph's name and increased sorrow.

32 I use the copy held at MBSB, 4 P.o.lat. 747, 50. The title page provides no details of place of publication but the text must have been printed in the Palatinate as the volume includes a poem dedicated to Johann Wilhelm, Elector Palatine from 1690 to 1716.

33 The full title of the volume reads *Post nubila Phoebus, sive Austriae luctus ex morte duorum augustissimorum Imp. Imp. patris et filii Leopoldi et Iosephi abstersus in electione felicissima Caroli VI in Romanorum imperatorem* ('After clouds the sun, or Austrian grief caused by the death of the most august emperors, Emperor father Leopold and Emperor son Joseph, dispelled by the most auspicious election of Charles VI as Holy Roman Emperor'), s.l., 1711, copy at ÖNB, 154704-B Alt Mag. For the image of the sun, a traditional metaphor for royalty, applied to Emperor Leopold I, see Schumann 2003.

34 The inclusion of an epitaph in honour of Louis, eldest son of Louis XIV, should come as no surprise. We know that, because of their family relationship, the Imperial court held funeral services in Vienna for the Grand Dauphin of France when he died, also of smallpox, on 14 April 1711 (Hengerer 2018: 222).

35 As noted by Casarotto 2020, funeral sermons given for Emperors Leopold I and Joseph I often portrayed French policy as Machiavellian.

36 *Epitaphium tertium ponunt equites aurei velleris, qui per signum ordinis, agnum, extollunt Leopoldi mansuetudinem* ('A third epitaph composed by the knights of the Order of the Golden Fleece, who, by means of the symbol of the order, the Lamb [of God], praise Leopold's clemency'), sign. B3r-3v.

37 Presented as a renewal, the founding of the Austrian Order of the Golden Fleece was an important element of Habsburgian ideology. In November 1712 the Swedish numismatist Carl Gustav Heraeus (1671-1725) was commissioned by the Imperial court to strike a medal to mark the occasion (Polleroß 2000: 146-7). The piece featured Charles on horseback with the Latin devices *Moribus antiquis* and *Aviti ordinis equitum torquator. Aurei velleris solemmnia restituta* ('The bearer of the collar of the ancestral order of the knights. The solemn restitution of the [Order] of the Golden Fleece'). The former is part of a verse by Ennius (*Annales*, 156: *Moribus antiquis res stat Romana virisque* – 'On the traditions and heroes of ancient times the Roman state stands firm') wrongly attributed to Virgil in numismatic histories of the reign of Charles VI.

38 It is worth noting that Joseph I's sarcophagus in the *Kapuzinergruft* ('Capuchin Crypt') in Vienna was decorated with scenes from his successful campaigns during the War of the Spanish Succession (Hawlik–van de Water 1993: 138–45).

39 The royal birth was commemorated with a firework display on the Seine on 28 August (La Gorce 2007) and with a Latin poem in elegiacs (*Hispaniae ad Galliam epistola*) written by the Jesuit Eustache Lebrun (1680–1732). The child's death nine months later also elicited the anonymous *Hispaniae ad Galliam epistola consolatoria*. Surviving in rare copies held at BnF, both compositions celebrate the union of the two Bourbon crowns at a time when the tide of events in the war in Europe became unfavourable to the French.

40 In the town of La Seu d'Urgell in northern Catalonia, under Bourbon control since the autumn of 1713, the sovereign's death was marked with a volume of occasional verse in Latin, Catalan and Spanish, which was subsequently published in Barcelona, most likely after the fall of the Catalan capital in September 1714 (Comas 1964: 556–7). In the Latin poems included in the book there are no references whatsoever to the dynastic conflict. The same is true of Luis Gómez de Parada's Latin oration for the late queen, pronounced at the University of Salamanca in 1714 (I owe this reference to the *Catálogo colectivo del patrimonio bibliográfico español*, no. CCPB000170575-X, accessed on 30 November 2021).

41 See, for example, Johann Caspar Khun, *Oratio funebris consecrandae memoriae serenissimi Delphini, Ludovici magni filii* ('A funerary oration to immortalize the memory of the most serene Dauphin [of France], son of Louis XIV'), Strasbourg, 1711, and Noël-Étienne Sanadon, *Laudatio funebris Ludovici Delphini, nepotis Ludovici magni, dicta in regio Ludovici magni Collegio Societatis Iesu* ('A funerary eulogy of Louis Dauphin [of France], grandson of Louis XIV, pronounced at the Royal Collège Louis-le-Grand of the Society of Jesus'), Paris, 1712. Interestingly, a version in verse of Khun's oration by Günther Preußer was published also in Strasbourg in 1711.

42 I have inspected the copy of Pestel's poem available on *NuBIS* (accessed on 23 August 2021).

43 *Iacobo tertio, magnae Britanniae regi, pro strenuis offeruntur corda et brachia Hibernicae gentis* ('The hearts and the arms of the Irish people are offered to James III, king of Great Britain, on behalf of active men'), Paris, 1704, and *In diem natalem Iacobi tertii, magnae Britaniae regis, Musae Hibernicae plausus* ('Applause from the Irish Muse for the birthday of James III, king of Great Britain'), Paris?, 1705. Copies of the poems are held at BnF Yc. 4091 and Yc. 950 (6). Saint-John's pro-Bourbon propagandist Latin works also include *Verus heros, seu Dux de Barwick, carmen*, published to commemorate Berwick's triumph at Almansa in 1707 (BnF Yc. 4093). James Fitzjames, first duke of Berwick, was the illegitimate son of James II.

44 Although often referred to as the Treaty of Utrecht, the result of the negotiations was the Peace of Utrecht which comprised a series of discrete treaties negotiated and signed between the different warring parties between April 1713 and February 1715.
45 First printed at Paris in 1713 (copy at BnF, 8-Z Le Senne-4706), the text was included in Porée's collection of speeches (Porée 1747: 166–202, copy at BnF, X-18191), from which I quote.
46 The episode refers to an unsuccessful incursion into the Champagne province by Imperial troops under the command of Major-General Grovestein in June 1712.
47 *Gallica fortitudo ludos hosti luctuosos, Gallis laetissimos exhibet, silente Anglia, plaudente Hispania, flente Batavia, fremente Germania, Lusitania pavente, Sabaudia eventum expectante, tota circum adstante Europa et propter spectaculi magnitudinem attonita* (p. 198).
48 I use the copy of the text held at the Bibliothèque des Fontaines, Chantilly, available on Google books (accessed on 13 April 2021).
49 *Sponte concordes tibi ponit aras / ultimi potor Thamesis Britannus / quique captivum Batavus flagellat / molibus aequor* ('Of his own free will the drunken Briton of the remotest Thames erects peaceful altars to you and the Dutchman beats the captive sea with dams', ll. 9–12). In the reprint of the poem included in Sanadon's complete works (pp. 77–81) the adjective *ultimi* ('remotest') was replaced by *infidi* ('treacherous'), pointing to a more confrontational tone on the part of the poet after the new Whig government in Britain had taken retaliatory measures against several politicians for their part in the negotiations over the Peace of Utrecht (Hoppit 2014: 17).
50 *Te nimis duro data praeda Marti / poscit Europe. Tibi vota Gallus, / vota certatim tibi mille supplex / fundit Iberus*, ll. 5–8.
51 [*Allobrox et*] *quem Tagus invidenda / ditat arena. / Otii blanda vice turbulentos / pelle vesani strepitus Gradivi / et metum et curam procul inquietas / transfer in Arctos* (ll. 15–20). For Ursa Major, the Great Bear, and Ursa Minor, its twin constellation, which both revolve around the pole star, see Virgil, *Georgics* 1.245–6. In Neo-Latin poetry the nation under the noble Arctos is commonly associated with Sweden (Helander 2004: 345–9).
52 See stanza 9: *Dextera postquam rutilus tonante / Iupiter mundi tremefecit axes, / saepe depulsis pluvium serenat / aethera nimbis* (ll. 33–6), possibly alluding to Horace, *Od.* 1.2.1–4: *Iam satis terris nivis atque dirae / grandinis misit pater et rubente / dextera sacras iaculatus arces / terruit Urbem* ... ('The Father has loosed upon earth sufficient snow and hail, smitten with his livid right hand the sacred heights and terrorized Rome our city') and Virgil, *Aen.* 9.106: *annuit et totum nutu tremefecit Olympum* ('[Jupiter] nodded and with his nod he caused all Olympus to tremble').
53 *Te suis, virgo, Lodoix amicam / sentiat longum populis favere, / et triumphali placidos in umbra / exigat annos* ('May Louis perceive that you, maiden, as his friend will long

be favourable to his people, and may he spend peaceful years in triumphant leisure', ll. 45–8). As with other writers of Neo-Latin verse, here Sanadon prefers *Lodoix* as the Latin version of Louis rather than *Ludovicus* or *Lodovicus*, presumably for metrical reasons.

54 These lines, *Iam fides et fas metuensque fraudis / candor et comis redit*, are modelled on Horace, *Carmen saeculare*, 57–9: *Iam fides et pax et honos pudorque / priscus et neglecta redire virtus / audit* ('Now faith, and peace, and honour, and venerable modesty, and neglected virtue, dare to return'), a normative classical poem on the motif of the Golden Age.

55 Lines 73–4, *Te sub arguta resupinus ulmo / concinet molli Corydon cicuta* ('Lying under a whispering elm tree Corydon will sing of you with his soft pipe'), draw on several passages in Virgil's pastoral poems (*Ecl.* 1.1: *Tityre, tu patulae recubans sub tegmine fagi* – 'Tityrus, while you lie there at ease in the shade of a broad beech tree'; 5.85: *Hac te nos fragili donabimus ante cicuta* – 'I will first give you this delicate pipe'; and 7.1: *Forte sub arguta consederat ilice Daphnis* – 'Daphnis had by chance sat down under a whispering oak tree').

56 Recited at the Collège des Augustins and published in Paris on 20 March 1713, this 68-line ode in Asclepiads survives in at least two copies held in Lyon and Paris (copy used: BnF Yc.13153).

57 *Codrum grata suum Graecia iactitet, / mirabunda suos Gallia principes, / queis orbis habet dignius exhibet, / ut sint nostra quies, salus* ('Grateful Greece may show off her own Codrus but France, full of wonder, has her own princes; there is nothing in the world more worthy of display, that they may be a source of tranquillity and prosperity for us', ll. 1–4).

58 See Burman 1746: 338. I am grateful to Susanna de Beer and Floris Verhaart for drawing my attention to Burman's distich.

59 *Petri Burmanni oratio de pace inter potentissimum Galliarum regem et praepotentes foederati Belgii ordines composita*, Utrecht, 1713a, and *Redevoering over den vrede, gesloten tusschen den allermagtisten koning van Vrankryk en de hogmogende Heren Staten der Verenigde Nederlanden*, Utrecht, 1713b. For the brief analysis of Burman's oration which follows, I draw on Koen Stapelbroek's excellent summary of the Dutch text (2011: 137–8).

60 *Academiae Oxoniensis comitia philologica in theatro Sheldoniano decimo die Iulii A.D. 1713 celebrata in honorem serenissimae reginae Annae pacificae* ('Literary assembly of the University of Oxford held in the Sheldonian Theatre on 10 July 1713, in honour of the most serene and peace-loving Queen Anne'), Oxford, 1713, available in ECCO. The volume also includes an ode in English by Joseph Trapp, placed at the end. The book is unpaginated.

61 It is worth pointing out that, as early as 1712, Robinson – together with his French counterpart at Utrecht, Cardinal Melchior de Polignac (1661–1742) – was praised

for his efforts to end the war by practitioners of Neo-Latin verse elsewhere in Europe, such as the Swedish poet Magnus Rönnow, 1665–1735 (Dahlberg 2018: 412–13).

62 On Alleyn's *Commercium ad mare Australe* ('The South Sea trade') and Maynard's *Assiento, sive commercium Hispanicum* ('The Asiento, or Spanish trade'), see Money 1998: 237–8 and, above all, Gilmore 2010 and 2021.

63 *Illa nimirum auspicante, tot principum, tot heroum animi in bello plane concordes, in pace demum formanda felicius coalescunt: utinam vero omnium ita concordassent animi! Caeterum usque viribus suis nimium fisus bellum producit Austriacus; qui si tuis, regina, consiliis auscultasset, sicut olim Britannicis armis, ita nunc quoque pace Britannica securum tenuisset imperium* ('Without doubt under Anne's auspices the minds of so many princes, of so many heroes, clearly as one in war, come together more favourably in finally preparing peace: if only the minds of everybody had agreed! For the rest, the Austrian [Eugene, or the Emperor], who always has too much confidence in his own forces, prolongs the war; had he heeded your advice, Queen, as he once heeded British arms, he would also now have kept his realm secure in British peace').

64 *Ipse testatur Ludovicus . . . iam senio confectus protractique belli laboribus pene fractus, Annae ultro efflagitet amicitiam et securam demum agat senectutem; testatur Hispania, quae, dum te miratur pacis ferentem munera, sponte tibi aureos suos expandit sinus ac congestas utriusque Indiae suae opes in Britannicum quotannis aerarium lubens effundit.*

65 *Gratulatio Academiae Cantabrigiensis de pace serenissimae reginae Annae auspiciis feliciter constituta anno MDCCXIII* ('A celebration offered by the University of Cambridge on the happy agreement of peace under the auspices of most serene Queen Anne in the year 1713'), Cambridge, 1713. The volume, which is unpaginated, is also available in ECCO.

66 For the interaction between diplomacy and poetry in the work of Matthew Prior, see Jensen and Corporaal 2016: 378.

67 *Haec* [Minerva for Queen Anne] *dedit ingenium nobis, haec otia fecit*, alluding to Virgil, *Ecl.* 1.6 (*O Meliboee, deus nobis haec otia fecit*) against the backdrop of the Roman civil war. For the identification of this god who 'gave us this peace' as Octavian, see Büchner 1956: 161–4.

68 *crescentes lauros reprimat matura Britannum / gens superis dilecta, decoro / ne pigeat ramo ornari pacalis olivae. / Se vincat, quae caetera vincit* (ll. 21–4). Here metaphors from the plant kingdom (the laurel crown and the olive tree) are used by the poet to denote military triumphs and peace respectively. The last line appears to be an adaptation from a maxim by the Roman mime-writer and actor Publilius Syrus (fl. 85–43 BCE): *Bis vincit qui se vincit in victoria* – 'He who conquers himself in victory conquers twice' (1. 64). Publilius Syrus' *sententiae* were largely quoted in antiquity,

had enjoyed a wide circulation since the Renaissance (Wölfflin 1869: 23–33) and must have been known to Elliot.

69 See Hoppit 2000: 300–12 and Farguson 2015: 208.

70 See the first five lines of the poem: *Anna duas gentes (queis Magna Britannia nomen) / uniit, unitas et regit Anna duas. / Imperiis regit una aequis; hanc Gallia vidit / dictantem populo iura fidemque suo; / vidit et obstupuit* ... ('Anne united two peoples – whose name is Great Britain – and, once united, she governs both of them. She governs them as one with equal rule; France watched how she brought justice and fidelity to her people; France watched and wondered').

71 *Civis et miles feret et sacerdos / parta felici sibi servitute* (ll. 17–18). The monarch is also presented as restoring tranquillity to the British people: *Sic Deo pacis, tibi et obsequentes / regna confirmans, repares Britannos* ('By confirming your royal power, you will restore the British people, obsequious to you and the god of peace', ll. 25–6).

72 Martial, *Epigrams*, 1.3.11–12: *aetherias, lascive, cupis volitare per auras: / i, fuge; sed poteras tutior esse domi* ('You are eager, wanton one, to fly through the airs of heaven. Go! Fly! Yet you would have been safer at home'). Two lines earlier Bolder encourages his enemy to tread other paths in Europe as 'you shall be welcome to the remote Muscovites, Swedes, and Turks' (*Gratus eris Moschis, Suedis Turcisque remotis*, l. 45), alluding to the Great Northern War (1700–21) being fought between Sweden and Russia, and to the most recent episodes of the long-running Russo-Turkish War.

73 See Frey and Frey 1995: 375.

74 *Laudis vectigal serenissimo Eugenio Sabaudiae principi bello et pace magno* (Graz, 1714). I use the copy at ÖNB, 297552- A. Adl. The passage from *Pro lege Manilia*, 28 in which Cicero describes the perfect general is reproduced separately on p. 4.

75 *Eugenius auctoritate magnus* ('Eugene distinguished by his prestige'): ... *auctoritate tua, qua gravissimam belli molem hactenus sustentasti, pacis negotium feliciter compone*, p. 36.

76 On this text see Schwarz 1991.

4 Latin Propaganda beyond the Dynastic Conflict (1715–1740)

1 *Disputatio politica de praerogativa iuris in coronam Hispanicam, qua Leopolodus Dei gratia electus Romanorum imperator gaudet eminetve prae Ludovico XIV rege Galliarum, ut vult vocari, Christianissimo* ('A political debate on the legal prerogative regarding the Spanish crown, which Leopold, elected Holy Roman Emperor by God's grace, enjoys and in which he takes precedence over Louis XIV, most Christian king of France, as he wishes to be named'), Stargard, 1719. I use the copy held at MBSB, 4 Diss. 520.

2 On p. 19 Desnovius quotes, for example, one of the riddles included in Engelbert Bischoff's chronogrammatic collection *Austriacum vale et Hispanicum ave* ('An Austrian farewell and a Spanish greeting') discussed in Chapter 1 (p. 20). Elsewhere in the text (p. 20) a *Certamen de corona Hispanica* ('A contest for the Spanish crown') purported to have been held in 1701 features all the protagonists in the dynastic dispute, alongside the pope and Fame, who lay claim to the throne of Spain also through chronogrammatic verse.
3 The only copy known to exist is held at Sächsische Landesbibliothek – Staats- und Universitätsbibliothek, Dresden, Hist. Germ. D. 243.
4 A close aid to Charles in Barcelona – where he married into the Catalan nobility –, Stella followed Charles on his return to Vienna in 1712 and soon became a prominent member of the Imperial administration (León Sanz 2020: 164).
5 Charles VI is, for example, praised for his ability to speak Latin and for his knowledge of several modern languages: ... *nunc quinque idiomata linguam / expediunt; Germanus, Gallus ab ore loquentis, / Italus, Hispanus pendent sinul atque Latinus, / quisque suo putat ore loqui* ... ('Now five languages trip off his tongue: Germans, French, Italians and Spaniards listen attentively when he speaks, as do those who speak Latin; everyone thinks he speaks their own language', ll. 205–8). Kalmár's findings (2020: 66–7) seem to confirm that Charles's linguistic proficiency and command of Latin were no poetic licence on San Marco's part.
6 Though the Allies were forced to retreat from Toulon after sustaining heavy losses, Louis XIV ordered the French fleet inside the harbour to be partially sunk to prevent it being completely destroyed.
7 Ovid's words *Est deus in nobis* (*Fasti*, 6.5) are reproduced verbatim in l. 436.
8 A copy of the engraving is held at the Arxiu Històric de la Ciutat de Barcelona (reg. 18265) and is reproduced and discussed in Alcoberro 2013: 126–31. For the Virgilian source (*Georgics* 2.173) of the title, see González Germain 2017.
9 The text of the prefatory *Explicatio Ichnographiae* [sic] also emphasizes the resilience shown by the people of Barcelona and portrays the besieging army as a foreign enemy: *Oppugnatio et defensio urbis Barcinonensis, tuentibus eam indigenis contra exercitum Hispanico-Gallicum, quatuordecim mensium obsidione, inchoata die vigesimo quinto Iulii anno millesimo septingentesimo decimo tertio usque ad undecimum diem Septembris, anno millesimo septingentesimo decimo quarto. Describuntur castrametationes et munimenta tam oppugnantium quam defendentium, adductis quibusdam eruptionibus et dimicationibus pro meliori notitia eventuum; ut ex literis et numeris sequentibus patebit* ('Assault and defence of Barcelona, whilst its citizens protected it against the Spanish and French army, under a siege of fourteen months, begun on 25 July 1713 and lasting until 11 September 1714. Camps and fortifications of both the assailants and the defenders are also depicted, with an

indication of breakthroughs and combats to provide a better knowledge of the events, as will become apparent from the following letters and numbers').

10 The *Discursus* is included in the *Tractatus de tacita onerum et conditionum repetitione* ('A treatise on the secret reclamation of goods and stipulations'), Vienna, 1721, from the copy at ÖNB, 35 G. 12. The volume was reprinted two years later in Venice by Niccolò Pezzana.

11 This is dealt with in the chapter entitled *Quid sub nomine Generalitatis Cathaloniae contineatur?* ('What does the Generalitat of Catalonia comprise?' pp. 8–10). In a contemporary tract on the history of the Royal Palace in Barcelona written in Spanish (Vienna, 1725), Aguirre declares Catalonia an independent entity, based on the principle of a contractual agreement between the king and his subjects, which could only be amended or confirmed at meetings of the Catalan parliament (see De Montagut i Estragués 2004–2006, who also provides detailed information on Aguirre's biography).

12 The texts are preserved in Biblioteca Nazionale Bridense, MS AF XI 12. An annotated Catalan translation of *De Cataloniae Principatu* can be read in Plantí 2019 (with the original Latin text available online at https://de.scribd.com/document/437502888/De-Cathalauniae-principatu-de-Josep-Planti); Plantí 2022 has a bilingual edition (Latin and Catalan) of the *De morte Caroli secundi*, from which I quote. Both volumes include extremely well-informed introductions to Plantí and his work. I am grateful to Martí Duran for procuring me a copy of his transcription of the Latin text of the *De Cataloniae Principatu*.

13 *De rebus nostrae Cataloniae tractaturus, in quantum potero exterorum notitiis vel eorum approbationibus ac dictis concedam, iuxta illud proverbium 27:* '*Laudet te alienus et non os tuum; extraneus et non labia tua*'; *talibus meliori de ratione tanquam minus suspectis creditur istique vero sine afectione loquuntur* ('I am about to deal with matters relating to our Catalonia and, as much I can, I shall give precedence to the knowledge of foreigners or to their opinions and remarks, according to *Proverbs* 27 [verse 2]: "Let someone else praise you, and not your own mouth; an outsider, and not your own lips"; for such men are credited as much with better reasoning as they are regarded with less suspicion and they tell the truth without feeling', f. 117r). Use of the future participle *tractaturus* at the beginning of Plantí's account may be reminiscent of the opening words in Livy's *History of Rome* (*Facturusne operae pretium*).

14 Significantly, the chapter entitled *De litteris, scientiis ac artibus Catalanorum* ('On Catalan letters, sciences and arts', ff. 193r–6v) contains a eulogy of the eight 'Catalan' universities (including the one in Perpignan), at a time when the new Bourbon administration had abolished all the universities in the Principality and created a new one in Cervera, near Lleida.

15 These positive features are discussed in the chapters *De genio Catalanorum* ('On the spirit of Catalans', f. 150r) and *De fidelitate Catalanorum et amicitia in amicos* ('On the loyalty and friendship of Catalans towards their friends', ff. 181r–6v).

16 Interestingly, Plantí alludes to the propaganda campaign undertaken by the Habsburg dynasty in support of Charles following the publication of Charles II's will, which I examined in Chapter 1: *ad suum ius ostendendum iustitiamque monstrandam, plura ad publica ediderunt iuridica scripta* ('[Emperor Leopold and his son Joseph] published many legal documents to show his rights and to prove justice', Plantí 2022: 58).

17 It is tempting to speculate about the reasons why Plantí's works were never brought to the press. The tone, at times very critical of the emperor and the Allies, and the change in the wider geopolitical scenario after the signing of the Peace of Vienna in 1725 may have been deterrents to publication.

18 *Qua vero ratione ab aliquibus scriptoribus impropriis indecorosis ac criminosibus verbis tractentur Catalani pro ista defensione, non intellego* ('Yet, I do not understand why Catalans, on account of this defence [of Barcelona], should be discussed with disgraceful and slanderous words by some unsuitable writers', Plantí 2022: 134).

19 See, for example, Plantí's personal statement in his *De Cataloniae Principatu*: *aliquid de mea patria Barcinone non tacere et connaturalis ratio filiationis exigit, praesens tempus expostulat; utique impulsiva huius operis causa cogit, vindicando ab iniuriis scribentium iustitia, veritas amorque constringunt* ('A natural affiliation also compels me to speak up about my fatherland Barcelona, and this is demanded by the present situation: certainly, the impelling cause of this work also compels me, and with justice vindicating me of the wrongdoings of those who write, truth and love keep me in check', f. 133v).

20 Oxford [but this is clearly a fabrication], 1736, from the copy at Barcelona, Biblioteca Pública Episcopal, 946.71 Rec. Agustí Alcoberro (2007: 171) suggests the Low Countries as the place of publication. The Catalan version of the text is also available in Torras i Ribé 1996: 61–83, where 'the voluminous critical apparatus of the original Latin text, currently anachronistic for most of the quotations', is significantly omitted. For her part, Alabrús seems not to have consulted the eighteenth-century original volume but only a modern Catalan edition, for she claims that the text 'was written in Catalan, with the odd insertion in Latin' (2001: 408).

21 In the Latin text, for example, Grotius's work is quoted by the presumed editor to prove that Queen Anne's instructions to her ministers to engage in negotiations with the Catalan delegates present at Genoa were not 'only the personal acts of the queen but formal regal acts, meaning the entire kingdom and her successors were bound by the queen in perpetuity' (*Nec acta haec fuere tantum reginae personalia, sed rite regalia, obligandis regno integro reginaque successoribus perpetuo*, sign. b1r). The source is explicitly acknowledged in note 23 (*De iure belli et pacis*, 2.14.1, 2).

22 The passage in the main text reads as follows: *Imperantes Austriaci, neutiquam arrogato sibi absoluto dominatu (quem praedicti Ludovici XIV magisterium videtur tradidisse regibus in morem communem), ubi esset hic legibus regulandus, iusta*

lenitate firmabant sceptrum monarchicum; quod eo debilius fit in aliis, quo plus sibi plaudit acquirere roboris ('Austrian masters, having by no means claimed absolute rule for themselves [which the teachings of the aforesaid Louis XIV seem to have customarily handed over to kings], when rule should have been regulated with the aid of laws, strengthened the royal sceptre with fair lenience; the more power they are happy to amass for themselves, the weaker the royal sceptre becomes for others', sign. a3v).

23 At the end of his prefatory letter the putative annotator expresses his hope that 'Catalans should hear the poet who speaks on behalf of the English on earth' (*audiant Catalani in terra vatem pro Anglis loquentem*) and quotes the following lines from Virgil's poem: *Alter erit tum Typhis, et altera quae vehat / Argo delectos heroas: erunt etiam altera bella / atque iterum ad Troiam magnus mittetur Achilles* ('With a new Tiphys at the helm, a second Argo will set out, manned by a picked crew of heroes. There will even be other wars and the great Achilles must be despatched to Troy once more', *Eclogues* 4.34–6).

24 The *Record de la aliança* and other contemporary anti-Bourbon texts in the vernacular were, for example, published again in Barcelona in the late 1890s alongside reprints of Latin and Catalan texts related to the anti-Castilian War of Separation between 1640 and 1652 (Marfany 1995: 191–6).

25 Charles's accession to the throne of Sicily was also disputed by the rival camp. A prominent Bourbon propagandist in Sicily, Giovanni Battista Palermo rebuked Pope Innocent XIII's investiture of Charles VI in 1721 as king of Sicily in his *Libellus defensivus ad Philippum V regem Hispaniarum et ad Principem Asturiarum super nullitate investiturae concessae a Innocentio XIII imperatori Carolo VI regnorum utriusque Siciliae* ('A booklet in defence of Philip V, king of Spain, and of the Prince of Asturias on the matter of the nullity of the investiture of Emperor Charles VI as king of the two Sicilies [Sicily and Naples] granted by Innocent XIII'), BNE, MS 6771. Palermo is also the author of *Tractatus de successione regni Galliae ad tenorem legis Salicae et de nullitate renunciationis serenissimi regis Philippi V* ('A treatise on the succession of the kingdom of France in Salic law and on the nullity of the renunciation of most serene King Philip V'), BNE, MS 6561.

26 Palermo, 1720, copy available on Google books (accessed on 11 March 2022).

27 The last line in Turano's poem is an adaptation from Martial *Epigr.* 2.2.6: *quae datur ex Chattis laurea, tota tua est* ('the laurel which is given from the conquest of the Catti is all your own').

28 On Philip V's abdication, which had been subject to discussion since at least 1719, see Kamen (2000: 173–7), for whom the renunciation on religious grounds is only the official explanation, the main reason being the king's bipolar disorder.

29 Among those who fully accepted Philip's religious reasons was, for example, Noël-Étienne Sanadon, the author of the ode *Ad religionem, quum Philippus V,*

Hispaniae rex, imperio abdicaret ('To religion, as Philip V, king of Spain, abdicated'), Paris, 1724, copy at BnF, YC-920 (25), which praises the monarch's spiritual motives for abdication. In this edition the Latin text is followed by a French translation of the poem by the Jesuit Pierre Brumoy (1688–1742).

30 I have consulted the Spanish and Latin copies of Bacallar's *Comentarios* held at BUB, C-212/5/29–30 and B-69/9/38 respectively, one of the only two libraries (alongside BNE) which hold copies of both the Latin and vernacular texts. The Latin translation was also published in Genoa in 1725 but the volume provides no details of the printer's name. A modern edition of the Spanish text, in which significantly no mention whatsoever is made of the Latin translation, is easily accessible in Bacallar 1957.

31 Vienna, 1728, from the copy at ÖNB, 676151-A; the text is mentioned by Matsche 1981: 44–5 and Klecker 2008: 84.

32 I owe this information to Alcoberro 2003: 340.

33 The text is available in a modern edition with translations of the poems for each month and of the paratexts 'in a multitude of languages illustrating the cultural diversity of the Danubian monarchy and the European networks of the Habsburg family' (*Fasti* 1736 [2015]: 11). The volume includes my Spanish translation of October (*Fasti* 1736 [2015]: 117–27).

34 Abylla and Calpe are the Pillars of Hercules on the Strait of Gibraltar and 'further beyond' (*plus ultra*) is a reference to Charles V's personal motto. The Herculean work he commissioned might be the *Decades* of Pietro Martire d'Anghiera (1457–1526), accounts of the recently discovered territories in Central and South America (first complete edition in 1530). I am grateful to David Barnett for drawing my attention to this point.

35 The paratexts to lines 43–4 and lines 45–8 shed light on these allusions: *Vide 14. Octobr. Anno 1705. CAROLUS III. Hisp. Rex, nunc Aug. Rom. Imp. Barcinonem Catalauniae metropolim, terra marique acerrime oppugnatam, deditione occupat* ('See 14 October 1705. Charles III, king of Spain, now august Holy Roman Emperor, seizes Barcelona, capital of Catalonia, after having fiercely attacked it by land and sea') and *Vide 12. Octobr. Anno 1711. Eadem, qua Genuam ex Hispania appulsus est, die Francofurti unanimi imperii electorum assensu Romanorum rex dicitur CAROLUS VI* ('See 12 October 1711. On the very same day on which he was driven from Spain to Genoa, with the unanimous approval of the electors of the Empire, he was declared in Frankfurt king of the Romans with the name of Charles VI').

36 *Repraesentatio ac descriptio sacri rogi quem Carolo VI . . . erigendum curavit antiquissima Universitas Vindobonensis* ('Representation and description of the sacred grave which the most ancient University of Vienna undertook to erect for Charles VI'), Vienna, 1741, copy at MBSB, Res/2 Or. fun. 398,17. The description of the inscriptions is included on pp. 1–5 and the oration, on pp. 7–54. A German version of both texts was published in Vienna later that year.

37 The two references to Elisabeth Christine's sojourn in Catalonia read as follows: (top inscription) *MDCCVIII. I AVG. CAROLO BARCINONAE FELICI CONNVBIO IVNCTAE* ('[To Elisabeth Christine] joined on 1 August 1708 in happy matrimony with Charles in Barcelona') and (bottom inscription) *[FEMINA] SVB EXPEDITIONE HISPANICA COMES LABORVM, SOLLICITVDINVM, CVRARVM IN SVMMO FASTIGIO REGIO PRIVATORVM SORTEM EXPERTA* ('[This woman], as partner in exertion, disquiet and concern during the Spanish campaign, experienced the fortunes of the common folk at the peak of royal power'). Here I reproduce both inscriptions only partially.

38 It should be noted that Charles's victory at Saragossa – one of the last Allied successes on Spanish soil – had been a recurring theme within the Habsburg propaganda machine since the end of the War of the Spanish Succession. As an example, a German poem in praise of Charles's valour during the battle featured in *Vermischte Nebenarbeiten Hn. Carl Gustafs Heraei, Käyserl. Raths und Antiquitäten-Inspectors* ('Various additional works by Carl Gustav Heraeus, Imperial councillor and antiques inspector', Vienna, 1715, sign. B1r–D1r, copy at MBSB, 4 P.o.germ. 90). This miscellaneous volume includes a small collection of vernacular and Latin panegyric verse on behalf of Charles VI and Elisabeth Christine, several Latin inscriptions related to the Habsburg dynasty as well as samples of medals relating to Charles's reign minted by the Imperial numismatist. I owe this information to Klecker 2015: 25, who also shows how a manuscript copy of the Saragossa piece (now ÖNB, Cod. 8322) was presented by Heraeus as a token for Emperor Charles VI on his thirtieth birthday.

Appendix 3 Two Eighteenth-Century Latin Poets at Work

1 Lines 1–3 = *LVO*, 69–71 (*Hic vir ... aequis*).
2 Lines 9–10 = *Ligurinus,* VIII.535–6 (*hic ... reducit*).
3 Lines 11–25 = *LVO*, 72–86 (*Si dotes ... se limine promit*).
4 *Aen.* 7.279 reads ... *fulvum mandunt sub dentibus aurum.*
5 Lines 27–33 = *LVO*, 88–94 (*portat equus ... ictusque lacessit*).
6 Lines 34–5 = *Ligurinus,* I.315–6 (*Qualis erit ... sub principi surget*).
7 Line 37 = Ausonius, *Epistles*, 24.89 (*Tarraco ... ponto*).
8 Line 40 = *Ligurinus,* VI.388 (*agnoscit ... fatetur*).
9 Lines 44–6 = Riccardo Bartolini, *Austrias*, 6.535–7 (*non fuit hoc animo ... iura volo imperii*).
10 Lines 48–9 = *Ligurinus,* III.92–3 (*ulcisci scelerum ... fraenare superbos*).
11 Lines 51–2 = *Ligurinus,* IV.515–6 (*sancta et plena ... iure recursum*).
12 Lines 53–6 = *Ligurinus,* I.100–4 (*O vere magni ... subtenditur undas*).

13 Lines 59–60 = *LVO*, 108–9 (*Omnia virtutis sunt . . . insignia laudis*).
14 Lines 61–2 = *Ligurinus*, IV.594–5 (*Nec de tam . . . tentanda Camaena*).
15 Lines 63–6 = *Ligurinus*, IV.603–6 (*Non est exigui . . . sub fasce laborem*).
16 Lines 69–70 = *Ligurinus*, VI.119–20 (*cum sit cunctorum . . . cessurus in orbe*).
17 *Aen*. 4.584–5: *Et iam prima novo spargebat lumine terras / Tithoni croceum linquens Aurora cubile.*
18 *Aen*. 3.589: *umentemque Aurora polo dimoverat umbram.*
19 *Aen*.7.25–6: *Iamque rubescebat radiis mare et aethere ab alto / Aurora in roseis fulgebat lutea bigis*, and 12.77: *puniceis invicta rotis Aurora rubebit.*

Bibliography

Primary sources

Except for individual medals and inscriptions, the present list includes all primary sources mentioned in this volume. Anonymous and collective works come first, followed by individual authors listed alphabetically. Spelling of *Rex, Regina, Imperator* or *Archidux* is not consistent, but it reproduces the way in which these words feature on the cover pages, at times in capital letters and at times in lower case.

Anonymous and collective works

Academiae Oxoniensis comitia philologica in theatro Sheldoniano decimo die Iulii A.D. 1713 celebrata in honorem serenissimae reginae Annae pacificae (1713), Oxford.
Achilles germanicus, seu Otho I imperator ad Augustam Vindelicorum pius et fortis Vandalorum debellator (1702), Vienna.
Ad serenissimum ac potentissimum Carolum tertium Hispaniarum et utriusque Indiae monarcham, regem Catholicum, Archiducem Austriae, dum ad capessendum haereditarium Hispaniarum regnum Vienna discederet, suprema ac festiva acclamatio ab antiquissima ac celeberrima Universitate Viennensi (1703), Vienna.
Affectus Musarum Viennensium (1705), Vienna.
Anagrammatismus augustissimo et sacratissimo imperatori Carolo VI, Hispaniarum et Indiarum regi, sacer (1712), Brunswick.
Anathema serenissimi Caroli tertii regis Catholici in Monte serrato ad Beatae Virginis aram ab eodem affixum, nunc paraphrasi elegiaca plenius explicatum (1706), Vienna.
Apparatus et symmetria exequialium inscriptionum, quibus tum soluto, tum ligato stylo omnifariam distinctum et illustratum fuit Iosephi primi Imperatoris cenotaphium, iussu Caroli tertii Regis Hispaniarum extructum in basilica Sanctae Mariae ad Mare Barcinone pridie nonas Quintiles et nonis Quintilibus currentis anni Christi Domini (1711), Barcelona.
Barcelona atacada pels francesos (2014), A. Coroleu and M. Paredes (eds), Martorell.
Carolus III invictissimus Hispaniarum rex (s.d. but surely 1706), s.l.
Carta con la qual la magestad del rey...Carlos III...participa a la...ciudad de Barcelona su feliz y dichoso casamiemto (1706), Barcelona.

Clamors de Barcelona al tirà govern de Velasco (1705?), Barcelona.
Copia de carta escrita por un vezino de Barcelona, amonestandola...a que se entregue a su legítimo rey Phelipe V (1713?), Madrid.
Copia de la real carta que Carlos III...ha escrito à la imperial ciudad de Çaragoça (1706), Barcelona.
Coronatio Philipi [sic] quinti, Hispaniae regis, ab auctore quodam veridico conscripta et in partes digesta (c. 1700, manuscript copy).
Elegiaca narratio auspicatae obsidionis cum deditione excellentissimae civitatis Barcinonensis totiusque Principatus Cathaloniae (1705), Barcelona.
Elogia heroum Caesareorum in Italia (1702), Vienna.
Epinicion Oxoniense (1702), Oxford.
Exequias del augustissimo señor emperador Josepho primero, celebradas por el magnifico magistrado de la Lonja del Mar de la ciudad de Barcelona en su capilla de dicha Lonja el dia 21 de iulio de 1711 e ilustradas con varias inscripciones latinas (1711), Barcelona.
Exortació catholica dirigida a la nació catalana (1711?), s.l.
Fasti Austriae (1736 [2015]), *Ein neulateinisches Gedicht in fünfzehn europäischen Sprachen*, F. Römer, H. Bannert, E. Klecker and Ch. Gastgeber (eds), Vienna.
Germania vetus selectis quaestionibus illustrata (1712), Vienna.
Goigs de la Purissima Concepcio de Maria Santissima collocada en la Real Columna, que en lo Born de la Excellentissima Ciutat de Barcelona erigí la Catolica Magestat de Carlos Tercer (que Deu guarde) Rey de las Espanyas (1706), Barcelona.
Gratulatio Academiae Cantabrigiensis de pace serenissimae reginae Annae auspiciis feliciter constituta anno MDCCXIII (1713), Cambridge.
Hispania terque quaterque beata in septem Austriacis regibus (1704), Vienna.
Hispaniae ad Galliam epistola consolatoria (1704), Paris.
Invectiva al político govierno de don Francisco Velasco (1705), Barcelona.
La bonaventura que diguè la gitana imaginaria al duch de Anjou al partirse de Paris per lo regnat de Espanya (1707), Barcelona.
Laudis vectigal serenissimo Eugenio Sabaudiae principi bello et pace magno (1714), Graz.
Laureae novi saeculi a Marte Austriaco hoc in bello relatae (1708), Vienna.
Lessus funebris super praematura et inopinata morte Iosephi primi (1711), s.l.
Lettre à leurs hautes puissances, de l'armee a la chapelle de Montplaquet le 11. Septembre 1709 (1709), s.l.
Lettre de messieurs les deputez à leurs hautes puissances escrite de l'armee devant Mons, le 14. Septembre 1709 (1709), s.l.
Lletres curioses de la bonaventura que diguè una gitana a Carlos tercer quant partí de Viena a Espanya (1707), Barcelona.
Memoria posthuma Iosephi primi in magnifico Caesarearum virtutum monumento adumbrata (1711), Vienna.
Musae iuveniles rhetorum in regio Ludovici magni Collegio Societatis Iesu Philippo Andegavensium duci ad Hispaniarum regna evocato felicitatem gratulantur (1701), Paris.

Nummi augustorum Caroli VI et Elisabethae Christinae Viennae Austriae cusi (1728), Vienna.
Ode Sapphica serenissimo Eugenio sacra (1709), Vienna.
Philippo Franciae Hispaniarum regi dum iter in Hispanias Aurelia faceret comitantibus regiis principibus fratribus suis duce Burgundiae et duce Bituricensi offerebat Collegium regium Aurelianense Societatis Iesu (1700), s.l.
Philippo quinto Hispaniarum regi et serenissimis eius fratribus Blesis transeuntibus regium Blesense Societatis Iesu Collegium gratulatur (1700), s.l.
Philippo V Hispaniarum regi Catholico ob caesos acie pulsosque occupatis urbibus ac regnis hostes epinicia in regio Ludovici magni Collegio (1711), Paris.
Plausus Musarum Oxoniensis sive gratulatio Academiae ob res prospere terra marique gestas (1704), Oxford.
Post nubila Phoebus, sive Austriae luctus ex morte duorum augustissimorum Imp. Imp. patris et filii Leopoldi et Iosephi abstersus in electione felicissima Caroli VI in Romanorum imperatorem (1711), s.l.
Record de la aliança: fet a. serm. Jordi–Augusto, rey de la Gran–Bretaña...ab una carta del Principat de Cataluña y ciutat de Barcelona (1736), Oxford?
Relation und Continuation Diarii Ihrer Königl. Majest. in Spanien Karl des Dritten vom 29 Mertz biß 15 May 1706 (1706?), s.l.
Repraesentatio ac descriptio sacri rogi quem Carolo VI...erigendum curavit antiquissima Universitas Vindobonensis (1741), Vienna.
Repraesentatio belli ob successionem in regno Hispanico...victoriosis armis usque ad pacem Badensem felicissime et fortissime gesti (1724), Augsburg.
Serenissimo ac potentissimo Hispaniarum ac Indiarum neo-regi Carolo III, Archiduci Austriae, principi ac domino domino suo clementissimo dum Viennae in Austria declaratus regnum adiret (1703), Vienna.
Synopsis quorundam iurium Austriacorum in successionem Hispanicam (after 1700), s.l.
Theatrum bellicum (1707), Amsterdam.
Theatrum gloriae Iosephi primi (1711), Vienna.
To Plus ultra columnae Herculis in Carolo VI augustissimo Romanorum imperatore figuratae (1712), Prague.
Vota orientis anni Caesareae Maiestati dicata Ratisbonae (1705), s.l.

Individual authors

Abad, A. (1711), *Oracion funebre en las exequias del emperador Joseph primero*, Barcelona.
Affatighi, B. (*c.* 1706), *Invictissimae Anglorum regnatrici* (manuscript copy).
Aguirre, D. (1721), *Discursus super officiis venalibus Generalitatis Cathaloniae*, in: *Tractatus de tacita onerum et conditionum repetitione*, Vienna.

Álvares da Costa, J. (1705), *Aquila augusta trisulco obarmata fulmine seu Carolus tertius Austriacus rex Hispaniarum assertus*, Lisbon.

[Álvares da Costa, J.] (1707), *Gründliche Anzeige und Vorstellung des Frantzösischen Unfugs und der Oesterreichischen Befugniß zur Spanischen Succession*, Vienna?

Ancioni, G. B. (1711), *Nell'essequie di Gioseppe il generoso re di Germania e romano imperatore orazione funebre panegirica*, Barcelona.

Bacallar, V. (1725a), *Comentarios de la guerra de España e historia de su rey Phelipe V el animoso*, Genoa.

Bacallar, V. (1725b), *De foederatorum contra Philippum quintum, Hispaniarum regem, bello commentaria*, Genoa.

Bacallar, V. (1957), *Comentarios de la guerra de España e historia de su rey Felipe V, el animoso*, C. Seco Serrano (ed.), Madrid.

Barceló, T. (1706), *Pindáricas flores*, Palma de Mallorca.

Bartolini, R. (1516), *Austrias*, Strasbourg.

Beckmann, J. Ch. (1704), *Ius Austriacum in successione regnorum Hispaniae vindicatum*, Vienna?

Biscardi, S. (1703), *Epistola pro augusto Hispaniarum monarcha Philippo V*, Naples.

Bischoff, E. (1703), *Austriacum vale et Hispanicum ave*, Vienna.

Böhmer, J. Ch. (1711), *Serenissimo, potentissimo invictissimoque principi ac domino domino Carolo VI electo Romanorum imperatori...gratulatur...*, Helmstedt.

Burman, P. (1713a), *Petri Burmanni oratio de pace inter potentissimum Galliarum regem et praepotentes foederati Belgii ordines composita*, Utrecht.

Burman, P. (1713b), *Redevoering over den vrede, gesloten tusschen den allermagtisten koning van Vrankryk en de hogmogende Heren Staten der Verenigde Nederlanden*, Utrecht.

Burman, P. (1746), *Petri Burmanni poematum libri IV*, Amsterdam.

Caracciolo, G. (1704), *De Philippo V potentissimo Hispaniarum rege...carmina*, Naples.

Commire, J. (1700), *Philippo quinto regi Catholico in Hispaniam abeunti Musarum gratulatio in regio Ludovici magni Collegio Societatis Iesu*, Paris.

Densovius, Ch. and Engelken, T. H. (1719), *Disputatio politica de praerogativa iuris in coronam Hispanicam, qua Leopolodus Dei gratia electus Romanorum imperator gaudet eminetve prae Ludovico XIV rege Galliarum, ut vult vocari, Christianissimo*, Stargard.

Estarrués, M. (1701), *Festiva, gratulatoria proclamatio pro regali et Oscensi Divi Vincentii Martyris Collegio, ex Philippis quinto Hispaniarum regi Philippo, Ibereos praecurrenti, dicata*, Huesca.

Haake, J. (1706), *Carolo III Austriaco, Hispaniarum atque Indiarum regi, regnorum avitorum vindici ac assertori, terra marique triumphanti, sacrum*, s.l.

Hackemann, F. A. (1711a), *Programma orationi solenni in obitum...Werlhofii*, Helmstedt.

Hackemann, F. A. (1711b), *Programma solenni orationi in coronationem augustissimi et sacratissimi imperatoris Caroli sexti*, Helmstedt.

Heraeus, C. G. (1715), *Vermischte Nebenarbeiten Hn. Carl Gustafs Heraei, Käyserl. Raths und Antiquitäten-Inspectors*, Vienna.

Hunoldt, T. A. (1703), *Ad serenissimum ac potentissimum Carolum tertium Hispaniarum et utriusque Indiae monarcham, regem Catholicum, Archiducem Austriae, dum ad capessendum haereditarium Hispaniarum regnum Vienna discederet, suprema ac festiva acclamatio ab antiquissima ac celeberrima Universitate Viennensi*, Vienna.

Khun, J. C. (1711), *Oratio funebris consecrandae memoriae serenissimi Delphini, Ludovici magni filii*, Strasbourg.

Lebrun, E. (1704), *Hispaniae ad Galliam epistola*, Paris.

Le Camus, A. (1701), *Hispanis et Gallis gratulatio, habita Parisiis, cum Philippus, dux Andegavensis, Hispaniarum rex renuntiatus est*, Paris.

Le Camus, A. (1703), *Imago nascentis herois*, Paris.

Le Comte, J. (1701), *Ad iustitiam cum ob delatam Philippo, duci Andegavensi, Ludovici Magni nepoti, Hispanicorum regnorum hereditatem M. Baltazar Gibert, rhetorum alter, utrique regi oratione publica gratularetur in Collegio Mazarinaeo die ultima Decembris anni 1700 ode*, Paris.

Leibniz, G. W. (1704), *Manifeste contenant les droits de Charles III, Roi d'Espagne, et les justes motifs de son expédition*, The Hague.

Le Jay, G. (1708), *Res prosperas hostibus minus gloriae, quam adversas Gallis peperisse*, Paris.

May, J. B. (1711), *De augustae domus Austriacae fatis commentatio historica*, Kiel.

Mongitore, A. (1701), *Il Trionfo Palermitano, nella solenne acclamazione del cattolico re delle Spagne e di Sicilia Filippo V, festeggiata in Palermo a 30 di Gennaro 1701*, Palermo.

Montefortino, G. de (1704), *Pro Philippo quinto catholico, Hispaniarum ac Indiarum monarcha piissimo, oratio panegirica*, Naples.

Müller, J. (1708), *Vota academica*, s.l.

Newton, H. (1710), *Epistolae, orationes et carmina*, Lucca.

Noriega, B. de (1705), *Iniustitia belli Austriaci contra Catholicum Hispaniarum regem Philippum V gliscentis*, Naples.

Öttl, A. J. von (1708a), *Festiva acclamatio serenissimae ac potentissimae Elisabethae Christinae...dum ad ineundum cum Carolo III rege Catholico connubium Vienna discederet*, Vienna.

Öttl, A. J. von (1708b), *Syncharisticon amoris imperio reginae Mariae Annae archiduci Austriae, dum felici nuptiali faedere serenissimo ac potentissimo Lusitaniae et Algarbiae regi Ioanni V illigata sub idem amoris imperium iret ter fausto connubio orbi gaudium paritura*, Vienna.

Pairis, Gunther of (c. 1150–c. 1220), *Ligurinus*.

Palladio, O. (1702), *Oratio panegirica de Philippo V, invictissimo Neapolitani regni atque Hispaniarum rege*, Naples.

Pérez, D. (1711), *Oratio in augustissimi imperatoris Iosephi primi regio fraterno funere*, Barcelona.

Pestel, P. (1702), *Iacobo secundo magnae Britanniae regi mausoleum*, Paris.

Petersen, J. W. (1711), *Corona Austriaca augustissimo Carolo sexto, Romanorum imperatori gloriosissimo...Europa applaudente...subiectissime cantata*, Coloniae Brandenburgicae.

Plantí, J. (2019), *El Principat de Catalunya*, A. Alcoberro and M. Duran (eds), Barcelona.

Plantí, J. (2022), *La desfeta de Catalunya i la destrucció de Barcelona*, pròleg de C. Puigdemont; A. Alcoberro and M. Duran (eds), Martorell.

Porée, Ch. (1747), *Gallis ob victoriam reducem gratulatio*, in *Caroli Porée orationes*, Paris.

Pretis, S. de (1583), *De ultimarum voluntatum interpretatione tractatus amplissimus*, Frankfurt am Main.

Reusch, E. (1707), *Oratio solennis qua felicissimam summorum foederatorum expeditionem bellicam in Catalonia, Brabantia et Italia, anno seculi huius sexto confectam, in illustri Academia Altdorfina...prosecutus est Erhardus Reusch*, Nuremberg.

Rodrigues da Costa, A. (1704), *Iusta Lusitanorum arma pro vindicanda Hispanorum libertate Gallico dominatu oppressa asserendoque Hispaniae imperio*, Lisbon.

Rönick, J. T. (1749), *Recentiorum poetarum Germanorum carmina latina selectiora*, Helmstedt.

Saint-John, P. of (1704), *Iacobo tertio, magnae Britanniae regi, pro strenuis offeruntur corda et brachia Hibernicae gentis*, Paris.

Saint-John, P. of (1705), *In diem natalem Iacobi tertii, magnae Britaniae regis, Musae Hibernicae plausus*, Paris?

Saint-John, P. of (1707), *Verus heros, seu Dux de Barwick, carmen*, Paris.

San Marco, M. A. (1706), *Carmen historico-genethliacum*, Vienna.

San Marco, M. A. (1712), *In celebratione coronationis Caroli sexti...In laudem Elisabeth Christinae...oratio panegyrica*, Barcelona.

Sanadon, N. E. (1712a), *Laudatio funebris Ludovici Delphini, nepotis Ludovici magni, dicta in regio Ludovici magni Collegio Societatis Iesu*, Paris.

Sanadon, N. E. (1712b), *Villartio, liberata Victoria, castigata Fortuna, ode*, Paris.

Sanadon, N. E. (1713), *Ad pacem ode*, Paris.

Sanadon, N. E. (1715), *Natalis Stephani Sanadonis e Societate Iesu carminum libri quatuor*, Paris.

Sanadon, N. E. (1724), *Ad religionem, quum Philippus V, Hispaniae rex, imperio abdicaret*, Paris.

Santacruz i Gener, F. de (1718), *Barcino magna parens*, Vienna.

Scharff, F. F. (1700), *Serenissimo principi...Carolo archiduci Austriae...hoc genethliacum munusculum...dicatur et consecratur*, Vienna.

Schlittern, P. Ch. (1712a), *Oratio gratulatoria ob auspicatum in Austriam reditum ad Carolum sextum*, Vienna.

Schlittern, P. Ch. (1712b), *Divinae providentiae cura singularis in erigenda, conservanda augendaque augustissima domo Habsburgo-Austriaca*, Vienna.

Schönwetter, J. B. (1707), *Eugenio, duci Sabaudiae,...post expeditionem in Italia feliciter peractam, in urbem Viennam...reduci applausus emblematicus*, Vienna?

Segarra, E. (1711), *Panegyrico funeral que de orden del excelentissimo y fidelissimo consistorio de la Deputación del Principado de Cathaluña predicó Fray Esteve Segarra, predicador de su Magestad en las ostentosas exequias por la muerte del augustissimo Emperador Joseph primero de Austria*, Barcelona.
Seilern, F. von (1701), *Ius Austriacum in monarchiam Hispanicam assertum*, Vienna.
Sicardo, J. B. (1711), *Oratio in obitu augustissimi Caesaris Iosephi huius nominis primi*, Barcelona.
Solanes, F. (1700 and 1706), *El emperador político y política de emperadores*, Barcelona.
Staindl, F. (1702), *Annus primus belli Italici serenissimo Eugenio Caesarearum in Italia copiarum supremo duce ter secundus Suada panegyrica celebratus*, Graz.
Steyerer, A. (1708), *Mariae Annae archiduci ad augustas Portugalliae coronas ex Austria proficiscenti felix iter!*, Vienna.
Tann, F. von (1712), *Oratio solennis, qua...Carolo VI Romano imperatori...gratulatur...*, Meiningen.
Tolstoy, L. (1869), *War and Peace*, Moscow [anonymous English translation, Everyman's Library Classics, London, 1932].
Truchseß, H. (1711), *Causae doloris in obitu Iosephi I Romanorum imperatoris oratio*, Rome.
Turano, D. (1720), *Apparato fatto in Palermo...in occasione della solenne acclamazione dell'imnperator Carlo VI e III re delle Spagne e di Sicilia*, Palermo.
Ubilla y Medina, A. (1704), *Succession del rey D. Phelipe V, nuestro Señor en la corona de España: diario de sus viages desde Versalles a Madrid, el que executó para su feliz casamiento, jornada a Nápoles, a Milan, y a su exercito, successos de la campaña, y su buelta a Madrid*, Madrid.
Verderosa, M. G. (1703), *Philippi V Catholici regis Neapolis ac totius Hesperiae in imperium de successione*, Naples.
Vico, G. (after 1701), *De coniuratione principum Neapolitanorum*, Naples.
Vitale, P. (1711), *Le simpatie dell'allegrezza tra Palermo e la Castiglia*, Palermo.
Voltaire (François Marie Arouet) (1775), *Histoire de Jenni ou le sage et l'athée*, Paris.
Waltrin, C. L. (1713), *In solemnem abdicationem regnorum Franciae et Hispaniae factam in Parisiensi senatu die Mercurii 15 Martii 1713 ode*, Paris.
Werlhof J. (1708), *Epithalamium potentissimi Hispaniarum regis Catholici Caroli III et serenissimae principis Brunsuico-Luneburgicae Elisabethae Christinae augusto connubio*, Helmstedt.

Secondary sources

In the interests of concision, when different chapters from the same collective work are listed, I give full details of the source volume only once.

Alabrús, R.-M. (2001), *Felip V i l'opinió dels catalans*, Lleida.

Alabrús, R.-M. (2007), 'El eco de la batalla de Almansa en la publicística', *Revista de Historia moderna*, 25: 113-27.
Alabrús, R.-M. (2010), 'La opinión sobre las mujeres austracistas y el imaginario religioso en los sitios de 1706 y 1713-1714 en Barcelona', *Cuadernos de Historia Moderna*, 35: 15-34.
Albareda, A. M. (1924), *La congregació benedictina de Montserrat a l'Àustria i la Bohèmia*, Montserrat.
Albareda, J. (2005), *El 'cas dels catalans': La conducta dels aliats arran de la Guerra de Successió (1705-1742)*, Barcelona.
Albareda, J. (2010), *La Guerra de Sucesión de España (1700-1714)*, Barcelona.
Alcoberro, A. (2002), *L'exili austriacista, 1713-1747*, Barcelona.
Alcoberro, A. (2003), 'Memòria, història i pensament polític a l'exili austriacista. La crònica de la Guerra de Successió de Josep Plantí', *Pedralbes: Revista d'història moderna*, 23: 325-44.
Alcoberro, A. (2007), *Catalunya i la Guerra de Successió*, Barcelona.
Alcoberro, A. (2013), *Barcelona 1714. Els gravats de la Guerra de Successió*, Barcelona.
Álvarez-Ossorio Alvariño, A., García García, B. J. and León Sanz, V. (eds) (2017), *La pérdida de Europa: la guerra de Sucesión por la Monarquía de España*, Madrid.
Angulo, R. and Pons, A. (eds) (2017), *Sebastián Durón (1660-1716), Coronis: Zarzuela*, Madrid.
Auer, L. (2018), 'A Habsburg overseas empire after 1700? Contemporary Austrian views on the colonial dimension of the Spanish Succession', in: Pohling and Schaich (eds), *The War of the Spanish Succession: new perspectives*, 431-42.
Barbosa Machado, D. (1786), *Summario da Bibliotheca luzitana*, Lisbon.
Ben Messaoud, S. (2005), 'L'enseignement rhétorique de Gibert', *Recherches sur Diderot et sur l'Encyclopédie*, 38: 93-123.
Binns, J. (2008), 'Sir Henry Newton and the war', in: Money (ed.), *1708: Oudenarde and Lille*, 102-5.
Boge, B. and Bogner, R. G. (eds) (1999), *'Oratio funebris': Die katholische Leichenpredigt der frühen Neuzeit*, Leiden.
Borreguero, C. (2003), 'Imagen y propaganda de guerra en el conflicto sucesorio, 1700-1713', *Manuscrits: Revista d'història moderna*, 21: 95-132.
Bouza, F. (2008), *Papeles y opinión: Políticas de publicación en el Siglo de Oro*, Madrid.
Braun, L. (2007), *Ancilla Calliopeae: Ein Repertorium der neulateinischen Epik Frankreichs, 1500-1700*, Leiden-Boston.
Brix, M. (1973), 'Trauergerüste für die Habsburger in Wien', *Wiener Jahrbuch für Kunstgeschichte*, 26: 208-65.
Bruin, R. de, Haven, C. van der, Jensen, L. and Onnekink, D. (eds) (2015), *Performances of Peace: Utrecht 1713*, Leiden.
Bruin, R. de, Haven, C. van der, Jensen, L. and Onnekink, D. (2015), 'Introduction', in: Bruin et al. (eds), *Performances of Peace*, 1-24.
Büchner, K. (1956), *P. Vergilius Maro: Der Dichter der Römer*, Stuttgart.

Burke, P. (2004), 'Latin: a language in search of a community', in *Languages and Communities in Early Modern Europe*, 43-60, Cambridge.
Campabadal i Bertran, M. (2003), *El pensament i l'activitat literària del Setcents català*, Barcelona.
Camprubí, X. (2018), *L'impressor Rafael Figueró (1642-1726) i la premsa a la Catalunya del seu temps*, Barcelona.
Cardim, P. (2009), 'Portugal en la Guerra de Sucesión de la Monarquía española', in: F. García González (ed.), *La Guerra de Sucesión en España y la Batalla de Almansa: Europa en la encrucijada*, 231-82, Madrid.
Carreras i Bulbena, J. R. (1902), *Carles d'Àustria i Elisabet de Brunswick a Barcelona i Girona*, Barcelona.
Casademunt i Fiol, S. (2011), 'La Capella Reial de Carles III a Barcelona. Nova documentació sobre la música a la ciutat durant la Guerra de Successió (1705-1713)', *Revista Catalana de Musicologia*, 4: 81-100.
Casarotto, P. (2020), '*Plumer le coq gaulois*: éloge du prince, guerre des images et stratégies médiatiques dans les oraisons funèbres et les catafalques éphémères en l'honneur de Léopold Ier († 1705) et Joseph Ier de Habsbourg († 1711), dans l'Empire et les territoires de la Maison d'Autriche', *Études Épistémè*, 38 (accessed on 15 July 2022).
Cilleßen, W. (ed.) (1997), *Krieg der Bilder: Druckgraphik als Medium politischer Auseinandersetzung im Europa des Absolutismus*, Berlin.
Classen, C. J. (2003), *Antike Rhetorik im Zeitalter des Humanismus*, Munich.
Comas, A. (1964), *Història de la literatura catalana: Part moderna*, Barcelona.
Compère, M. M. and Pralon-Julia, D. (eds) (1992), *Performances scolaires de collégiens sous l'Ancien Régime. Études d'exercices latins rédigés au collège Louis-le-Grand vers 1720*, Paris.
Coreth, A. (1982), *Pietas Austriaca. Österreichische Frömmigkeit im Barock*, Vienna.
Coroleu, A. (2006), 'The siege of Barcelona of 1706 in three Latin texts', in: Verbeke et al. (eds), *Ramillies*, 91-8.
Coroleu, A. (2019), 'Bodas reales entre Viena y Barcelona: un epitalamio latino de 1708', *Liburna*, 14: 143-54.
Coroleu, A. and Paredes, M. (2014), 'Llatí i consciència política a la Catalunya setcentista', *Caplletra: Revista internacional de Filologia*, 57: 215-31.
Crispi, G. (1720), *Notizie istoriche degli Arcadi morti*, Rome.
Dadson, T. J. and Elliott, J. H. (eds), *Britain, Spain and the Treaty of Utrecht, 1713-2013*, London.
Dahlberg, E. (ed.) (2014), *The voice of a waning empire: selected Latin poetry of Magnus Rönnow from the Great Northern War*, Uppsala.
Dahlberg, E. (2016), 'National, religious and cultural identity in Latin poetry from the Great Northern War (1700-1721)', in: T. Hass, N. Humble and M. Pade (eds), *Latin and the Early Modern World: linguistic identity and the polity from Petrarch to the Habsburg novelists*, Special issue of *Renaessanceforum*, 10, 193-217.

Dahlberg, E. (2018), 'String your lyre promptly: Magnus Rönnow's Latin poetry from the Great Northern War as literary news reports', in: Gwynne and Schirg (eds), *The economics of poetry*, 409–42.

Darder Lissón, M. (1996), *De nominibus equorum circensium: Pars Occidentis*, Barcelona.

Dauga-Casarotto, P. (2018), 'La *Douceur* autrichienne contre la superbe des Bourbons: un éloge funèbre en images à la gloire de l'empereur Léopold Ier (Vienne, 1705)', *Exercices de Rhétorique*, 11: 1–33.

De Beer, S. (2014), 'Poetic genres—Occasional poetry: practice', in: P. Ford, J. Bloemendal and C. Fantazzi (eds), *Brill's Encyclopaedia of the Neo-Latin World*, Leiden-Boston, 2, 1142–4.

De Montagut i Estragués, T. (2004–6), 'El jurista Domènec d'Aguirre i la memòria del dret públic català', *Ivs Fvgit*, 13–14: 231–49.

Deneire, T. (2006), 'Some overlooked chronograms and epigrams following the battle of Ramillies, collected by Gisbert Cuper (1644–1716)', in: Verbeke et al. (eds), *Ramillies*, 79–90.

De Smet, I. (2014), 'Poetic genres—Occasional poetry: theory', in: Ford et al. (eds), *Brill's Encyclopaedia of the Neo-Latin World*, 2, 1144–6.

Di Fede, M. S. (2005–6), 'La festa barocca a Palermo: città, architetture, istituzioni', *Espacio, Tiempo y Forma*, 18–19: 49–75.

Dörrie, H. (1968), *Der heroische Brief: Bestandsaufnahme, Geschichte, Kritik einer humanistisch-barocken Literaturgattung*, Berlin.

Dünnhaupt, G. (1990), 'Anton Ulrich, Herzog zu Braunschweig und Lüneburg. Werk- und Literaturverzeichnis', in: G. Dünnhaupt (ed.), *Personalbibliographien zu den Drucken des Barock*. Band 1, 294–313, Stuttgart.

Enenkel, K. A. E., Laureys, M., and Pieper, Ch. (eds) (2012), *Discourses of Power: Ideology and Politics in Neo-Latin Literature*, Hildesheim.

Farguson J. (2015), 'Promoting the peace: Queen Anne and the Public Thanksgiving at St Paul's Cathedral', in: Bruin et al. (eds), *Performances of Peace*, 207–22.

Fernández-Xesta y Vázquez, E. (2018), 'Comunicación del Archiduque Don Carlos de Austria, como 'Carlos III de España', a su General de batalla Francisco de Asprer y Talric, Gobernador de Tarragona, sobre su próxima boda con la Princesa de Brunswick-Wolfenbüttel', *Emblemata: Revista aragonesa de emblemática*, XXIV: 49–70.

Flood, J. (2006), *Poets Laureate in the Holy Roman Empire: A Bio-bibliographical Handbook*, Berlin.

Fogel, M. (1989), *Les cérémonies de l'information dans la France du XVIe au XVIIIe siècle*, Paris.

Fontcuberta i Famadas, C. (2014), 'De la Guerra dels Segadors a la Guerra de Successió: Catalunya a les medalles de Lluís XIV i de l'Arxiduc Carles', in: VV.AA., *Històries metàl·liques: art i poder a la medalla europea*, 94–103, Barcelona.

Frey, L. and Frey, M. (1995), *The Treaties of the War of the Spanish Succession: An Historical and Critical Dictionary*, London.

Frijhof, W. (2015), 'Fiery Metaphors in the Public Space: Celebratory Culture and Political Consciousness Around the Peace of Utrecht', in: Bruin et al. (eds), *Performances of Peace*, 223–50.

Garcés Manau, C. (2002), 'Quinto Sertorio, fundador de la Universidad de Huesca. El mito sertoriano oscense', *Alazet*, 14: 243–56.

Geelhaar, M. (2010), *Maria Theresia und der Österreichische Erbfolgekrieg im Spiegel neulateinischer Huldigungsliteratur. Anton Palmers 'Mars accusatus' und Leopold Heizlers 'Austria liberata'*, PhD dissertation, Vienna.

Gilmore, J. (2008), 'Schoolboy patriotism and gender perspectives', in: Money (ed.) *1708: Oudenarde and Lille*, 106–9.

Gilmore, J. (2010), '*Sub herili venditur hasta*: an early eighteenth-century justification of the slave trade by a colonial poet', in: Y. Haskell and J. F. Ruys (eds), *Latinity and Alterity in the Early Modern Period*, 221–39, Turnhout.

Gilmore, J. (2021), '*Justaque cupidine lucri ardentes*: A Barbadian poet celebrates the Peace of Utrecht', in: M. Feile Tomes, A. Goldwyn and M. Duques (eds), *Brill's Companion to Classics in the Early Americas*, 146–80, Leiden.

Goloubeva, M. (2000), *The glorification of Emperor Leopold I in image, spectacle and text*, Mainz.

Gómez Uriel, M. (1884), *Bibliotecas antigua y nueva de escritores aragoneses de Félix Latassa, aumentadas y refundidas en forma de diccionario bibliográfico-biográfico por. . .*, Saragossa.

González Cruz, D. (2002), *Guerra de religión entre príncipes católicos: el discurso del cambio dinástico en España y América (1700–1714)*, Madrid.

González Cruz, D. (2009a), *Propaganda e información en tiempos de guerra: España y América (1700–1714)*, Madrid.

González Cruz, D. (2009b), 'Propaganda y estrategias de legitimación de la sucesión en los dominios de la Monarquía Hispánica (1700–1714)', in: J. M. de Bernardo Ares (ed.), *La sucesión de la Monarquía Hispánica, 1665–1725*, 167–208, Madrid.

González Germain, G. (2017), '*Barcino magna parens*: mutacions i pervivència de Virgili al setge de Barcelona de 1714', *Faventia*, 39: 101–10.

González Tornel, P. (2021), 'Proclamations and coronations in Palermo (1700–1735): performing kingship and celebrating civic power', in: A. Kalinowska and J. Spangler (eds), *Power and Ceremony in European History: Rituals, Practices and Representative Bodies Since the Late Middle Ages*, 33–48, London.

Griffin, D. (2005), *Patriotism and Poetry in Eighteenth-Century Britain*, Cambridge.

Grönert, A. (2011), 'Independence in the imperial realm: political iconography and urbanism in eighteenth-century Palermo', in: Ch. Chastel-Rousseau (ed.), *Reading the Royal Monument in Eighteenth-Century Europe*, 131–52, Farnham.

Gwynne, P. and Schirg, B. (2018), 'Introduction', in: Gwynne and Schirg (eds), *The Economics of Poetry*, 1–20.

Gwynne, P. and Schirg, B. (2018), *The Economics of Poetry: The Efficient Production of Neo-Latin Verse, 1400–1720*, Oxford.

Hartmann, G. and Schnith, K. (eds) (1996), *Die Kaiser: 1200 Jahre europäische Geschichte*, Augsburg.

Haskell, Y. (2003), *Loyola's Bees: Ideology and Industry in Jesuit Latin Didactic Poetry*, Oxford.

Haskell, Y. (2013), *Prescribing Ovid: The Latin works and networks of the enlightened Dr Heerkens*, London – New York.

Hawlik-van de Water, M. (1993), *Die Kapuzinergruft: Begräbnisstätte der Habsburger in Wien*, Vienna.

Helander, H. (2004), *Neo-Latin Literature in Sweden in the Period 1620–1720*, Uppsala.

Hengerer, M. (2018), 'The War of the Spanish Succession and Habsburg politics of representation', in: Pohling and Schaich (eds), *The War of the Spanish Succession: new perspectives*, 205–33.

Hoppit, J. (2000), *A Land of Liberty?: England, 1689–1727*, Oxford.

Hoppit, J. (2014), 'Party politics and war weariness in the reign of Queen Anne', in: Dadson and Elliott (eds), *Britain, Spain and the Treaty of Utrecht*, 9–17.

Jensen, L. (2015), 'Visions of Europe: Contrasts and Combinations of National and European Identities in Literary Representations of the Peace of Utrecht (1713)', in: Bruin et al. (eds), *Performances of Peace*, 159–80.

Jensen, L. and Corporaal, M. (2016), 'Poetry as an act of international diplomacy: English translations of Willem van Haren's political poetry during the War of the Austrian Succession', *Journal for Eighteenth-Century Studies*, 39, 3: 377–94.

Johnstone, C. A. (2018), *A very murdering year: the Duke of Marlborough's 1709 campaign and the experience of battle at Malplaquet*, PhD dissertation, Birmingham.

Kalmár, J. (2020), 'Zur Erziehung Kaiser Karls VI. Sein Ajo, seine Lehrer und Mitschüler', in: Seitschek and Hertel (eds), *Herrschaft und Repräsentation in der Habsburgermonarchie*, 57–70.

Kamen, H. (1969), *The War of Succession in Spain, 1700–15*, London.

Kamen, H. (2020), *Felipe V: El rey que reinó dos veces*, Madrid.

Klecker, E. (2008), 'Neulatein an der Universität Wien. Ein Forschungsdesiderat', in: Ch. Gastgeber and E. Klecker (eds), *Neulatein an der Universität Wien. Ein literarischer Streifzug*, 11–88, Vienna.

Klecker, E. (2015), 'Einleitung. Streiflichter zur barocken Buchkultur in Wien', in: Ch. Gastgeber and E. Klecker (eds), *Geschichte der Buchkultur: Barock*, 9–42, Graz.

Klecker, E. and Römer, F. (1994), 'Poetische Habsburg–Panegyrik in lateinischer Sprache: Bestände der Österreichischen Nationalbibliothek als Grundlage eines Forschungsprojekts', *Biblos*, 43, 3–4, 183–98.

Koch, A. (2004), '*Viva la reyna*': *Die Brautreise der spanischen Königin Elisabeth Christine von Braunschweig–Wolfenbüttel von Wien nach Barcelona im Spiegel zeitgenössischer Berichte*, Graz.

Korenjak, M. (2008), '*Applausus ad Principem Eugenium*: Ein neulateinisches Ereignislied', *Neulateinisches Jahrbuch*, 10: 177–94.

Krasser, H. and Schmidt, E. A. (eds) (1996), *Zeitgenosse Horaz: Der Dichter und seine Leser seit zwei Jahrtausenden*, Tübingen.

Krüssel, H. (2011, 2015 and 2020), 'Napoleo Latinitate vestitus': Napoleon Bonaparte in lateinischen Dichtungen vom Ende des 18. bis zum Beginn des 20. Jahrhunderts (3 volumes), Hildesheim.

La Gorce, J. de (2007), 'Le triomphe de la Seine et du Tage sur les autres fleuves de l'Europe, affermi par la naissance du Duc de Bretagne: Une fête organisée à Paris pendant la guerre de Succession d'Espagne', in: Álvarez-Ossorio Alvariño et al. (eds), La pérdida de Europa, 49–63.

Laird, A. (2020), The epic of America: An introduction to Rafael Landívar and the 'Rusticatio Mexicana', London – New York.

Lauffer, C. G. (1742), Das Laufferische Medaillen-Cabinet. Oder Verzeichniß aller Medaillen, welche sowohl die historischen Begebenheiten von A. 1679. bis A. 1742 als auch andere christlich- und moralische Betrachtungen, nebst der vollkommenen Reise der Römischen Päbste enthalten, Nuremberg.

León Sanz, V. (2003), Carlos VI: El Emperador que no pudo ser Rey de España, Madrid.

León Sanz, V. (2008), 'Una Habsburgo en el Portugal de los Braganza: el matrimonio de Juan V con la Archiduquesa María Ana de Austria', in: J. Martínez Millán and M. P. Marçal Lourenço (eds), Las relaciones discretas entre las monarquías hispana y portuguesa: Las casas de las reinas (siglos XV–XIX), 395–416, Madrid.

León Sanz, V. (2020), 'Der Hof und die Regierung von Karl VI. in Barcelona', in: Seitschek and Hertel (eds), Herrschaft und Repräsentation in der Habsburgermonarchie, 141–70.

Levantal, Ch. (1996), La Route royale: Le voyage de Philippe V et de ses frères de Sceaux à la frontière d'Espagne (décembre 1700–janvier 1701) d'après la relation du Mercure Galan, Paris.

Lynn, J. A. (1999), The Wars of Louis XIV, 1667–1714, London.

MacDowall, S. (2020), Malplaquet 1709: Marlborough's bloodiest battle, Oxford.

Maestre Maestre, J. M. (1994), 'Un supuesto poema de Nebrija sobre la Peña de los Enamorados de Antequera: su correcta atribución a Fabián de Nebrija', in: C. Codoñer Merino and J. A. González Iglesias (eds), Antonio de Nebrija: Edad Media y Renacimiento, 491–504, Salamanca.

Marfany, J.-L. (1995), La cultura del catalanisme: El nacionalisme català en els seus inicis, Barcelona.

Marshall, D. L. (2006), 'The impersonal character of action in Vico's De coniuratione principum Neapolitanorum', New Vico Studies, 24: 81–128.

Martín Marcos, D. (2011), El Papado y la Guerra de Sucesión española, Madrid.

Martínez Gil, F. (2011), 'Los sermones como cauce de propaganda política: la Guerra de Sucesión', Obradoiro de Historia Moderna, 20: 303–36.

Matsche, F. (1981), Die Kunst im Dienst der Staatsidee Kaiser Karls VI: Ikonographie, Ikonologie und Programmatik des Kaiserstils, Berlin.

Mertz, J. J., Murphy, J. P. and IJsewijn, J. (eds) (1989), Jesuit Latin Poets of the Seventeenth and Eighteenth Centuries: An Anthology of Neo-Latin Poetry, Wauconda, IL.

Mínguez Cornelles, V. M., González Tornel, P., Chiva, J. and Rodríguez Moya, I. (eds) (2014), *La fiesta barroca: los reinos de Nápoles y Sicilia (1535–1713)*, Castelló de la Plana.

Miralpeix, F. (2012), 'Simbologia austriacista. Tipologies, usos i interpretacions', in: VV. AA., *Barcelona 1700: Política, economia i guerra*, 242–67, Barcelona.

Mollfulleda, C. (2007), '*In futuri operis signum*. La piràmide de la Inmaculada i el setge de Barcelona de 1706', in: M. Morales (ed.), *L'aposta catalana a la Guerra de Successió (1705–1707)*, 109–24, Barcelona.

Money, D. (1998), *The English Horace: Anthony Alsop and the Tradition of British Latin Verse*, Oxford.

Money, D. (ed.) (2008), *1708: Oudenarde and Lille (A Tercentenary Commemoration in Prose and Verse)*, Cambridge.

Money, D. (2013), 'New Year books, University verses, and Neo-Latin works', in: I. Gadd (ed.), *History of Oxford University Press, I: Beginnings to 1780*, 385–98, Oxford.

Mörschbacher, T. (2015), *Helden- und Heldinnenbriefe aus dem Hause Habsburg. Anton Kiffers 'Epistolae heroum et heroidum' als Beispiel der Heroides-Rezeption im Jesuitenorden*, Graz.

Muth, R. (1954), 'Hymenaios und Epithalamion', *Wiener Studien*, 67: 5–45.

Naddeo, B. A. (2011), *Vico and Naples: The urban origins of modern social theory*, Ithaca, NY and London.

Olivas, A. A. (2015), 'Performance and Propaganda in Spanish America During the War of the Spanish Succession', in: Bruin et al. (eds), *Performances of Peace*, 197–208.

O'Reilly, W. (2011), 'A life in exile: Charles VI (1685–1740) between Spain and Austria', in: P. Mansell and T. Riotte (eds), *Monarchy and Exile: The Politics of Legitimacy from Marie de Médicis to Wilhem II*, 66–90, London.

O'Reilly, W. (2023), 'The Phoenix and the Eagle: Catalan Political Economy and the Habsburg Monarchy of Charles III/VI', in: V. Hyden-Hanscho and W. Stangl (eds), *Formative Modernities in the Early Modern Atlantic and Beyond: Identities, Polities and Global Economies*, 95–123, London.

Oury, C. (2020), *La Guerre de Succession d'Espagne: La fin tragique du Grand Siècle*, Paris.

Pasolini, A. (2008), 'Un coleccionista sardo en la Europa del siglo XVIII', *Boletín de la Real Academia de la Historia*, 205, 2: 251–82.

Peinlich, R. (1864), *Geschichte des Gymnasiums zu Graz*, Graz.

Peper, I. (2010), *Konversionen im Umkreis des Wiener Hofes um 1700*, Vienna.

Pérez Álvarez, M. (2012), *Aragón durante la guerra de Sucesión*, Saragossa.

Pérez i Durà, J. and Estellés, J. M. (eds) (1985), *La Guerra de Sucesión en Valencia (el 'De bello rustico Valentino' de José Manuel Miñana)*, Valencia.

Pérez Picazo, M. T. (1966), *La publicística española en la Guerra de Sucesión*, Madrid.

Pohling, M. and Schaich, M. (2018), 'Revisiting the War of the Spanish Succession', in: Pohling and Schaich (eds), *The War of the Spanish Succession: New Perspectives*, 1–27.

Pohling, M. and Schaich, M. (eds) (2018), *The War of the Spanish Succession: New Perspectives*, Oxford.

Polleroß, F. (2000), 'Hispaniarum et Indiarum rex. Zur Repräsentation Kaiser Karls VI. als König von Spanien', in: J. Jané (ed.), *Denkmodelle: Akten des achten Spanisch-Österreichischen Symposions, 13.-18. Dezember in Tarragona*, 121–75, Tarragona.

Popelka, L. (1970), 'Das Trauergerüst der Wiener Universität für Kaiser Joseph I', *Wiener Jahrbuch für Kunstgeschichte*, 23: 239–352.

Popelka, L. (1999), 'Trauer-Prunk und Rede-Prunk: Der frühneuzeitliche Trauerapparat als rhetorische Leistung auf dem Weg zur virtuellen Realität', in: Boge and Bogner (eds), '*Oratio funebris*', 9–80.

Race, W. H. (1982), *The Classical Priamel from Homer to Boethius*, Leiden.

Ricuperati, G., (1968), 'Serafino Biscardi', in: *Dizionario biografico degli Italiani*, 10, 654–7, Rome.

Robertson, J. (2005), *The Case for the Enlightenment: Scotland and Naples, 1680–1760*, Cambridge.

Römer, F. (1997), 'Poetische Habsburg-Panegyrik in lateinischer Sprache vom 15. bis ins 18. Jahrhundert', in: F. Römer (ed.), *1000 Jahre Österreich – Wege zu einer österreichischen Identität. Vorträge anläßlich des Dies academicus der Geisteswissenschaftlichen Fakultät der Universität Wien am 10. Jänner 1996*, 91–9, Vienna.

Sabatier, G. (2007), '*Vacua melior nunc regnet in aula*: La guerre des médailles entre Philippe V de Bourbon et Charles III de Habsbourg pendant la guerre de Succession d'Espagne (1700–1711)', in: Álvarez-Ossorio Alvariño et al. (eds), *La pérdida de Europa*, 65–98.

Schaffenrath, F. and Tilg, S. (eds) (2004), *Achilles in Tirol: Der 'bayerische Rummel' 1703 in der 'Epitome rerum Oenovallensium'*, Innsbruck.

Schneidmüller, B. (2000), *Die Welfen. Herrschaft und Erinnerung (819–1252)*, Stuttgart.

Schumann, J. (2003), *Die andere Sonne: Kaiserbild und Medienstrategien im Zeitalter Leopolds I*, Berlin.

Schwarz, W. (1991), '*Repraesentatio belli*: Eine Kupferstichfolge zum Spanischen Erbfolgekrieg aus dem Augsburger Verlag Jeremias Wolff', *Zeitschrift des historischen Vereins für Schwaben*, 84: 129–84.

Scott, H. (2018), 'The War of the Spanish Succession: new perspectives and old', in: Pohling and Schaich (eds), *The War of the Spanish Succession: New Perspectives*, 29–52.

Seidel, R. (2015), 'The German-speaking countries', in: S. Knight and S. Tilg (eds), *The Oxford Handbook of Neo-Latin*, New York, 445–60.

Seitschek, S. and Hertel, S. (eds) (2020), 'Vorwort', in: Seitschek and Hertel (eds), *Herrschaft und Repräsentation in der Habsburgermonarchie*, 1–36.

Seitschek, S. and Hertel, S. (eds) (2020), *Herrschaft und Repräsentation in der Habsburgermonarchie (1700–1740): Die kaiserliche Familie, die habsburgischen Länder und das Reich*, Berlin.

Serrano Cueto, A. (2019), *El epitalamio neolatino: Poesía nupcial y matrimonio en Europa (siglos XV y XVI)*, Alcañiz–Lisbon.

Serrano Martín, E. (2014), 'Las exequias de María Luisa Gabriela de Saboya en Aragón (1714): Política y religión en los discursos funerales', *e-Spania*, 17 (accessed on 15 July 2022).

Serrano Méndez, A. (2008), 'Consideracions sobre Elisabeth Cristina de Brunswick-Wolfenbüttel en el tres-cents aniversari de la seva estada a Mataró', *Sessió d'estudis mataronins*, 25: 121–41.

Shaw, C. (2022), *Reason and Experience in Renaissance Italy*, Cambridge.

Stapelbroek, K. (2011), 'The emergence of Dutch neutrality: Trade, treaty politics and the peace of the Republic', in: A. Alimento (ed.), *War, Trade and Neutrality: Europe and the Mediterranean in the seventeenth and eighteenth centuries*, 129–45, Milan.

Steinhuber, A. (1895), *Geschichte des Collegium Germanicum Hungaricum in Rom*, Freiburg im Breisgau.

Sterling, B. L. (2009), *Do good fences make good neighbors? What history teaches us about strategic barriers and international security*, Washington, DC.

Stone, H. S. (1997), *The Production and Transmission of Ideas in Naples, 1685–1750*, Leiden.

Suárez Golán, F. (2017), 'Between Naples and Compostela: St James, St Januarius and the dispute about the patronage of the Hispanic Monarchy at the beginning of the XVIII century', in: G. Belli, F. Capano and M. I. Pascariello (eds), *La città, il viaggio, il turismo: Percezione, produzione e trasformazione*, 73–8, Naples.

Symcox, G. (1983), *Victor Amadeus II: Absolutism in the Savoyard State, 1675–1730*, Berkeley, CA.

Tanner, M. (1993), *The Last Descendant of Aeneas: The Hapsburgs and the Mythic Image of the Emperor*, New Haven, CT.

Thompson, A. C. (2014), 'The Utrecht settlement and its aftermath', in: Dadson and Elliott (eds), *Britain, Spain and the Treaty of Utrecht*, 57–70.

Torras i Ribé, J.-M. (ed.) (1996), *Escrits polítics del segle XVIII: Documents de la Catalunya sotmesa*, Vic.

Torras i Ribé, J.-M. (1999), *La Guerra de Successió i els setges de Barcelona, 1697–1714*, Barcelona.

Torrione, M. (2007), 'La imagen de Felipe V en el grabado francés de la Guerra de Sucesión' in: Álvarez-Ossorio Alvariño et al. (eds), *La pérdida de Europa*, 21–48.

Van Loon, G. (1717), *Histoire metallique des XVII provinces des Pays-Bas, depuis de l'abdication de Charles V jusqu'à la paix de Bade en 1716*, The Hague.

Verbeke, D., Money, D. and Deneire, T. (eds) (2006), *Ramillies: A commemoration in prose and verse of the 300th anniversary of the battle of Ramillies, 1706*, Cambridge.

Verhaart, F. and Brockliss, L. (eds) (2023), *The Latin Language and the Enlightenment*, Liverpool.

Viiding, K. (2006), 'Zum Formengrundbestand der neulateinischen Propemptikadichtung', in: R. Schnur, C. Kallendorf, G. H. Tucker, P. Galand-Hallyn, H. Wiegand, A. Iurilli and J. Pascual Barea (eds), *Acta Conventus Neo-Latini*

Bonnensis: Proceedings of the Twelfth International Congress of Neo-Latin Studies (Bonn, 2003), 871–80, Binghampton, NY.
Vissac, J. A. (1862), *De la poésie latine en France au siècle de Louis XIV*, Paris.
Voltes Bou, P. (1963), *Barcelona durante el gobierno del Archiduque Carlos de Austria, 1705–1714*, Barcelona.
Waquet, F. (2001), *Latin, or the empire of a sign: from the sixteenth to the twentieth century*, tr. John Howe, London.
Wölfflin, E. von (1869), *Publilii Syri mimi sententiae*, Leipzig.

Index

Numbers in *italics* refer to illustrations. Biblical references are listed under Bible, literary works under authors. People's names that include 'von' are listed under the word following the preposition: so, for example, Anton Joseph von Öttl is at Öttl, Anton Joseph von. This index was compiled by David Barnett.

Achilles 30, 194 n.23
Aeneas 19–20, 23, 61, 66, 95
Aeolus 59, 75
Affatighi, Basilius 58
Aguirre, Domènec, count of Massot
 (fl. 1683–1734) 125–7
Albert VII, archduke of Austria (1559–1621; r. 1598–1621) 94
Alembert, Jean le Rond d' (1717–83) 165 n.9
Almansa, Battle of (1707) 62, 71–3, 124
Almenar, Battle of (1710) 80
Altdorf 68–9
Álvares da Costa, João, jurist 33–4
Anchises 23, 31
Anjou, duke of, *see* Philip V of Spain
Anne (1665–1714), queen of England, Scotland and Ireland (1702–7), of Great Britain and Ireland (1707–14) 23, 53, 58–62, 85–7, 106, 112–15, 130
Anton Ulrich, prince of Brunswick-Wolfenbüttel (1633–1714) 36, 94, 96, 98, 118
Antons, Thomas Maria des 83–4
Augustus 30, 63, 83
Ausonius
 Epistles 65
Austrian Succession, War of the 6, 12

Bacallar, Vincenzo (1669–1726) 130, 134–6
Baden, Treaty of (1714) 3, 106, 111, 116
Barceló, Tomàs (d. 1723) 66–7
Barcelona 2–3, 36, 65, 84, 95, 100–2, *125*, 174 n.19, 177 n.56

 sieges (1705 and 1706) 39, 51–8, 59, 68–9, 74–6, 94, 124, 128, 135–6, 138, 159–60
 surrender (11 September 1714) 3, 122, 124–5, 132
 see also Montjuïc
Bartolini, Riccardo
 Austrias 66
Berwick, duke of, *see* Fitzjames, James
Bible
 Ecclesiastes 174 n.21
 Genesis 36
 Isaiah 61
 Judith 58
 Matthew 21
 Proverbs 192 n.13
 Song of Solomon 67
Biscardi, Serafino, jurist (1643–1711) 27
Bischoff, Engelbert (1654–1711) 20, 191 n.2
Blenheim (Höchstädt), Battle of (1704) 48, 50, 77
Böhmer, Justus Christoph, professor (1610–1732) 37–8, 182–3 n.15
Bolder, John 115–16
Bouchain, siege of (1712) 85–6, 105, 108
Bourbon, House of 1, 14, 24–5, 72, 79, 82, 127–8
 see also Philip V
Bourbon, Louis Joseph de, *see* Vendôme, duke of
Bowtell, John 115
Brihuega, Battle of (1710) 80–2, 179 n.65
Brunswick-Wolfenbüttel, principality of 36, 94, 98
Brusati, Giulio Cesare (d. 1743) 134–6

Burman, Pieter, professor (Petrus Burmannus, 1668–1741) 111–12
Butler, James, 2nd duke of Ormonde (1665–1745) 85, 113–14

Camarasa, Marqués de, viceroy of Aragon (Baltasar Cobos y Luna, 1651–1715) 18
Cambrai, Congress of (1722–25) 137
Cambridge, University of 114–15
Cannae, Battle of 73, 82
Caracciolo, Giovanni (d. 1707) 29, 48–9
Cardona, siege of (1711) 38, 40, 84, 122
Carpi, Battle of (1701) 44
Carthage 107, 113
Cassano, Battle of (1705) 77
Catinat, Nicolas, marshal (1637–1712) 44, 86, 180 n.76
Cato 30, 113
Caux de Montlebert, Gilles de (c. 1682–1733) 180 n.75
Cerda y Aragón, Luis Francisco de la, 9th duke of Medinaceli (1660–1711), viceroy of Naples 19, 27, 29, 31
Charlemagne, king of the Franks (747–814) 39, 40
Charles I, king of Spain (1500–58: r. 1516–56), Holy Roman Emperor (r. 1519–56) 14, 25, 37, 45, 98, 121, 166 n.12
Charles II, king of Spain (1661–1700; r. 1665–1700) 1, 2, 11, 25, 49, 128, 148
    will 2, 14, 15, 16–17, 27, 33–4, 103, 123, 169 n.32, 193 n.16
Charles III, pretender to the Spanish throne, *see* Charles VI, Holy Roman Emperor
Charles V, Holy Roman Emperor (r. 1519–56), *see* Charles I, king of Spain
Charles VI, Holy Roman Emperor (1685–1740; r. 1711–40) 1, 2, 4, 11, 64, 109, 113, 121
    arrival in Lisbon 2, 23, 124
    coronation as emperor (1711) 3
    death 9, 139
    election as emperor (1711) 3, 35, 85, 139
    genealogy 25, 33, 148
    marriage 89–98, 118, 123
    proclamation as King Charles III of Spain (1703) 2, 12, 19–24, 52, 60, 66, 167 n.22
    proclamation as king of Sicily (1720) 132–4
    return to Vienna 35, 38–9
    Spanish campaign 2, 39, 53, 58–62, 69–71, 77, 122, 124, 128, 136, 138
Charles of Austria, Archduke, *see* Charles VI, Holy Roman Emperor
Charles of France, duke of Berry (1686–1714) 13, 110–11
Chatillon, Nicolas 82
Chiari, Battle of (1701) 44
Churchill, John, 1st duke of Marlborough (1650–1722) 48, 68, 77, 107, 114
Cicero
    Pro lege Manilia 51, 116
Claudian 174 n.22
    Against Eutropius 137
    Panegyricus de Tertio Consulatu Honorii Augusti 59
Clement XI (1649–1721; pope 1700–21) 24, 26, 171 n.54
Codrus 69, 110
Commire, Jean (1625–1702) 14
Cortes (Castilian Parliament) 17
Corts (Catalan Parliament) 17, 51–2, 128
Corydon 110, 182 n.14
Cremona, Battle of (1702) 44–6, 50
Cuper, Gisbert (1644–1716) 72–3
Cupid 94, 95

d'Alembert, Jean le Rond (1717–83) 165 n.9
de Noriega, Benito, bishop (1650–1708) 31–3
de Roquette, Henri-Emmanuel (1655–1725) 105
de Santacruz i Gener, Francesc, *see* Santacruz i Gener, Francesc de
della Rovere, Francesco Maria II, duke of Urbino (1549–1631) 63, 157
Denain, Battle of (1712) 85–6, 105
Densovius, Christoph 121
D'Orival, Pierre 82–3
Douai 86, 108

Elisabeth Christine of Brunswick-
    Wolfenbüttel (1691–1750) 3, 36, 38,
    75, 123, 136, 139–40, 160–1
  marriage (1708) 3, 75–6, 89–98, 118,
    123, 176 n.45
Elliot, Adam 114–15
Engelken, Tobias Heinrich 121
Estarrués, Juan Miguel 17
Eugene of Savoy, Prince (1663–1736)
    44–6, 48–9, 51, 68, 72, 77–80, 85–6,
    116
Exton, John 115

Ferdinand II, king of Aragon (1452–1516;
    r. 1479–1516) 14, 167 n.18
Ferdinand III, Holy Roman Emperor
    (1608–57; r. 1637–57) 25, 57, 148,
    166 n.12
Fernández de Velasco, Francisco Antonio,
    duke of Frías, viceroy of Catalonia
    (1646–1716) 52–4, 135–6
Figueró, Rafael, printer 74, 76
Fitzjames, James, 1st duke of Berwick
    (1670–1734) 71, 73, 186 n.43
Flanders, Council of (1717) 123
Fortune (goddess) 81, 86
Francis I, king of France (1494–1547;
    r. 1515–47) 37, 45, 98
Frederick I Barbarossa, Holy Roman
    Emperor (1122–90; r. 1155–90)
    63, 97
Fresen, Christian Ernst von, colonel baron
    77, 180 n.74
Friedlingen, Battle of (1703) 48

Gambacorta, Gaetano, prince of Macchia
    (1657–1703) 167 n.20
Generalitat de Catalunya (Catalan
    government) 75, 100, 102,
    125–6
Genoa, Pact of (1705) 52, 130
George of Hesse-Darmstadt, Prince
    (1669–1705) 53–4, 74, 77
Gerstorff, Johann Adam Gerster von
    (1681–1747) 139
Gibert, Balthasar (1662–1741) 13
Gibraltar 50, 52, 60, 159–60
Girona, siege of (1711) 80, 83
Grand Alliance 1, 2, 29, 33, 44, 128

Portugal's incorporation (1703) 20, 23,
    48
Graz, University of 45, 116
Great Northern War (1700–21) 6, 109,
    190 n.72
Grotius, Hugo (1583–1645) 27, 131
Gunther of Pairis (c. 1150– c.1220)
    Ligurinus 63, 66, 157

Haake, Johann Jakob (J. I. Haakius de
    Bopfing, fl. 1699) 59–61, 151–4
Habsburg, House of 1, 11, 14, 36, 41, 57, 62,
    82, 90, 103–4, 123, 127, 133
  see also Charles II, Charles VI
Hackemann, Friedrich August 37
Hannibal 82, 107
Harley, Robert, earl of Oxford (1661–
    1724) 107, 110, 113–14
Hector de Villars, Claude Louis, *see* Villars,
    Claude Louis Hector de
Helen of Troy 90–1
Helmstedt 37, 94
Heraeus, Carl Gustav (1671–1725) 136,
    185 n.37, 196 n.38
Hercules 46, 79, 174 n.19
Höchstädt (Blenheim), Battle of (1704) 48,
    50, 77
Horace
  Carmen saeculare 188 n.54
  Epodes 110, 176 n.47
  Odes 38, 83, 114, 187 n.52
Hospitalet Agreement (1713) 122
Hunoldt, T. A. 21–3

Ibiza 3, 66
Ilbersheim, Treaty of (1704) 48
Ingoult, Nicolas Louis (1689–1754)
    83–4
Isabella Clara Eugenia (1566–1633) 94
Isham, Edmund 113

John V, king of Portugal (1689–1750; r.
    1706–50) 75, 90–2
Joseph I, Holy Roman Emperor (1678–
    1711; r. 1705–11) 2, 20, 48, 50, 61,
    75, 123, 148, 168 n.30
  death 3, 34, 37, 85, 98–104, 128, 139
  victory at Landau 77, 104
Joseph, Archduke, *see* Joseph I

Joseph Ferdinand of Bavaria, Prince (1692–9) 2, 148
Jupiter 30, 54, 75, 81, 94–6, 109

Khogler, Anton, professor 76

Laguerre, Louis (1663–1721) 78, 178 n.62
Landau, siege of (1702) 48, 50, 77 104
Landrecies, siege of (1712) 85–6
Le Camus, André, Father 13, 172 n.5
Le Comte, Jean 13, 149–51
Le Jay, Gabriel François, professor 73, 166 n.13
Le Quesnoy, siege of (1712) 85–6, 108
Leopold I, emperor of Austria (1640–1705; r. 1658–1705) 2, 20, 25, 29, 36, 45, 57, 75, 121, 123, 148
  death 33, 98, 103–4
Leopold Johann, archduke of Austria (Apr 1716–Nov 1716) 123–4
Lepanto, Battle of (1571) 58, 67
Levet, Richard 113
Libitina, goddess 86, 109
Liebpert, Ulrich, printer 36, 170 n.45
Lille, siege of (1708) 76
Lisbon 2, 23, 91–2
Lleida (Catalonia) 62, 73, 84
London 112, 113–14
Louis I, king of Spain (1707–24; r. Jan–Aug 1724) 71–2, 134
Louis XIV, king of France (1638–1715; r. 1643–1715) 1, 15, 16, 25, 36, 61, 69, 85, 98, 104, 106–8, 110–11, 113, 121, 128, 136, 148
Louis, duke of Brittany (1704–5) 105, 148
Louis, duke of Burgundy, Petit Dauphin of France (1682–1712) 105, 148, 172 n.5
Louis of Bourbon, Grand Dauphin of France (1661–1711) 103, 105, 148
Louis-le-Grand, Collège de (Paris) 13–16, 73, 82, 106, 109, 172 n.5
Loungueval, Jacques (1680–1735) 82–3
Lucan 16
  Pharsalia 177 n.57

Luxembourg, duke of (François Henri de Montmorency-Bouteville, 1628–95) 86, 180 n.76
Luzzara, Battle of (1702) 45, 48–9, 50

Macchia, Conspiracy of (1701) 19, 26, 30
Madrid 16, 29, 62, 66, 80
  Treaty of (1715) 106
Majorca 3, 66–7, 102, 118
Malaga, Battle of (1704) 52
Malplaquet, Battle of (1709) 77–80, 78
Mantua 44, 49, 133–4
Margaret Theresa of Spain, Holy Roman Empress (1651–73; r. 1666–73) 25–6, 28, 148
Maria Anna of Austria, queen consort of Portugal (1683–1754; r. 1708–50) 75, 90–2
Maria Anna of Neuburg, queen consort of Spain (1667–1740; r. 1689–1700) 34, 148
Maria Anna of Spain, Holy Roman Empress (1606–46; r. 1637–46) 32, 148
Maria Luisa Gabriella of Savoy, queen consort of Spain (1688–1714; r. 1701–14) 17–18, 104–5
Maria Theresa, Holy Roman Empress (1717–80; r. 1745–65) 140
Maria Theresa of Spain, queen of France (1638–83; r. 1660–83) 25–7, 33, 148
Mariana of Austria, queen of Spain (1634–96; r. 1649–65) 25–6, 28
Mariazell (Austria), Marian shrine 20, 57, 123
Marlborough, duke of, *see* Churchill, John
Mars 81, 109, 138
Martial 16, 116
  Epigrams 133, 190 n.72, 194 n.27
Maximilian I, Holy Roman Emperor (1459–1519; r. 1508–19) 37, 66, 90
Maximilian II Emanuel of Bavaria, elector (1662–1726) 35, 48, 61
May, Johann Burchard, professor (1652–1726) 35–6
Medinaceli, viceroy of Naples, *see* Cerda y Aragón
Ménestrier, Claude-François (1631–1705) 136

Mercury 16, 94, 137
Milan 3, 44, 122, 127
Mons, siege of (1709) 77–8
Montjuïc (Barcelona) 53–4, 74, 177 n.56
Montlebert, Gilles de Caux de (*c.* 1682–1733) 180 n.75
Montserrat 55–7, 62, *64*
Mordaunt, Charles, 3rd earl of Peterborough (1658–1735) 52–3

Naples 3, 12, 19, 29–30, 60, 80, 95, 122, 124, 133–4, 137, 143
Nemesis 60–1
Neptune 19, 74
Newton, Sir Henry (1651–1715) 73
Noailles, duke of (Adrien Maurice de Noailles, 1678–1766) 80, 83–4
Noriega, Benito de, bishop (1650–1708) 31–3

Orival, Pierre D' 82–3
Öttl, Anton Joseph von (1671–1750) 90–1, 118, *119*
Oudenarde, Battle of (1708) 76–7, 80, 163 n.5
Ovid 75, 124, 159
 Fasti 138, 191 n.7
 Heroides 173 n.14, 181 n.5
 Metamorphoses 18, 30, 54, 160, 177–8 n.57, 180 n.79, 182 n.13, 183 n.19
Oxford, University of 112–14

Palermo 18, 80–1, 132–3
Pallas 46–7, 106–7
Paris 13, 85, 105, 110
 see also Louis-le-Grand, Collège de
Pestel, Pierre, professor (1651– *c.* 1725) 105
Peter II, king of Portugal (1648–1706; r. 1683–1706) 48, 75
Petersen, Johann Wilhelm (1649–1727) 35–6
Philip, duke of Anjou, *see* Philip V, king of Spain
Philip I, the Handsome, king of Castile (1478–1506; r. 1506) 41, 90
Philip II, king of Spain (1527–98; r. 1556–98) 25, 104

Philip III, king of Spain (1578–1621; r. 1598–1621) 25, 32, 148
Philip III, the Good, duke of Burgundy (1396–1467) 104
Philip IV, king of Spain (1606–65; r. 1621–40) 25, 26, 98, 148
Philip V, king of Spain (1683–1746; r. 1700–46) 1, 2, 4, *15*, 71, 82, 107, 110–11, 121, 137, 169 n.31
 abdication (1724) 134
 campaign in northern Italy 48
 genealogy 18, 25, 32, 148
 king of Naples (1702) 27–8, 29
 marriage 104
 proclamation as king (1700) 2, 12, 13–19, 29
 Spanish campaign (1706) 29, 52, 61, 73, 122
Philippe II, duke of Orleans (1674–1723) 73, 110–11, 148
Piedmont 45, 68
Plantí, Josep, jurist (1681–1743) 127–30, 144
Porée, Charles, professor (1675–1741) 106–8
Portocarrero, cardinal (1635–1709) 34, 103
Prats de Rei, Battle of (1711) 38, 84
Preliminary Articles of London (1711) 85
Priaulx, Matthew 113
Purgstall, Albrecht (1671–1744) 99
Pyrenees, Treaty of (1659) 26, 98, 127

Quadruple Alliance (1718) 132–3, 136

Ramillies, Battle of (1706) 57, 61, 68, 163 n.5
Rastatt, Treaty of (1714) 3, 106, 111, 116, 121, 129, 136
Rauld, Robert 82
Rechteren, Adolf Hendrik van, count (1656–1731) 106
Reusch, Erhard, professor (1678–1740) 68–71, 98
Robinson, John (1650–1723) 113–15
Rodrigues da Costa, António (1656–1732) 24
Roquette, Henri-Emmanuel de (1655–1725) 105

Rovere, Francesco Maria II della, *see* della Rovere, Francesco Maria II
Rubens, Peter Paul (1577–1640) 94
Rüdiger, Guido Wald, count of Starhemberg (1657–1737) 46, *47*, 80, 82–3
Rudolf I, king of Germany (1218–91; r. 1273–91) 36, 133

Sallust
  Conspiracy of Cataline 170 n.40
  Jugurthine War 131
San Marco, Marco Antonio 38, 123–4, 128
Sanadon, Noël-Étienne (1676–1733) 71–2, 82–3, 85–7, 109–10, 154–5, 186 n.41, 194 n.29
Santa Vittoria, Battle of (1702) 45
Santacruz i Gener, Francesc de (d. 1730) 124–5, *125*
Saragossa 17–18, 62–3, 65–6
  Battle of (1710) 39, 80, 82, 124, 140
Sardinia 3, 127–8, 132
Savoy, duke of, *see* Victor Amadeus II
Scharff, Franz Ferdinand 11–12
Schellenberg, Battle of (1704) 48, 50
Schlittern, Paul Christoph von (d. 1715) 39, 41
Schloss Salzdahlum (Germany) 94
Segarra, Esteve 102
Seilern, Johannes Friedrich von 25
Sicily 18, 60, 80–1, 132–3, 136–7, 143
Spain, Council of (1713) 123–5, 143
Speyerbach, Battle of (1703) 48
Staindl, Franz, professor 45
Starhemberg, marshal, *see* Rüdiger, Guido Wald
Szatmár, Treaty of (1711) 36

Tann, Georg Friedrich von 39–40
Tethys 74–5
The Hague, Treaty of (1701) 43–4,
  Treaty of (1720) 106, 132
  see also Grand Alliance
Tories 3, 85, 107, 113–15
Toulon, siege of (1707) 71–3, 124
Tournai, siege of (1709) 77
Trelawney, Charles 112
Troy 46, 70

t'Serclaes, Claude Frédéric, count of Tilly (1648–1723) 78
Turano, Domenico 133–4
Turin, siege of (1706) 68, 77
Turenne, viscount of (Henri de La Tour d'Auvergne, 1611–75) 86, 180 n.76
Turnus 65–6

Utrecht, Peace of (1713–15) *also called* Treaties of Utrecht 1, 3, 9, 40, 85, 105–17, 121–2, 129–30, 132

Valencia 62, 65, 71
Van Loon, Gerard 111, *112*
Vendôme, duke of, marshal (Louis Joseph de Bourbon, 1654–1712) 45, 48–9, 80, 82, 84
Venus 81, 93–7
Veragua, duke of, viceroy of Sicily 18
Verderosa, Muzio Giuseppe 27–9
Vernulaeus, Nicolaus
  Historia Austriaca (1651) 36
Verrua, siege of (1704–5) 77, 84
Versailles 2, 13, *15*, 29, 61
Victor Amadeus II, duke of Savoy (1666–1732) 72, 104, 132
Victory (goddess) 86
Vienna 23, 36, 39, 48, 57, 95, 123, 127, 143, 174 n.23
  St Stephen's Cathedral 39, 99, 139
  Treaty of (1725) 3, 41, 126, 134, 136–7
  university 21, 39, 49–50, 76, 90–1, 99, 118, *119*, 139
Vigo Bay, Battle of (1702) 48
Villars, Claude Louis Hector de, marshal (1653–1734) 77, 85–6, 105, 108, 116
Villaviciosa, Battle of (1710) 80, 82, 124
Villeroy, duke of (François de Neufville, 1644–1730) 44–6
Virgil 49, 75, 118, 159
  Aeneid 20, 23, 31, 35, 46, 60, 61, 63–4, 66–7, 95, 144, 157–9, 164 n.3, 168 n.27, 177 n.56, 177 n.57, 187 n.52
  Eclogues 91–3, 131, 178 n.57, 182 n.14, 188 n.55, 189 n.67, 194 n.23
  Georgics 187 n.51, 191 n.8

Visconti, Annibale, general (1660–1747) 45, 173 n.9
Vitale, Pietro (1656–1728) 80
Vitale Orosio, Livio (Livius Vitalis Orosius, fl. 1538) 63, 157

Waltrin, Claude-Louis (fl. 1713) 110–11, 179 n.69
Welf, House of 96–7

Werlhof, Johann, professor (1660–1711) 93–8, 118, 159–61
Whigs 3, 107, 114–15, 187 n.49

Ypres, siege of (1709) 77

Zaragoza, *see* Saragossa
Zephyrus 16, 74, 110